Medieval Thought:
Augustine and Thomas Aquinas

THOMAS AQUINAS

AUGUSTINE

Medieval Thought

AUGUSTINE & THOMAS AQUINAS

MONUMENTS OF WESTERN THOUGHT

Edited by **Norman F. Cantor** and **Peter L. Klein,** Brandeis University

BLAISDELL PUBLISHING COMPANY

A Division of Ginn and Company

Waltham, Massachusetts | Toronto | London

FOREWORD

The basis of a university education is an understanding of the great writings that have shaped Western civilization. The aim of this twelve-volume series is to make these doctrines of Western thought available to the student in the most convenient and readily comprehensible form. Each volume presents carefully selected texts by the two major thinkers of a particular historical period. In choosing the texts, the entire works of each thinker have been drawn upon, and passages from both familiar and unfamiliar writings are presented to bring the reader to an understanding of the central thought of the author. Following the selections are commentaries by leading modern scholars on the works studied. Many of these statements are drawn from books which are available only in the very best libraries. Again, these modern commentaries are carefully edited to present the main points as succinctly as possible. The first two chapters of each volume delineate the relevant historical context and biographical information and suggest the main outlines of the two thinkers' arguments, thus providing a framework for the student's own analysis of the texts. The source texts are followed by study guide questions which challenge the student's understanding of the arguments he has been reading and force him to go back and analyze the texts again. These study guides will also serve as a basis for class discussion. The modern commentaries are similarly followed by study guides, requiring the student to consider the merits of the authors' critiques.

We believe that the richness of the material selected and the pedagogical principles that have determined the organization of each volume will enable the student to carry away from his study a sophisticated understanding of the imperishable ideas the two great thinkers have propounded. The student who studies all twelve volumes will have an excellent basis for comprehending the fundamental thought of Western civilization.

N. F. C.
P. L. K.

CONTENTS

1

THE HISTORICAL CONTEXT

Two creative eras of philosophical speculation flourished during the Middle Ages in the Christian West. The first lasted from the third through the fifth century A.D. and culminated in the work of Augustine; the second, from the twelfth through the fourteenth century, was dominated by the work of Thomas Aquinas. Within this entire period, philosophy was at once an obligation and a pastime for churchmen and philosophers who sought knowledge in order to understand their Christian beliefs. Thus, unlike the Greeks, medieval philosophers did not seek knowledge for its own sake but used knowledge as a supplement to faith. Nonetheless, medieval thinkers studied and imitated the pagan philosophy of Greece. Why did Christian theorists devote considerable time and effort to the work of Plato and Aristotle whose teachings often conflicted with the dogmas of Christian faith? The reason is simply that not only did Greek philosophy function as a catalyst for medieval thought, but, from the Greeks, Christian thinkers acquired the language and method of philosophical inquiry. Using these tools for their own purpose, medieval theorists fashioned an original Christian philosophy.

The development of this Christian medieval philosophy in both of its creative eras can be understood in terms of the same general model: in both cases the first stage was marked by a revival in Greco-Roman thought. This classical revival, however, stimulated strong hostility among many Church leaders, forcing the defenders of ancient wisdom to reevaluate and justify their position. Finally, reevaluation led in each case to the formulation of a new Christian world view founded on a synthesis of Greek philosophy and Christian dogma.

Within the context of their general similarity, each creative era of medieval philosophy was shaped by entirely different social and political forces. In Augustine's time—in the late fourth and early fifth centuries —Christianity still suffered the travails of growth and diffusion; one of the foremost problems was the conversion of educated pagans. While Greek literature and philosophy comprised the core of the Roman curriculum, they were studied with the bland enthusiasm typical of pedantic and formal education. Yet, in spite of intellectual torpor, they conditioned generations of students to expect and respect the Greek style of thought. Applying Greek literature and philosophy to the task of conversion and incorporating them within the Christian curriculum, church leaders subdued their adversaries by employing their own techniques. This practice was reinforced by the fact that most church leaders, coming to Christianity as converts, were conditioned by the same secular Roman curriculum.

During the High Middle Ages (1050–1300) the classical revival was given impetus by monarchical and papal reforms. By increasing the size and efficiency of their governments, monarchy and papacy created a demand for obedient bureaucrats and clear logical systems of law, the former to staff their offices and the latter to solidify their domains. The desire for position and power in both church and secular government led young men to study Roman law and Aristotelian logic, both of which had fallen into disrepute after the collapse of the Roman empire. Aristotle's work had been gradually neglected and ultimately lost in the West primarily because Christian thinkers of the first millennium A.D. found succor in the idealistic and hierarchic world of Platonic and Neoplatonic philosophy and were bored by the scientific approach of Aristotle. Fortunately for later generations of scholars, Aristotle's thought was studied and preserved in the Moslem world of the Southern Mediterranean. In the twelfth century, increased peace and prosperity, a surplus of unemployed young aristocrats, and the promise of position and power in the councils of the mighty prompted the curious and the ambitious to journey to Moslem Spain where they could study the ancient wisdom of Aristotle. As a consequence of these journeys, Aristotle's works, the physics and metaphysics, as well as the logic, found their way into the libraries and cloisters of the West. The advent of Aristotle in the West stimulated the second era of Christian philosophy.

Although the assimilation of Greek philosophy by Christian theologians in the first era almost seems inevitable, since both pagan and Christian thinkers were educated in the Greek style of thought, several of the foremost Christian theorists believed Greek and Christian thought to be fundamentally incompatible. Tertullian, the North African Christian theorist of the third century, denounced the Greco-Roman philosophers, telling Christians that "we have no need for curiosity after Jesus Christ, or for investigation after the Gospel." In face of such attacks, the primary question which the defenders of classical thought were compelled to answer was, "Can pagan thought be compatible with Christian belief?" The question was never definitely settled; at the end of the era, Augustine was still pondering it and still advocating a moderately conservative interpretation. Nonetheless, in the long course of debate, the concepts and methods of Greek philosophy had become the language of Christian theology. By the twelfth century few thinkers seriously entertained the possibility of excluding pagan thought from Christian philosophy. Rather, they were bothered by the influx of Aristotelian thought and the threat it posed for their Platonic world order. How could Aristotle's mechanistic god be compatible with the theistic and providential god who constantly determines the fate of the universe? How could Aristotle's assumption of the eternity of matter be reconciled with the creation of the world *ex nihilo*? And how could the Aristotelian denial of the immortality of individual existence be entertained when Christian belief offered the promise of immortality? These are the questions which troubled the conservative leaders of the twelfth- and thirteenth-century church, and which the advocates of Aristotelian thought had to resolve.

In addition to the difference in the social and political forces which shaped both periods, there was a fundamental difference in the personality and character of each period's most significant writer— Augustine and Thomas Aquinas. Augustine (354–430) was the Bishop of Hippo, a North African city, and was intimately involved in the day-to-day problems and sufferings of his parishioners. With the single exception of *On the Trinity*, all of his works were written to meet practical problems of Christian existence. Thomas Aquinas (1225–1274), on the other hand, was born into an aristocratic family and lived as a professor of theology at the University of Paris, far from the problems and sufferings of human existence. His primary concern was with the general principles which lay behind human existence and reality. Thus, in order to understand the work of Augustine, we must consider the problems of Christian existence in the late Roman empire and to understand Thomas Aquinas, the academic disputes of the High Middle Ages.

Fashioned by the blood of legions in the last two centuries B.C., the Roman empire was solidified by the same brutal means in the first two centuries of our era. By 100 A.D. the Roman emperor ruled a vast domain stretching from the Euphrates to Scotland and from the Danube to the Sahara. Although Rome was at its zenith in the second century, it suffered from incurable political and economic disorders. Foremost among its political deficiencies was the lack of a well-defined principle of succession to the emperorship. By the second century the emperor designated his own successor by adopting him into the royal family; but in the third century this system broke down, precipitating a long, bloody struggle in which the provincial legions vied for the imperial throne. Finally, in the latter half of the fourth century, the hereditary principle of succession was established; even then, there were periodic civil wars and revolutions. Economically the Roman empire suffered under the burden of a primitive system of productivity, slave labor. The empire not only curtailed the incentive to invent new means of production (to increase production it was necessary to increase the number of slaves at work), but also severely limited the quality of goods produced. And where there are no unique regional products, there is little inter-regional trade. Thus, at the end of the second century, not only was the empire divided by political intrigue, but it was slowly disintegrating as an economic unit.

During the second, third, and fourth centuries, while the empire rotted at its core, people increasingly turned to religion. In the third century, superstition and supernatural religion were rife; people were suffering from severe insecurity and sought a personal salvation. For most people in the late empire, life was short and miserable. In search of a religion to suit their needs, the lower classes, and eventually educated and wealthy men as well, turned to the mystery and sacramental religions which had been circulating in the Roman and Greek worlds for many centuries. The mystery religions all held to a savior god who died and was reborn, and to a sacramental rite which allowed the believer to gain immortality by associating himself with the triumph of the deity. Within this emotional and unstable context Christianity spread across the empire, but it by no means immediately conquered the Roman world. In the second and third centuries, the mystery religion of Mithra, the Unconquerable Sun, was unquestionably stronger, gaining many converts among the soldiers and officers of the legions. By the fourth century no more than a third of the Eastern, Greek-speaking half of the empire was Christian and less than a tenth of the Latin-speaking West. Nonetheless, Christianity exercised considerable appeal. This can be attributed to two causes. First, unlike most of the other supernatural religions, the Christian savior god had an historical concreteness; Jesus had appeared in the flesh at an historical time; and the reality of Christianity's origin gave credence to its promise of a heavenly end. Second, Christianity managed to absorb the best in all the religions of the time. From Judaism it acquired the Old Testament and a well-formulated moral code. From stoicism it borrowed the belief in the brotherhood of man. Christian thinkers also borrowed heavily from Platonism and Neoplatonism.

Two of the most significant characteristics of the early church were its concepts of "church" and "priesthood." Until the late fourth century Christianity was predominantly an urban faith and, in the most important cities such as Antioch and Alexandria, there was a particular, physical, local church; however, Christians believed that the church was both universal and eternal, stretching from creation to the last judgment, and, they believed that the priesthood was elevated above the common members of the church by the performance of the miracle of the Eucharist. Underlying this position was the view that the validity of the sacremental rite depends not on the personal qualities of the priest but on the priest's office in the church and his role as a representative of Christ. Because of their crucial position, both of these concepts gave rise to profound disputes within the church. Blood was shed over the question of whether sacraments performed by an evil priest could be valid, and men were deeply troubled by the implications of an eternal and universal church. But the most significant controversy in the fourth century involved the relationship of church and empire.

In the unstable world of the fourth century, the church probably would have perished along with the empire, if it had not unified its position and clarified its dogmas. The principal agent in achieving both of these goals and insuring the possibility that the church might survive the empire was the emperor Constantine. In a dramatic conversion before the battle of the Milvain bridge (in 213), one of the periodic internal quarrels among the generals of the legion, Constantine placed the standard of Christ on the shields of his soldiers. In light of his victory, he felt compelled to save the Roman state and further the Christian church by binding both to the same destiny. This move was also politically astute, for Constantine immediately acquired support from a large part of the population which had formerly turned its back on the affairs of the empire. From the beginning of his reign Constantine aided the church by granting her special privileges. But this was not enough, for the church was torn by doctrinal disputes. In 325 Constantine convened the Council of Nicaea in which he presided and tried, with limited success, to settle church dispute by imperial dictate. Although Constantine failed in his immediate objective, he created the precedent of the emperor's right to govern the affairs of the church, a precedent which was to have repercussions throughout the Middle Ages.

The two theological disputes with which Constantine attempted to deal were the Arian and Donatist heresies. Arianism, which arose from the Eastern insistence on philosophical definitions, had demanded a strong definition in the distinction between God and Christ. Arius, the founder of the movement, tried to distinguish different levels in the godhead. In the Western half of the empire, where the need for philosophical precision was not as keenly felt, there was greater concern over the polytheistic tendency of the movement. Since the dispute ultimately rested on national and cultural differences, the affair was settled in terms of political expediency. More important was the Donatist heresy, which was the fundamental doctrinal dispute in Western Christianity. Essentially the Donatists demanded a church of saints as opposed to the Catholic (universal) church. They insisted that the sacramants be administered by priests of pure spirit, holding that the rites performed by the unworthy were invalid.

Constantine took one more action which profoundly affected the course of Christianity. By building a second capital, Constantinople, in the Eastern half of the empire, he furthered the schism which had been gradually dividing the Eastern and Western halves of the empire. The eventual separation of Eastern and Western Christianity was to have an important effect on the course of medieval history. One of the results was the long absence of Greek science in the West.

After the death of Constantine only paganism remained a threat to Christianity. In the mid-fourth century, paganism enjoyed a revival when the emperor Julian, known as Julian the Apostate, reversed Constantine's course and converted from Christianity to paganism. Well-educated, sober, and austere, Julian had a grand vision of restoring pagan religion and classical culture to a new high level. Julian was well meaning, but ineffectual; however, he encouraged the Roman aristocracy, who, along with the academics, had always been the warmest defenders of paganism, to stubbornly resist Christianity. It was a catastrophe that the aristocracy and the intellectuals devoted their entire energies to the confrontation with Christianity: while preoccupied with the church they failed to notice the real threat of the Germanic invasions until it was too late.

For the fate of Christianity, it was essential that the church come to terms with the intellectual heritage of the ancient world. There were three reasons why the church fathers sought to absorb the classical tradition: First, as products of the same educational system and curriculum as the pagans, they could visualize no alternative, and, as products of the same system, they shared many of the same values in spite of their religious differences. Second, the acceptance of the double faith theory provided adequate justification for the study of classical thought. Initially enunciated by the early third-century Alexandrian theologian Origen and accepted by most church fathers including Augustine, the double faith theory maintained there was both a simple, uncritical, fundamentalist faith for the uneducated and a more philosophical doctrine for the leaders of the church. Third, the early first-century Jewish philosopher, Philo of Alexandria, had already demonstrated that it was possible to achieve harmony between biblical faith and the classical tradition. The principal ingredient in Philo's method was his demonstration that there was a hidden allegorical meaning behind the biblical text which was compatible with Platonism. Philo's interpretation of the Bible could be justified by the double faith theory; thus, a prolific school of apologetics and theology flourished in Alexandria between the second and third centuries. In the Latin half of the empire, church fathers were more cautious, paying heed to the advice of Tertullian. They argued that it was one thing to read Plato but quite another to read the lewd literature produced by some Roman writers. But the presence of a pagan revival, the educational background of the church fathers, and the double faith theory all moved Western Christian leaders to accept and absorb the classical tradition. However, it was Augustine who provided an adequate intellectual synthesis of the two worlds.

The enormous influence of Augustine's thought was insured primarily by virtue of his intellect and also by the cataclysmic events which shook the Roman empire shortly after his death. It is not insignificant that while Augustine lay on his deathbed, Vandal invaders battered the doors of Hippo. Between the fourth and tenth century, Western Christendom suffered internal anarchy and foreign invasion. By the fourth century the Roman empire had virtually collapsed—as Gibbon said, "under its own weight"; the successive waves of Goths, Visigoths, and Vandals which engulfed the Roman empire in the fifth and sixth centuries were a symptom of the empire's internal anarchy. Social, political, and economic life was fragmented. The idea of "empire" persisted, but power resided within the hands of petty warlords. Between the eighth and tenth century Europe was invaded on three fronts: in the South by the followers of Mohammed, in the East by the Hungarians, and in the North by the Scandinavians. Because of the political and social turmoil, education and learning were reduced within narrowly circumscript boundaries, and curriculum took the form of summaries and encyclopedias of knowledge. Thus, not until the twelfth century did intellectuals of sufficient stature criticize Augustine and the other church fathers, and not until the thirteenth century did Thomas Aquinas erect an edifice to rival the Augustinian synthesis.

Beginning in the tenth century there was a general awakening of European society. Foreign invasions had subsided and a modest degree of peace and order prevailed. Commerce was steadily increasing and once again after a long hiatus there was a resurgence of urban society. The gradual solidification and organization of secular monarchies transformed the political landscape, particularly in Germany where the Ottonian and Salian rulers of the tenth and eleventh centuries effectively usurped power from the local barons. The fundamental basis for Ottonian power was the king's control over the German church. They exercised this control by means of the institution which came to be called "lay-investiture": the king, by asserting the right to invest bishops and abbots with the symbols of their office, gained effective control over the election of the higher clergy. Thus, the Ottonians filled the ranks of the episcopate with their own relatives and with their own royal chancery clerks. The rise of monarchical power stimulated a similar reorganization within the papacy. Church leaders were particularly annoyed by the German ruler's encroachment on their power and, under the leadership of Gregory VII (1073–1085), the papacy provoked a direct confrontation with the German king, Henry IV. The fundamental question which had to be resolved was, "Who should rule in this world, the church or state?"

The controversy between Pope Gregory VII and Henry IV of Germany was a continuation of the struggle between church and empire which began with the ascension of Constantine to the imperial throne. In the century after Constantine's death, when the empire no longer represented any real power, the papacy tried to reverse the trend which Constantine had initiated. Pope Leo I created the official doctrine of the medieval papacy by arguing that the Roman see had been granted by St. Peter supremacy in all matters pertaining to the church. This was the so-called Petrine doctrine and represented a direct challenge to the political monotheism which Constantine and his successors represented. St. Leo's affirmation of the church's and the pope's supremacy was more a matter of faith than fact, for he wielded little actual power. The main theme in the history of the medieval papacy, however, was the attempt to turn the Petrine doctrine into a practical reality. In the last decade of the fifth century another pope, Gelasius I, added a theory, appropriately known as the Gelasian Doctrine, to the theoretical props which supported the papacy. In defining the relationship between secular and spiritual authority, he said that there could be found in the Bible figures such as Melchizedek and Christ who were both kings and priests, but since the time of Christ authority had been divided between church and state. Thus, there were two institutions of authority in the world: the prelates exercising divine power and the kings holding royal power, with the latter beneath the former. Although Gelasius separated church and state, he clearly implied that the church should rule in any matters of dispute. Besides the Petrine and Gelasian doctrines, the medieval papacy also had the authority of Augustine, who maintained that the state was no more than a band of robbers and, if all else failed, the papacy could drag out a fictitious document known as the Donation of Constantine which purported to be Constantine's profession of subordination to the papacy. In the early Middle Ages the papacy asserted its theoretical supremacy at every opportunity; however, medieval kings did little more than tolerate such illusions of grandeur, recognizing the impotence of the papacy. In the third quarter of the eleventh century the papacy finally had the opportunity to realize its goal. Peace, prosperity, the rise of urban communities, and the inspiration of devout kings all stimulated a new wave of popular piety. Emerging from this milieu, Pope Gregory

VII and his fellow reformers reiterated the church's supremacy over the state. For a brief moment they were successful, bringing Henry to their feet begging for absolution. But, the actual domination of the state by the church was short-lived; Henry counterattacked, and the reforming party in Rome gave way to a more moderate faction. However, a practical lesson was not lost on the medieval kings—papal ideology was always a potential threat to their effective leadership in society. In the course of the investiture controversy, monarchy had lost all theoretical justification for its position of dominance. It was not until the work of Thomas Aquinas that the secular state once again acquired a theoretical justification for its existence and function.

As the countryside grew more prosperous in the eleventh century, urban life also began to flourish. While in the ninth and tenth centuries, towns had been inhabited by a handful of people, scraping a precarious living within crumbling walls of once prosperous communities, by the eleventh century people were rebuilding their fortifications, offering security, and demanding rights for their citizens. The rise of urban life and its middle class mentality served as a catalyst for the intellectual resurgence of the High Middle Ages; frequently destructive in its effects, it also was a source of vitality and creativity. Urban life was an anomaly in medieval society. Medieval life was founded on the twin pillars of the monastery and the castle; the hero of the time was the contemplative saint, living secure from mundane distractions in the solitude of his cell. To be sure, few men in medieval society actually tried to live up to this ideal, fewer succeeded, but those who did were held in the highest esteem. The landed nobility, who had traditionally wielded the most power, were also rewarded by their share of public regard. Initially the more successful members of the burgher class tried to compete with the nobility, but the lavish, carefree, and frequently violent, lives of the landed rich were incompatible with the banking house mentality of the merchants. Thus, the urban class was forced to form its own ideal: in place of contests of arms they substituted oral combat. Debate was deemed mightier than the sword; in place of the art of leisure, they idealized the rigorous demands of hard work and rational thought; and in place of sumptuous banquets and lavish parties, they cultivated the fine arts. The combined efforts of this new ideal placed a premium on intellectual dexterity and led to the foundation of institutes for the study of law and rhetoric. Students came from all over Europe, for not only did the urban communes see value in the study of Roman law, but both church and state were in need of a more efficient and more civilized code of law than the German system which came into general use after the barbarian invasions of the Roman empire.

Twelfth-century Europe was a vital and creative era; in every area of thought and feeling men daily opened new frontiers. For the history of philosophy the most significant change was the transition from rhetoric to logic as the primary method of disputation. Since the early Roman empire rhetoric had occupied an increasingly prominent place in the educational curriculum, and philosophers such as Augustine were actually trained rhetoricians. The rigorous demands of legal studies, and the gravity of the theological issues raised during the investiture controversy, created an urgent demand for a more effective method of arbitrating disputes. The logic of Aristotle had been preserved in the encyclopedias of the early Middle Ages, along with all the other miscellanea; and in the eleventh century lawyers and theologians employed the syllogism of Aristotle more frequently than the invective of Cicero to clinch their point. Around 1050 a celebrated ecclesiastical scholar named Berengar of Tours demonstrated the superiority of dialectic in disentangling the web of theological controversies, and a half century later the universally admired St. Anselm of Canterbury also used dialectic in his theological work. By the end of the eleventh century, churchmen, liberal and conservative, were all dabbling in the art of logic. However, in the twelfth century the appearance of Peter Abelard (d. 1142), a brilliant but egotistical and headstrong logician, reawakened the latent fears of more spiritual and conservative churchmen. Abelard had absolute confidence in dialectic as the means for resolving all controversies, and by sheer force of intellect and personality he devastated anyone who would dispute with him. The frightening specter of Abelard divided the intellectual world into two camps: there were those who would follow Abelard and idolize the syllogism; and those who would find greater truth in the depths of piety and spiritual revelation. The twelfth century was so rich and fecund that both tendencies found a place and an opportunity to develop.

While the twelfth-century creativity ran its course, scholars were being gradually inundated by a vast wealth of Greek, Islamic, and Jewish philosophy. The revival of logic had created a great demand for the works of Aristotle, most of which had been lost to the West in the late years of the empire through indifference and neglect. Some Islamic and Greek scientific treatises had already found their way into the West during the eleventh century when the study of medicine was revived in the Italian cities. There were four centers where Western scholars could discover these lost works: Syria, Constantinople, Sicily, and Spain. In each of the first three places, Westerners could acquire the Greek philosophical works written in Greek; in Spain, the Greek texts had been translated into Arabic. Although lines of direct access were open, most of Aristotle's work crossed over into the West from Spain, where Latin translations of the Arabic translation of the Greek were made. Spain was chosen principally because, except for Rome, it had been the most frequent object of Christian pilgrimages which over the course of years had developed lines of communication.

Because of its source, Aristotle's work came to the West veiled in the garb of Islamic and Jewish commentaries. The Aristotelian corpus was translated into Arabic in the eighth century by Moslem scholars in Syria. It spread slowly throughout the Moslem world and in the tenth century reached Spain, where it was intensively studied in the great schools of philosophy and science in Cordoba and elsewhere. The greatest of the Moslem philosophers was a Spaniard named Ibn Rushd, whom the West called Averroes. He interpreted Aristotle in a materialistic and deterministic manner; the world of science as represented by Aristotle inexorably demonstrates that God is the mechanistic mover of the universe. At the same time Averroes was a devout Moslem and met the contradiction between science and revelation by insistence on a double truth. There is one truth for science and another for revelation.

Not only did the Western scholars acquire a vast amount of knowledge from the works of Aristotle, but they also acquired an equally imposing corpus of commentaries. The influx of this material presented two overwhelming problems for Western scholars: first, they had to distinguish between what was Aristotle and what was interpretive comment; second, they had to digest the new information and theories. The combined effect of these two tasks altered the course of twelfth-century creativity. Creativity was dampened, and in its place universities became sorting houses of knowledge.

When Thomas Aquinas began his career in the middle of the thirteenth century, there was still considerable confusion among philosophers and theologians. There were those who still supported the older Augustinianism and Neoplatonism. A few openly advocated the Averroist position, whose determinism and denial of creation *ex nihilo* contradicted Christian revelation. And the German Dominican thinker at the University of Paris, Albertus Magnus, was attempting to establish a Christian Aristotelian position. Beginning his career at this point, Thomas Aquinas set as his life task the problem of resolving the differences between Aristotelian science and Christian revelation and forming a synthesis of the two.

2

AN INTRODUCTION TO THE LIFE AND WORK OF AUGUSTINE AND THOMAS AQUINAS

An Introduction to Augustine

It would not be an exaggeration to say that Augustine was the conscience of the dying classical civilization and of the emerging Christian world. All of the issues which divided the late Roman empire and all of the problems which tortured men's souls found their way into the work of Augustine. Even from birth—the offspring of a pagan father and a Christian mother—he seemed destined to partake of both worlds. " O God, always one and the same, if I know myself, I shall know Thee," said Augustine and in this remark he indicates the two primary poles of his thought: "God and my soul." Like Plato, Augustine begins his quest for the universal and eternal good by turning inward; his first concern is for man. It has already been noted that Augustine's deep concern for the daily problems of his parishioners was essential to his works. Similarly, there was a personal, existential commitment to his works: whenever pointing to the wickedness of man, he pointed first to his own base and nefarious life. But, unlike Plato, he did not believe that man can achieve his goal through his own power. Plato had identified knowledge with virtue: if a man truly knows what is good, he will do good. For Augustine it is obvious that not only do men often act against their knowledge but that man is not a rational animal. The will, according to Augustine, has primacy. If man is to achieve his salvation, he must turn his will to God; however, the Augustinian man, unlike his Greek counterpart, has not even the power to turn his own will to the good. It is by God's gift that man achieves salvation.

"God and my soul" might also be considered the subtitle of Augustine's *Confessions*. The work is both autobiographical and theological, personal and symbolic. It begins with an affirmation of God's goodness and omnipotence; the theme of the work is the quest of man for the love and understanding of God, whose existence and power he has already affirmed. In order to reach God, Augustine must pass through the misery of his own soul. His sins have a symbolic character, for they are the sins of every man. This is the theological side of the work. In describing his selfishness as an infant, Augustine is at the same time expounding the doctrine of original sin. In the famous story of the theft of the pears, Augustine steals fruit, even though he is not hungry, merely to enhance himself in the eyes of his friends. The purpose of this story is to demonstrate the nature of sin as rebellion.

In the seventh book, when Augustine finally arrives at the point where he must explain the nature of sin, he gives not merely his own interpretation, but also depicts the three theological positions that rivaled his view in the ancient world as three stages in his life's journey, three stages which he wandered through before arriving at the truth of Christianity. The basic question of the chapter is, "How can there be evil in the world if God is good and all-powerful?" First, Augustine presents the psychologically naive view of God as some kind of material substance. If God were like space, Augustine imagines, then his goodness would be spread evenly throughout the world—but an elephant would possess more of God's goodness than the sparrow, and a large man would be more godly than a small one. This is untenable, for our ethic would become: eat and be good! If God is not some kind of material substance, then perhaps his nature and the presence of evil can be explained by postulating two forces in the world, a force of good and a force of evil. This is the second view and it is in part autobiographical. When Augustine was a young man he was sent by his parents to Carthage to study rhetoric. While he was there, he acquired a mistress, kept her for fifteen years, fathered a son by her, and abandoned her after his later conversion to Christianity. The impressionable young Augustine also underwent his first great religious crisis. Augustine had been studying Christian doctrine and preparing for baptism, while he pursued his study of rhetoric; but his first taste of classical literature and philosophy led him away from his mother's faith. He became a Manichee. Manichaeism was related to the old Persian Zoroastrian religion and postulated an absolute dualism, an eternal struggle between the god of light and the god of darkness. Thus, the Manichees affirmed evil as an independent substance. Augustine personally abandoned Manichaeism, mostly at his mother's insistence. Theologically, he rejected Manichaeism because it was too naive and contradicted the goodness and omnipotence of God.

In 383, shortly after his arrival in Italy where he had journeyed to teach rhetoric, Augustine became a Neoplatonist. From Neoplatonism he found inspiration for the solution of the problem of evil. God is good, and all the things in this world, more or less, possess some good. Evil is not a thing; it is not a substance; it resides in the will of man. Evil comes into the world when man willingly turns away from the word of God. Conversely, however, man cannot turn towards God without divine aid, and divine aid comes only through the word disseminated by the church.

As bishop of Hippo, Augustine's greatest problem was the suppression of the Donatists, and from this conflict he derived his doctrine of the nature of the church and the sacraments. Claiming that the validity of the holy rites was independent of the morality or perfection of the priest administering them, Augustine argued that the validity of the sacraments depends upon the priesthood's divine office. As long as the priest is officially ordained by the church, the administration of the sacraments is valid. For Augustine, the Christian church was universal, ecumenical, and catholic. In the last judgment God would judge all men, separating the wheat from the chaff; the church on earth, however, was only a prelude to the heavenly city. There were good men outside the church and bad ones within. It was the church's obligation to bring all men within the fold. And since Christ said, "Compel them to come in," Augustine believed that physical force was justified in the task of conversion. When the Donatists would not renounce their heresies, Augustine marshalled all the force he could to compel them to abdicate. Along with his other doctrines, Augustine's sanction of force was also accepted as authoritative and became the justification for the Christian soldier.

The relationship of church and state was always a crucial question in the medieval world, but it was particularly acute in Augustine's day. After the empire had become Christian, people tended to associate their destinies. Had not Christ been born in the reign of the first Roman emperor? Thus, when the Germans sacked Rome, Christians were dismayed. Augustine began his longest work, *The City of God*, to dismiss the fears of his contemporaries. The work, however, took fifteen years to write, and before he was finished it was necessary for him to delve deeply in the philosophy of history and to reconsider the whole question of the relationship between the course of secular affairs and Christian faith. In the ancient world the principal view of history was cyclical: the universe as a whole perpetually passes through the same stages. Against the cyclical theory Augustine argued that the incarnation of Christ was a unique event in history. In the Augustinian view, Christian faith implies that human history is a definite development from the creation of the world to the last judgment. Within this linear scheme, the life of Christ was a unique event to which all history must relate.

The most important event in history is moral, theological, and metaphysical in Augustine's view: in each individual there is a struggle within the soul between the spiritual and the carnal will. Those men in whom the carnal will prevails love themselves and neglect God; and those men in whom the spiritual will predominates love God to the point of contempt for self. Thus, humanity may be grouped into two communities, two cities. One is the city of God in which the spiritual will prevails, and the other is the earthly city. The life of the two cities extends from the beginning of time to the end of the world. During this period of human history the two societies are mixed physically but separated spiritually and morally. The two cities are not intended to represent any existing societies, for the struggle occurs within the individual soul; nonetheless, the implication is obvious: the affairs of men are meaningless and mundane when compared to the love of God.

An Introduction to Thomas Aquinas

Thomas Aquinas' initial assumption was that the conclusions of Averroes did not necessarily follow from the principles of Aristotle. The vast corpus of his work is designed to show that a great part of revelation is confirmed by rational science. The accomplishment of this task by Thomas was an achievement of the first magnitude, but in spite of its intrinsic worth it has been popular to overemphasize his achievement; it is far from true to say that his philosophy was immediately acclaimed by all in the Middle Ages as a final answer to the church's intellectual problem. Aquinas' work was like a great Gothic cathedral, held together by the mortar of logic; if you accepted the principles, everything else followed. But there were many Christians in the thirteenth century who were unwilling to accept his starting point, principally those who had taken the course of piety and revelation in the twelfth century.

In 1225 Thomas was born a younger son in the large family of the Count of Aquino, and he was related through his mother to the German-Sicilian Emperor Frederick II. Little of his personal life is known. At the age of five he was offered by his parents as a child of the cloister and destined for the monastic life. Taking the Dominican habit in 1244, he shortly thereafter became a pupil of Albertus Magnus at the university in Paris. The rest of his life was devoted to scholastic pursuits and he died in 1274. Similarly, little is known about his appearance and personality, except for the fact that he was known as "the angelic doctor," a reference to his unusually benevolent disposition even in the most heated debate, a characteristic which probably stemmed from his aristocratic provenance and perhaps also from his renowned obesity.

The primary characteristic of Thomas' approach was that, like his master, Albertus, he believed in an absolute separation of reason and revelation, the natural and the supernatural. Mysteries, such as the trinity and the incarnation, he believed, were not susceptible of proof or of comprehension. The human mind was bounded by its contacts with the external world, and it was from contact with external reality, not divine illumination or divine ideas, that knowledge of truth was acquired. From sense experience of external reality, not through the soul's direct consciousness of its own existence or even of God's existence, a proof of the first cause could be deduced. Thus, it was from an empirical epistemology that Thomas' system derived, and this was his principal debt to Aristotle. Aquinas countenanced neither the double truth theory, nor the Platonic conception of the world as a mere image of reality. There is only one truth and we can recognize it when we experience it, but there are also ultimate realms of truth to which the unaided human mind cannot attain.

Aquinas wrote two systematic treatises, the *Summa Contra Gentiles* and the *Summa Theologica*. The first was purportedly written to help in the conversion of the Moors in Spain, but it was principally written against those who supported a naturalistic philosophy; the latter was written as a systematic and summary exposition of theology. The organization of the *Summa Theologica* is overwhelming and deserves special comment. The work is divided into three parts, and the second part itself is divided into two parts, known respectively as the *Prima Secundae* and the *Secunda Secundae*. The first part is devoted to God and creation, though it includes a treatment of human nature and man's intellectual life. In the second part Aquinas considers man's moral life, dealing in the first sub-part with man's final end and general moral themes; in the second sub-part, with particular virtues and vices; finally, in the third part, with Christ and the sacraments. The *Summa* is broken down even further. Each part is divided into questions and each question contains several articles. In each article Aquinas follows the procedure of first citing objections against the doctrine which he intends to present. He, then, presents the doctrine in the body of the article, and finally replies to the objection in light of the doctrine which he has just developed. It is no wonder that scholars often compare the *Summa* to a Gothic cathedral.

Because their style and method differed so markedly, Augustine and Aquinas almost seem to belong to two totally different ages, and in many respects this is true, but they were both medieval thinkers and were united not only by a similar heritage, but by the common problems which confronted them. One of these was the problem of church-state relations; and Aquinas, like Augustine, played a fundamental role in shaping the doctrine of future generations. Political Augustinianism reached its fullest expression in the pronouncements and actions of Pope Gregory VII. In the twelfth and thirteenth centuries canon lawyers perpetuated this ecclesiastical political theory, but the actual entrenchment of secular power in society belied the established tradition. From the middle of the twelfth century a new current in political speculation tried to delineate a theory of the state which would conform more realistically with the actual social conditions. Aquinas' political theory represents a significant step in this movement. The starting point of Thomas' theory was, as in other cases, the science of Aristotle. Thus, he accepted the Greek view of the moral necessity of the state. At the same time he wanted to maintain the ultimate supremacy of the church in society. He reconciled both positions by asserting that the law of the state had to conform with natural law, which, in turn, was a reflection of divine law, and, when the positive law of the state thus conformed with the law of God, its moral sanction was complete and unmitigated.

In essence, Thomas' place in the history of Western thought is that of the founder of liberal humanism. He believed that man's rational power is sufficient to understand the nature of the universe and to live a good (if not saintly) life. The state, in the Thomist view, is necessary for the good life and its laws have a moral sanction insofar as they accord with the natural law of reason. Thomas' careful dialectic does not allow us to appreciate the heroism and passion that inspired his work. Attacked by church officials on the one side who feared the new Aristotelian science, and by intellectuals on the other who claimed that reason could not support faith, he went his lonely way, trying to establish a bridge between revelation and philosophic truth.

3

SELECTIONS FROM AUGUSTINE'S WORK

In Praise of God

Great *art Thou, O Lord, and greatly to be praised; great is Thy power, and of thy wisdom there is no number.* And man desires to praise Thee. He is but a tiny part of all that Thou hast created. He bears about him his mortality, the evidence of his sinfulness, and the evidence that *Thou dost resist the proud:* yet this tiny part of all that Thou has created desires to praise Thee.

Thou dost so excite him that to praise Thee is his joy. For Thou hast made us for Thyself and our hearts are restless till they rest in Thee. Grant me, O Lord, to know which is the soul's first movement toward Thee—to implore Thy aid or to utter its praise of Thee; and whether it must know Thee before it can implore. For it would seem clear that no one can call upon Thee without knowing Thee, for if he did he might invoke another than Thee, knowing Thee not. Yet may it be that a man must implore Thee before he can know Thee? But, *how shall they call on Him in Whom they have not believed? or how shall they believe without a preacher?* And, *they shall praise the Lord that seek Him;* for those that seek shall find; and finding Him they will praise Him. Let me seek Thee, Lord, by praying Thy aid, and let me utter my prayer believing in Thee: for Thou hast been preached to us. My faith, Lord, cries to Thee, the faith that Thou hast given me, that Thou hast inbreathed in me, through the humanity of Thy Son and by the ministry of Thy Preacher.

But how can I call unto my God, my God and Lord? For in calling unto Him, I am calling Him to me: and what room is there in me for my God, the God who made heaven and earth? Is there anything in me, O God, that can contain You? All heaven and earth cannot contain You for You made them, and me in them. Yet, since nothing that is could exist without You, You must in some way be in all that is: [therefore also in me, since I am]. And if You are already in me, since otherwise I should not be, why do I cry to You to enter into me? Even

SOURCE: *The Confessions of Saint Augustine*, translated by F. J. Sheed (New York: Sheed and Ward, 1943), pp. 1–4. Reprinted with permission of the publishers.

if I were in Hell You would be there *for if I go down into hell, Thou art there also.* Thus, O God, I should be nothing, utterly nothing, unless You were in me—or rather unless I were in You, *of Whom and by Whom and in Whom are all things.* So it is, Lord; so it is. Where do I call You to come to, since I am in You? Or where else are You that You can come to me? Where shall I go, beyond the bounds of heaven and earth, that God may come to me, since He has said: *Heaven and earth do I fill.*

But if You fill heaven and earth, do they contain You? Or do You fill them, and yet have much over since they cannot contain You? Is there some other place into which that overplus of You pours that heaven and earth cannot hold? Surely You have no need of any place to contain You since You contain all things, and fill them indeed precisely by containing them. The vessels thus filled with You do not render You any support: for though they perished utterly, You would not be spilt out. And in pouring Yourself out upon us, You do not come down to us but rather elevate us to You: you are not scattered over us, but we are gathered into one by you. You fill all things: but with Your whole being? It is true that all things cannot wholly contain You: but does this mean that they contain part of You? and do they all contain the same part at the same time? or do different parts of creation contain different parts of You—greater parts or smaller according to their own magnitude? But are there in You parts greater and smaller? Or are you not in every place at once in the totality of Your being, while yet nothing contains You wholly?

What then is my God, what but the Lord God? *For Who is Lord but the Lord, or Who is God but our God?* O Thou, the greatest and the best, mightiest, almighty, most merciful and most just, utterly hidden and utterly present, most beautiful and most strong, abiding yet mysterious, suffering no change and changing all things: never new, never old, making all things new, *bringing age upon the proud and they knew it not;* ever in action, ever at rest, gathering all things to Thee and needing none; sustaining and fulfilling and protecting, creating and nourishing and making perfect; ever seeking though lacking nothing. Thou lovest without subjection to passion, Thou art jealous but not with fear; Thou canst know repentance but not sorrow, be angry yet unperturbed by anger. Thou canst change the works Thou hast made but Thy mind stands changeless. Thou dost find and receive back what Thou didst never lose; art never in need but dost rejoice in Thy gains, art not greedy but dost exact interest manifold. Men pay Thee more than is of obligation to win return from Thee, yet who has anything that is not already Thine? Thou owest nothing yet dost pay as if in debt to Thy creature, forgivest what is owed to Thee yet dost not lose thereby. And with all this, what have I said, my God and my Life and my sacred Delight? What can anyone say when he speaks of Thee? Yet woe to them that speak not of Thee at all, since those who say most are but dumb.

Who shall grant me to rest in Thee? By whose gift shalt Thou enter into my heart and fill it so compellingly that I shall turn no more to my sins but embrace Thee, my only good? What art Thou to me? Have mercy, that I may tell. What rather am I to Thee, that Thou shouldst demand my love and if I do not love Thee be angry and threaten such great woes? Surely not to love Thee is already a great woe. For Thy mercies' sake, O Lord my God, tell me what Thou art to me. *Say unto my soul, I am Thy salvation.* So speak that I may hear, Lord, my heart is listening; open it that it may hear Thee say to my soul *I am Thy salvation.* Hearing that word, let me come in haste to lay hold upon Thee. Hide not Thy face from me. Let me see Thy face even if I die, lest I die with longing to see it.

The house of my soul is too small to receive Thee: let it be enlarged by Thee. It is all in ruins: do Thou repair it. There are things in it that muŝt offend Thy gaze, I confess and know. But who shall cleanse it? or to what other besides Thee shall I cry out: *From my secret sins cleanse me, O Lord, and from those of others spare Thy servant? I believe and therefore do I speak.* Lord Thou knowest, *Have I not confessed against myself my transgressions against Thee, and Thou, my God, hast forgiven the iniquities of my heart? I contend not in judgment with Thee,* who art the truth; and I have no will to deceive myself, *lest my iniquity lie unto itself.* Therefore I contend not in judgment with Thee, for *if Thou, O Lord, wilt mark iniquities, who shall endure it?*

Conversion

Why this monstrousness? And what is the root of it? Let Your mercy enlighten me, that I may put the question: whether perhaps the answer lies in the mysterious punishment that has come upon men and some deeply hidden damage in the sons of Adam. Why this monstrousness? And what is the root of it? The mind gives the body an order, and is obeyed at once: the mind gives itself an order and is resisted. The mind commands the hand to move and there is such readiness that you can hardly distinguish the command from its execution. Yet the mind is mind, whereas the hand is body. The mind commands the mind to will, the mind is itself, but it does not do it. Why this monstrousness? And what is the root of it? The mind I say commands itself to will: it would not give the command unless it willed: yet it does not do what it commands. The trouble is that it does not totally will: therefore it does

SOURCE: *The Confessions of Saint Augustine,* translated by F. J. Sheed (New York: Sheed and Ward, 1943), pp. 136–142. Reprinted with permission of the publishers.

not totally command. It commands in so far as it wills; and it disobeys the command in so far as it does not will. The will is commanding itself to be a will—commanding itself, not some other. But it does not in its fullness give the command, so that what it commands is not done. For if the will were so in its fullness, it would not command itself to will, for it would already will. It is therefore no monstrousness, partly to will, partly not to will, but a sickness of the soul to be so weighted down by custom that it cannot wholly rise even with the support of truth. Thus there are two wills in us, because neither of them is entire: and what is lacking to the one is present in the other.

Let them perish from thy presence, O God, as perish vain talkers and seducers of the soul, who observing that there are two wills at issue in our coming to a decision proceed to assert [as the Manichees do] that there are two minds in us of different natures, one good, one evil. For they are evil themselves in holding such evil opinions; and they will become good only if they perceive truth and come to it as your Apostle says to them: *You were heretofore darkness but now light in the Lord.* But these men though they want to be light, want to be light in themselves and not in the Lord, imagining the nature of the soul to be the same as God. Thus they become not light but deeper darkness, since in their abominable arrogance they have gone further from You, *the true Light that enlightens every man that comes into this world.* Take heed what you say and blush for shame: *draw near unto Him and be enlightened, and your faces shall not be ashamed.* When I was deliberating about serving the Lord my God, as I had long meant to do, it was I who willed to do it, I who was unwilling. It was I. I did not wholly will, I was not wholly unwilling. Therefore I strove with myself and was distracted by myself. This distraction happened to me though I did not want it, and it showed me not the presence of some second mind, but the punishment of my own mind. Thus it was not I who caused it but *the sin that dwells in me,* the punishment of a sin freely committed by Adam, whose son I am.

For if there be as many contrary natures in man as there are wills in conflict with one another, then there are not two natures in us but several. Take the case of a man trying to make up his mind whether he would go to the Manichees meeting-house or to the theatre. The Manichees would say: "Here you have two natures, one good, bringing him to the meeting-house, the other evil, taking him away. How else could you have this wavering between two wills pulling against each other?" Now I say that both are bad, the will that would take him to the Manichees and the will that would take him to the theatre. But they hold that the will by which one comes to them is good. Very well! Supposing one of us is trying to decide and wavering between two wills in conflict, whether to go to the theatre or to *our* church, will not the Manichees be in some trouble about an answer? For either they must admit, which they do not want to, that a good will would take a man to our church as they think it is a good will that brings those who are receivers of their sacrament and belong to them to their church; or they must hold that there are two evil natures and two evil wills at conflict in one man, and what they are always saying will not be true—namely, that there is one good will and one evil will. Otherwise, they must be converted to the truth and not deny that when a man is taking a decision there is one soul drawn this way and that by diverse wills.

Therefore, when they perceive that there are two wills in conflict in man, they must not say that there are two opposing minds in conflict, one good, one bad, from two opposing substances and two opposing principles. For you, O God of truth, refute them and disprove them and convict them of error: as in the case where both wills are bad, when, for instance, a man is deliberating whether he shall kill another man by poison or by dagger; whether he should seize this or that part of another man's property, when he cannot seize both; whether he should spend his money on lust or hoard his money through avarice; whether he should go to the games or the theatre if they happen both to come on the same day. Let us add a third possibility to this last man, whether he should go and commit a theft from someone else's house, if the occasion should arise: and indeed a fourth, whether he should go and commit adultery, if the chance occurs at the same time. If all four things come together at the same point of time, and all are equally desired, yet all cannot be done, then they tear the mind by the conflicting pull of four wills—or even more, given the great mass of things which can be desired. Yet the Manichees do not hold such a multitude of different substances.

The same reasoning applies to wills that are good. For I ask them whether it is good to find delight in the reading of the Apostle, and good to find delight in the serenity of a Psalm, and good to discuss the Gospel. To each of these they answer that it is good: but, if all these things attract us at the same moment, are not different wills tugging at the heart of man while we deliberate which we should choose? Thus they are all good, yet they are all in conflict until one is chosen, and then the whole will is at rest and at one, whereas it had been divided into many. Or again, when eternity attracts the higher faculties and the pleasure of some temporal good holds the lower, it is one same soul that wills both, but not either with its whole will; and it is therefore torn both ways and deeply troubled while truth shows the one way as better but habit keeps it to the other.

. . . .

Thus I was sick at heart and in torment, accusing myself with a new intensity of bitterness, twisting and turning in my chain in the hope that it might be utterly broken, for what held me was so small a thing! But it still held me. And You stood in the secret places of my soul, O Lord, in the harshness of Your mercy redoubling the scourges of fear and shame lest I should give way again and that small slight tie which remained should not be broken but should grow again to full strength and bind me closer even than before. For I kept saying within myself: "Let it be now, let it be now," and by the mere words I had begun to move towards the resolution. I almost made it, yet I did not quite make it. But I did not fall back into my original state, but as it were stood near to get my breath. And I tried again and I was almost there, and now I could all but touch it and hold it: yet I was not quite there, I did not touch it or hold it. I still shrank from dying unto death and living unto life. The lower condition which had grown habitual was more powerful than the better condition which I had not tried. The nearer the point of time came in which I was to become different, the more it struck me with horror; but it did not force me utterly back nor turn me utterly away, but held me there between the two.

Those trifles of all trifles, and vanities of vanities, my one-time mistresses, held me back, plucking at my garment of flesh and murmuring softly: "Are you sending us away?" And "From this moment shall we not be with you, now or forever?" And "From this moment shall this or that not be allowed you, now or forever?" What were they suggesting to me in the phrase I have written "this or that," what were they suggesting to me, O my God? Do you in your mercy keep from the soul of Your servant the vileness and uncleanness they were suggesting. And now I began to hear them not half so loud; they no longer stood against me face to face, but were softly muttering behind my back and, as I tried to depart, plucking stealthily at me to make me look behind. Yet even that was enough, so hesitating was I, to keep me from snatching myself free, from shaking them off and leaping upwards on the way I was called: for the strong force of habit said to me: " Do you think you can live without them?"

But by this time its voice was growing fainter. In the direction towards which I had turned my face and was quivering in fear of going, I could see the austere beauty of Continence, serene and indeed joyous but not evilly, honourably soliciting me to come to her and not linger, stretching forth loving hands to receive and embrace me, hands full of multitudes of good examples. With her I saw such hosts of young men and maidens, a multitude of youth and of every age, grey widows and women grown old in virginity, and in them all Continence herself, not barren but the fruitful mother of children, her joys, by You, Lord, her Spouse. And she smiled upon me and her smile gave courage as if she were saying: "Can you not do what these men have done, what these women have done? Or could men or women have done such in themselves, and not in the Lord their God? The Lord their God gave me to them. Why do you stand upon yourself and so not stand at all? Cast yourself upon Him and be not afraid; He will not draw away and let you fall. Cast yourself without fear, He will receive you and heal you."

. . . .

Yet I was still ashamed, for I could still hear the murmuring of those vanities, and I still hung hesitant. And again it was as if she said: "Stop your ears against your unclean members, that they may be mortified. They tell you of delights, but not of such delights as the law of the Lord your God tells." This was the controversy raging in my heart, a controversy about myself against myself. And Alypius stayed by my side and waited in silence the issue of such agitation as he had never seen in me.

When my most searching scrutiny had drawn up all my vileness from the secret depths of my soul and heaped it in my heart's sight, a mighty storm arose in me, bringing a mighty rain of tears. That I might give way to my tears and lamentations, I rose from Alypius: for it struck me that solitude was more suited to the business of weeping. I went far enough from him to prevent his presence from being an embarrassment to me. So I felt, and he realized it. I suppose I had said something and the sound of my voice was heavy with tears. I arose, but he remained where we had been sitting, still in utter amazement. I flung myself down somehow under a certain fig tree and no longer tried to check my tears, which poured forth from my eyes in a flood, *an acceptable sacrifice to Thee*. And much I said not in these words but to this effect: "*And thou, O, Lord, how long? How long, Lord; wilt Thou be angry forever? Remember not our former iniquities.*" For I felt that I was still bound by them. And I continued my miserable complaining; "How long, how long shall I go on saying tomorrow and again tomorrow? Why not now, why not have an end to my uncleanness this very hour?"

Such things I said, weeping in the most bitter sorrow of my heart. And suddenly I heard a voice from some nearby house, a boy's voice or a girl's voice, I do not know: but it was a sort of sing-song repeated again and again, "Take and read, take and read." I ceased weeping and immediately began to search my mind most carefully as to whether children were accustomed to chant these words in any kind of game, and I could not remember that I had ever heard any such thing. Damming back the flood of my tears I arose, interpreting the incident as quite certainly a divine command to open my book of Scripture and read the passage at which I should open. For it was part of what I had been told about Antony, that from the Gospel which he happened to be reading he had felt that he was being admonished as though what he read was spoken directly to himself: *Go, sell what thou hast and give to the poor and thou shalt have treasure in heaven; and come follow me.* By this experience he had been in that instant converted to You. So I was moved to return to the place where Alypius was sitting, for I had put down the Apostle's book there when I arose. I snatched it up, opened it and in silence read the passage upon which my eyes first fell: *Not in rioting and drunkenness, not in chambering and impurities, not in contention and envy, but put ye on the Lord Jesus Christ and make not provision for the flesh in its concupiscences.* [*Romans* xiii, 13.] I had no wish to read further, and no need. For in that instant, with the very ending of the sentence, it was as though a light of utter confidence shone in all my heart, and all the darkness of uncertainty vanished away. Then leaving my finger in the place or marking it by some other sign, I closed the book and in complete calm told the whole thing to Alypius and he similarly told me what had been going on in himself, of which I knew nothing. He asked to see what I had read. I showed him, and he looked further than I had read. I had not known what followed. And this is what followed: "*Now him that is weak in faith, take unto you.*" He applied this to himself and told me so. And he was confirmed by this message, and with no troubled wavering gave himself to God's good-will and purpose—a purpose indeed most suited to his character, for in these matters he had been immeasurably better than I.

Then we went in to my mother and told her, to her great joy. We related how it had come about: she was filled with triumphant exultation, and praised You who are mighty beyond what we ask or conceive: for she saw that You had given her more than with all her pitiful weeping she had ever asked. For You converted me to Yourself so that I no longer sought a wife nor any of this world's promises, but stood upon that same rule of faith in which You had shown me to her so many years before. Thus You changed her mourning into joy, a joy far richer than she had thought to wish, a joy much dearer and purer than she had thought to find in grandchildren of my flesh.

Man's Love for God

God must first be known by an unerring faith, that He may be loved.

But it is by love that we must stand firm to this and cleave to this, in order that we may enjoy the presence of that by which we are, and in the absence of which we could not be at all. For as "we walk as yet by faith, and not by sight," we certainly do not yet see God, as the

SOURCE: "On the Trinity," translated by A. W. Hadden and revised by W. G. J. Shedd, in *Nicene and Post-Nicene Fathers*, edited by Philip Schaff (Buffalo, N. Y.: The Christian Literature Co., 1887), *3*, pp. 118–124.

same [apostle] saith, "face to face:" whom however we shall never see, unless now already we love. But who loves what he does not know? For it is possible something may be known and not loved: but I ask whether it is possible that what is not known can be loved; since if it cannot, then no one loves God before he knows Him. And what is it to know God except to behold Him and steadfastly perceive Him with the mind? For He is not a body to be searched out by carnal eyes. But before also that we have power to behold and to perceive God, as He can be beheld and perceived, which is permitted to the pure in heart; for "blessed are the pure in heart, for they shall see God;" except He is loved by faith, it will not be possible for the heart to be cleansed, in order that it may be apt and meet to see Him. For where are there those three, in order to build up which in the mind the whole apparatus of the divine Scriptures has been raised up, namely Faith, Hope, and Charity, except in a mind believing what it does not yet see, and hoping and loving what it believes? Even He therefore who is not known, but yet is believed, can be loved. But indisputably we must take care, lest the mind believing that which it does not see, feign to itself something which is not, and hope for and love that which is false. For in that case, it will not be charity out of a pure heart, and of a good conscience, and of faith unfeigned, which is the end of the commandment, as the same apostle says.

But it must needs be, that, when by reading or hearing of them we believe in any corporeal things which we have not seen, the mind frames for itself something under bodily features and forms, just as it may occur to our thoughts; which either is not true, or even if it be true, which can most rarely happen, yet this is of no benefit to us to believe in by faith, but it is useful for some other purpose, which is intimated by means of it. For who is there that reads or hears what the Apostle Paul has written, or what has been written of him, that does not imagine to himself the countenance both of the apostle himself, and of all those whose names are there mentioned? And whereas, among such a multitude of men to whom these books are known, each imagines in a different way those bodily features and forms, it is assuredly uncertain which it is that imagines them more nearly and more like the reality. Nor, indeed, is our faith busied therein with the bodily countenance of those men; but only that by the grace of God they so lived and so acted as that Scripture witnesses: this it is which it is both useful to believe, and which must not be despaired of and must be sought. For even the countenance of our Lord Himself in the flesh is variously fancied by the diversity of countless imaginations, which yet was one, whatever it was. Nor in our faith which we have of our Lord Jesus Christ, is that wholesome which the mind imagines for itself, perhaps far other than the reality, but that which we think of man according to his kind: for we have a notion of human nature implanted in us, as it were by rule, according to which we know forthwith, that whatever such thing we see is a man or the form of a man. . . .

Of true love, by which we arrive at the knowledge of the Trinity. God is to be sought, not outwardly, by seeking to do wonderful things with the angels, but inwardly, by imitating the piety of good angels.

No other thing, then, is chiefly to be regarded in this inquiry, which we make concerning the Trinity and concerning knowing God, except what is true love, nay, rather what is love. For that is to be called love which is true, otherwise it is desire; and so those who desire are said improperly to love, just as they who love are said improperly to desire. But this is true love, that cleaving to the truth we may live righteously, and so may despise all mortal things in comparison with the love of men, whereby we wish them to live righteously. For so we should be prepared also to die profitably for our brethren, as our Lord Jesus Christ taught us by His example. For as there are two commandments on which hang all the Law and the prophets, love of God and love of our neighbor; not without cause the Scripture mostly puts one for both: whether it be of God only, as is that text, "For we know that all things work together for good to them that love God;" and again, "But if any man love God, the same is known of Him;" and that, "Because the love of God is shed abroad in our hearts by the Holy Ghost which is given unto us;" and many other passages; because he who loves God must both needs do what God has commanded, and loves Him just in such proportion as he does so; therefore he must needs also love his neighbor, because God has commanded it: or whether it be that Scripture only mentions the love of our neighbor, as in that text, "Bear ye one another's burdens, and so fulfill the law of Christ;" and again, "For all the law is fulfilled in one word, even in this, Thou shalt love thy neighbor as thyself;" and in the Gospel, "All things whatsoever ye would that men should do to you, do ye even so to them; for this is the Law and the prophets." And many other passages occur in the sacred writings, in which only the love of our neighbor seems to be commanded for perfection, while the love of God is passed over in silence; whereas the Law and the prophets hang on both precepts. But this, too, is because he who loves his neighbor must needs also love above all else love itself. But "God is love; and he that dwelleth in love, dwelleth in God." Therefore he must needs above all else love God.

Wherefore they who seek God through those Powers which rule over the world, or parts of the world, are removed and cast away far from Him; not by intervals of space, but by difference of affections: for they endeavor to find a path outwardly, and forsake their own inward things, within which is God. Therefore, even although they may either have heard some holy heavenly Power, or in some way or another may have thought of it, yet they rather covet its deeds at which human weakness marvels, but do not imitate the piety by which divine rest is acquired. For they prefer, through pride, to be able to do that which an angel does, more than, through devotion, to be that which an angel is. For no holy being rejoices in his own power, but in His from whom he has the power which he fitly can have; and he knows it to be more a mark of power to be united to the Omnipotent by a pious will, than to be able, by his own power and will, to do what they may tremble at who are not able to do such things. Therefore the Lord Jesus Christ Himself, in doing such things, in order that He might teach better things to those who marvelled at them, and might turn those who were intent and in doubt about unusual temporal things to eternal and inner things, says, "Come unto me, all ye that labor and are heavy laden, and I will give you rest. Take my yoke upon you." And He does not say, Learn of me, because I raise those who have been dead four days; but He says, "Learn of me; for I am meek and lowly in heart." For humility, which is most solid, is more powerful and safer than pride, that is most inflated. And so He goes on to say, "And ye shall find rest unto your souls," for "Love is not puffed up;" and "God is Love;" and "such as be faithful in love shall rest in Him," called back from the din which is without to silent joys. Behold, "God is Love:" why do we go forth and run to the heights of the heavens and the lowest parts of the earth, seeking Him who is within us, if we wish to be with Him?

That he who loves his brother, loves God; because he loves love itself, which is of God, and is God.

Let no one say, I do not know what I love. Let him love his brother, and he will love the same love. For he knows the love with which he loves, more than the brother whom he loves. So now he can know God more than he knows his brother: clearly known more, because more present; known more, because more within him; known more, because more certain. Embrace the love of God, and by love embrace God. That is love itself, which associates together all good angels and all the servants of God by the bond of sanctity, and joins together us and them mutually with ourselves, and joins us subordinately to Himself. In proportion, therefore, as we are healed from the swelling of pride, in such proportion are we more filled with love; and with what is he full, who is full of love, except with God? Well, but you will say, I see love, and, as far as I am able, I gaze upon it with my mind, and I believe the Scripture, saying, that "God is love; and he that dwelleth in love, dwelleth in God;" but when I see love, I do not see in it the Trinity. Nay, but thou dost see the Trinity if thou seest love. But if I can I will put you in mind, that thou mayest see that thou seest it; only let itself be present, that we may be moved by love to something good. Since, when we love love, we love one who loves something, and that on account of this very thing, that he does love something; therefore what does love love, that love itself also may be loved? For that is not love which loves nothing. But if it loves itself it must love something, that it may love itself as love. For as a word indicates something, and indicates also itself, but does not indicate itself to be a word, unless it indicates that it does indicate something; so love also loves indeed itself, but except it love itself as loving something, it loves itself not as love. What therefore does love love, except that which we love with love? But this, to begin from that which is nearest to us, is our brother. And listen how greatly the Apostle John commends brotherly love: "He that loveth his brother abideth in the light, and there is none occasion of stumbling in him." It is manifest that he placed the perfection of righteousness in the love of our brother; for he certainly is perfect in whom "there is no occasion of stumbling." And yet he seems to have passed by the love of God in silence; which he never would have done, unless because he intends God to be understood in brotherly love itself. For in this same epistle, a little further on, he says most plainly thus: "Beloved, let us love one another: for love is of God; and every one that loveth is born of God, and knoweth God. He that loveth not, knoweth not God; for God is love." And this passage declares sufficiently and plainly, that this same brotherly love itself (for that is brotherly love by which we love each other) is set forth by so great authority, not only to be from God, but also to be God. When, therefore, we love our brother from love, we love our brother from God; neither can it be that we do not love above all else that same love by which we love our brother: whence it may be gathered that these two commandments cannot exist unless interchangeably. For since "God is love," he who loves love certainly loves God; but he must needs love love, who loves his brother. And so a little after he says, "For he that loveth not his brother whom he hath seen, how can he love God whom he hath not seen"? because the reason that he does not see God is, that he does not love his brother. For he who does not love his brother, abideth not in love; and he who abideth not in love, abideth not in God, because God is love. Further, he who abideth not in God, abideth not in light; for "God is light, and in Him is no darkness at all." He therefore who abideth not in light, what wonder is it if he does not see light, that is, does not see God, because he is in darkness? But he sees his brother with human sight, with which God cannot be seen. But if he loved with spiritual love him whom he sees with human sight, he would see God, who is love itself, with the inner sight by which He can be seen. Therefore he who does not love his brother whom he sees, how can he love God, whom on that account he does not see, because God is love, which he has not who does not love his brother? Neither let that further question disturb us, how much of love we ought to spend upon our brother, and how much upon God: incomparably more upon God than upon ourselves, but upon our brother as much as upon ourselves; and we love ourselves so much the more, the more we love God. Therefore we love God and our neighbor from one and the same love; but we love God for the sake of God, and ourselves and our neighbors for the sake of God.

Our love of the righteous is kindled from love itself of the unchangeable form of righteousness.

For why is it, pray, that we burn when we hear and read, "Behold, now is the accepted time; behold, now is the day of salvation: giving no offense in anything, that the ministry be not blamed: but in all things approving ourselves as the ministers of God, in much patience, in afflictions, in necessities, in distresses, in stripes, in imprisonments, in tumults, in labors, in watchings, in fastings; by pureness, by knowledge, by long-suffering, by kindness, by the Holy Ghost, by love unfeigned, by the word of truth, by the power of God, by the armor of righteousness on the right hand and on the left, by honor and dishonor, by evil report and good report: as deceivers, and yet true; as unknown, and yet well known; as dying, and, behold, we live; as chastened, and not killed; as sorrowful, yet always rejoicing; as poor, yet making many rich; as having nothing, and yet possessing all things?" Why is it that we are inflamed with love of the Apostle Paul, when we read these things, unless that we believe him so to have lived? But we do not believe that the ministers of God ought so to live because we have heard it from any one, but because we behold it inwardly within ourselves, or rather above ourselves, in the truth itself. Him, therefore, whom we believe to have so lived, we love for that which we see. And except we loved above all else that form which we discern as always steadfast and unchangeable, we should not for that reason love him, because we hold fast in our belief that his life, when he was living in the flesh, was adapted to, and in harmony with, this form. But somehow we are stirred up the more to the love of this form itself, through the belief by which we believe some one to have so lived; and to the hope by which we no more at all despair, that we, too, are able so to live; we who are men, from this fact itself, that some men have so lived, so that we both desire this more ardently, and pray for it more confidently. So both the love of that form, according to which they are believed to have lived, makes the life of these men themselves to be loved by us; and their life thus believed stirs up a more burning love towards that same form; so that the more ardently we love God, the more certainly and the more calmly do we see Him, because we behold in God the unchangeable form of righteousness, according to which we judge that man ought to live. Therefore faith avails to the knowledge and to the love of God, not as though of one altogether unknown, or altogether not loved; but so that thereby He may be known more clearly, and loved more steadfastly.

There are three things in love, as it were a trace of the Trinity.

But what is love or charity, which divine Scripture so greatly praises and proclaims, except the love of good? But love is *of* some one that loves, and *with* love something *is* loved. Behold, then, there are three things: he that loves, and that which is loved, and love. What, then, is love, except a certain life which couples or seeks to couple together some two things, namely, him that loves, and that which is loved? And this is so even in outward and carnal loves. But that we may drink in something more pure and clear, let us tread down the flesh and ascend to the mind. What does the mind love in a friend except the mind? There, then, also are three things: he that loves, and that which is loved, and love. It remains to ascend also from hence, and to seek those things which are above, as far as is given to man. But here for a little while let our purpose rest, not that it may think itself to have found already what it seeks; but just as usually the place has first to be found where anything is to be sought, while the thing itself is not yet found, but we have only found already where to look for it; so let it suffice to have said thus much, that we may have, as it were, the hinge of some starting-point, whence to weave the rest of our discourse.

Interpretation of Scriptures

The fulfilment and end of Scripture is the love of God and our neighbour.

Of all, then, that has been said since we entered upon the discussion about things, this is the sum: that we should clearly understand that the fulfilment and the end of the Law, and of all Holy Scripture, is the love of an object which is to be enjoyed, and the love of an object which can enjoy that other in fellowship with ourselves. For there is no need of a command that each man should love himself. The whole temporal dispensation for our salvation, therefore, was framed by the providence of God that we might know this truth and be able to act upon it; and we ought to use that dispensation, not with such love and delight as if it were a good to rest in, but with a transient feeling rather, such as we have towards the road, or carriages, or other things that

Source: "On Christian Doctrine" in *The Work of Aurelius Augustine,* edited by Marcus Dods (Edinburgh: T. & T. Clark, 1875–1895), *9,* pp. 30–33, 51–55, 75–79.

are merely means. Perhaps some other comparison can be found that will more suitably express the idea that we are to love the things by which we are borne only for the sake of that towards which we are borne.

**That interpretation of Scripture which builds us up in love
is not perniciously deceptive nor mendacious, even though
it be faulty. The interpreter, however, should be corrected.**

Whoever, then, thinks that he understands the Holy Scriptures, or any part of them, but puts such an interpretation upon them as does not tend to build up this twofold love of God and our neighbour, does not yet understand them as he ought. If, on the other hand, a man draws a meaning from them that may be used for the building up of love, even though he does not happen upon the precise meaning which the author whom he reads intended to express in that place, his error is not pernicious, and he is wholly clear from the charge of deception. For there is involved in deception the intention to say what is false; and we find plenty of people who intend to deceive, but nobody who wishes to be deceived. Since, then, the man who knows practises deceit, and the ignorant man is practised upon, it is quite clear that in any particular case the man who is deceived is a better man than he who deceives, seeing that it is better to suffer than to commit injustice. Now every man who lies commits an injustice; and if any man thinks that a lie is ever useful, he must think that injustice is sometimes useful. For no liar keeps faith in the matter about which he lies. He wishes, of course, that the man to whom he lies should place confidence in him; and yet he betrays his confidence by lying to him. Now every man who breaks faith is unjust. Either, then, injustice is sometimes useful (which is impossible), or a lie is never useful.

Whoever takes another meaning out of Scripture than the writer intended, goes astray, but not through any falsehood in Scripture. Nevertheless, as I was going to say, if his mistaken interpretation tends to build up love, which is the end of the commandment, he goes astray in much the same way as a man who by mistake quits the high road, but yet reaches through the fields the same place to which the road leads. He is to be corrected, however, and to be shown how much better it is not to quit the straight road, lest, if he get into a habit of going astray, he may sometimes take cross roads, or even go in the wrong direction altogether.

Dangers of mistaken interpretation.

For if he takes up rashly a meaning which the author whom he is reading did not intend, he often falls in with other statements which he cannot harmonize with this meaning. And if he admits that these

statements are true and certain, then it follows that the meaning he
had put upon the former passage cannot be the true one: and so it
comes to pass, one can hardly tell how, that, out of love for his own
opinion, he begins to feel more angry with Scripture than he is with
himself. And if he should once permit that evil to creep in, it will
utterly destroy him. "For we walk by faith, not by sight." Now faith
will totter if the authority of Scripture begin to shake. And then, if
faith totter, love itself will grow cold. For if a man has fallen from faith,
he must necessarily also fall from love; for he cannot love what he
docs not believe to exist. But if he both believes and loves, then
through good works, and through diligent attention to the precepts of
morality, he comes to hope also that he shall attain the object of his
love. And so these are the three things to which all knowledge and all
prophecy are subservient: faith, hope, love.

Love never faileth.

But sight shall displace faith; and hope shall be swallowed up in that
perfect bliss to which we shall come: love, on the other hand, shall wax
greater when these others fail. For if we love by faith that which as
yet we see not, how much more shall we love it when we begin to see!
And if we love by hope that which as yet we have not reached, how
much more shall we love it when we reach it! For there is this great
difference between things temporal and things eternal, that a temporal
object is valued more before we possess it, and begins to prove worthless
the moment we attain it, because it does not satisfy the soul, which
has its only true and sure resting-place in eternity: an eternal object,
on the other hand, is loved with greater ardour when it is in possession
than while it is still an object of desire, for no one in his longing for it
can set a higher value on it than really belongs to it, so as to think it
comparatively worthless when he finds it of less value than he thought;
on the contrary, however high the value any man may set upon it
when he is on his way to possess it, he will find it, when it comes into
his possession, of higher value still.

He who is mature in faith, hope, and love, needs
Scripture no longer.

And thus a man who is resting upon faith, hope, and love, and who
keeps a firm hold upon these, does not need the Scriptures except for
the purpose of instructing others. Accordingly, many live without
copies of the Scriptures, even in solitude, on the strength of these
three graces. So that in their case, I think, the saying is already
fulfilled: "Whether there be prophecies, they shall fail; whether there
be tongues, they shall cease; whether there be knowledge, it shall
vanish away." Yet by means of these instruments (as they may be

called), so great an edifice of faith and love has been built up in them, that, holding to what is perfect, they do not seek for what is only in part perfect—of course, I mean, so far as is possible in this life; for, in comparison with the future life, the life of no just and holy man is perfect here. Therefore the apostle says: "Now abideth faith, hope, charity, these three; but the greatest of these is charity:" because, when a man shall have reached the eternal world, while the other two graces will fail, love will remain greater and more assured.

What manner of reader Scripture demands.

And, therefore, if a man fully understands that "the end of the commandment is charity, out of a pure heart, and of a good conscience, and of faith unfeigned," and is bent upon making all his understanding of Scripture to bear upon these three graces, he may come to the interpretation of these books with an easy mind. For while the apostle says "love", he adds "out of a pure heart," to provide against anything being loved but that which is worthy of love. And he joins with this "a good conscience," in reference to hope; for, if a man has the burthen of a bad conscience, he despairs of ever reaching that which he believes in and loves. And in the third place he says: "and of faith unfeigned." For if our faith is free from all hypocrisy, then we both abstain from loving what is unworthy of our love, and by living uprightly we are able to indulge the hope that our hope shall not be in vain.

. . . .

The knowledge both of language and things is helpful for the understanding of figurative expressions.

In the case of figurative signs, again, if ignorance of any of them should chance to bring the reader to a stand-still, their meaning is to be traced partly by the knowledge of languages, partly by the knowledge of things. The pool of Siloam, for example, where the man whose eyes our Lord had anointed with clay made out of spittle was commanded to wash, has a figurative significance, and undoubtedly conveys a secret sense; but yet if the evangelist had not interpreted that name, a meaning so important would lie unnoticed. And we cannot doubt that, in the same way, many Hebrew names which have not been interpreted by the writers of those books, would, if any one could interpret them, be of great value and service in solving the enigmas of Scripture. And a number of men skilled in that language have conferred no small benefit on posterity by explaining all these words without reference to their place in Scripture, and telling us what Adam means, what Eve, what Abraham, what Moses, and also the names of places, what Jerusalem signifies, or Sion, or Sinai, or Lebanon, or Jordan, and whatever other names in that language we are not acquainted with. And when these names have been investigated and explained, many figurative expressions in Scripture become clear.

Ignorance of things, too, renders figurative expressions obscure, as when we do not know the nature of the animals, or minerals, or plants, which are frequently referred to in Scripture by way of comparison. The fact so well known about the serpent, for example, that to protect its head it will present its whole body to its assailants—how much light it throws upon the meaning of our Lord's command, that we should be wise as serpents; that is to say, that for the sake of our head, which is Christ, we should willingly offer our body to the persecutors, lest the Christian faith should, as it were, be destroyed in us, if to save the body we deny our God! Or again, the statement that the serpent gets rid of its old skin by squeezing itself through a narrow hole, and thus acquires new strength—how appropriately it fits in with the direction to imitate the wisdom of the serpent, and to put off the old man, as the apostle says, that we may put on the new; and to put it off, too, by coming through a narrow place, according to the saying of our Lord, "Enter ye in at the strait gate!" As, then, knowledge of the nature of the serpent throws light upon many metaphors which Scripture is accustomed to draw from that animal, so ignorance of other animals, which are no less frequently mentioned by way of comparison, is a very great drawback to the reader. And so in regard to minerals and plants: knowledge of the carbuncle, for instance, which shines in the dark, throws light upon many of the dark places in books too, where it is used metaphorically; and ignorance of the beryl or the adamant often shuts the doors of knowledge. And the only reason why we find it easy to understand that perpetual peace is indicated by the olive branch which the dove brought with it when it returned to the ark, is that we know both that the smooth touch of olive oil is not easily spoiled by a fluid of another kind, and that the tree itself is an evergreen. Many, again, by reason of their ignorance of hyssop, not knowing the virtue it has in cleansing the lungs, nor the power it is said to have of piercing rocks with its roots, although it is a small and insignificant plant, cannot make out why it is said, "Purge me with hyssop, and I shall be clean."

Ignorance of numbers, too, prevents us from understanding things that are set down in Scripture in a figurative and mystical way. A candid mind, if I may so speak, cannot but be anxious, for example, to ascertain what is meant by the fact that Moses and Elijah, and our Lord Himself, all fasted for forty days. And except by knowledge of and reflection upon the number, the difficulty of explaining the figure involved in this action cannot be got over. For the number contains ten four times, indicating the knowledge of all things, and that knowledge interwoven with time. For both the diurnal and the annual revolutions are accomplished in periods numbering four each; the diurnal in the hours of the morning, the noontide, the evening, and the night; the annual in the spring, summer, autumn, and winter months. Now while we live in time, we must abstain and fast from all joy in time, for the sake of that eternity in which we wish to live; although by the passage of time we are taught this very lesson of despising time and seeking eternity. Further, the number ten signifies the knowledge of the Creator and the creature, for there is a trinity in the Creator; and the number seven indicates the creature, because of the life and the body. For the life consists of three parts, whence also God is to be loved with the whole heart, the whole soul, and the whole mind; and it is very clear that in the body there are four elements of which it is made up. In this number ten, therefore, when it is placed before us in connection with time, that is, when it is taken four times, we are admonished to live unstained by, and not partaking of, any delight in time, that is, to fast for forty days. Of this we are admonished by the law personified in Moses, by prophecy personified in Elijah, and by our Lord Himself, who, as if receiving the witness both of the law and the prophets, appeared on the mount between the other two, while His three disciples looked on in amazement. Next, we have to inquire in the same way, how out of the number forty springs the number fifty, which in our religion has no ordinary sacredness attached to it on account of the Pentecost, and how this number taken thrice on account of the three divisions of time, before the law, under the law, and under grace, or perhaps on account of the name of the Father, Son, and Holy Spirit, and the Trinity itself being added over and above, has reference to the mystery of the most Holy Church, and reaches to the number of the one hundred and fifty-three fishes which were taken after the resurrection of our Lord, when the nets were cast out on the right-hand side of the boat. And in the same way, many other numbers and combinations of numbers are used in the sacred writings, to convey instruction under a figurative guise, and ignorance of numbers often shuts out the reader from this instruction.

Not a few things, too, are closed against us and obscured by ignorance of music. One man, for example, has not unskilfully explained some metaphors from the difference between the psaltery and the harp. And it is a question which it is not out of place for learned men to discuss, whether there is any musical law that compels the psaltery of ten chords to have just so many strings; or whether, if there be no such law, the number itself is not on that very account the more to be considered as of sacred significance, either with reference to the ten commandments of the law (and if again any question is raised about that number, we can only refer it to the Creator and the creature), or with reference to the number ten itself as interpreted above. And the number of years the temple was in building, which is mentioned in the gospel—viz. forty-six—has a certain undefinable musical sound, and when referred to the structure of our Lord's body, in relation to which the temple was mentioned, compels many heretics to confess that our Lord put on, not a false, but a true and human body. And in several places in the Holy Scriptures we find both numbers and music mentioned with honour.

Origin of the legend of the nine Muses.

For we must not listen to the falsities of heathen superstition, which represent the nine Muses as daughters of Jupiter and Mercury. Varro refutes these, and I doubt whether any one can be found among them more curious or more learned in such matters. He says that a certain state (I don't recollect the name) ordered from each of three artists a set of statues of the Muses, to be placed as an offering in the temple of Apollo, intending that whichever of the artists produced the most beautiful statues, they should select and purchase from him. It so happened that these artists executed their works with equal beauty, that all nine pleased the state, and that all were bought to be dedicated in the temple of Apollo; and he says that afterwards Hesiod the poet gave names to them all. It was not Jupiter, therefore, that begat the nine Muses, but three artists created three each. And the state had originally given the order for three, not because it had seen them in visions, nor because they had presented themselves in that number to the eyes of any of the citizens, but because it was obvious to remark that all sound, which is the material of song, is by nature of three kinds. For it is either produced by the voice, as in the case of those who sing with the mouth without an instrument; or by blowing, as in the case of trumpets and flutes; or by striking, as in the case of harps and drums, and all other instruments that give their sound when struck.

No help is to be despised, even though it come from a profane source.

But whether the fact is as Varro has related, or is not so, still we ought not to give up music because of the superstition of the heathen, if we can derive anything from it that is of use for the understanding of Holy Scripture; nor does it follow that we must busy ourselves with their theatrical trumpery because we enter upon an investigation about harps and other instruments, that may help us to lay hold upon spiritual things. For we ought not to refuse to learn letters because they say that Mercury discovered them; nor because they have dedicated temples to Justice and Virtue, and prefer to worship in the form of stones things that ought to have their place in the heart, ought we on that account to forsake justice and virtue. Nay, but let every good and true Christian understand that wherever truth may be found, it belongs to his Master; and while he recognises and acknowledges the truth, even in their religious literature, let him reject the figments of superstition, and let him grieve over and avoid men who, "when they knew God, glorified him not as God, neither were thankful; but became vain in their imaginations, and their foolish heart was darkened. Professing themselves to be wise, they became fools, and changed the glory of the uncorruptible God into an image made like to corruptible man, and to birds, and four-footed beasts, and creeping things."

. . . .

Whatever has been rightly said by the heathen, we must appropriate to our uses.

Moreover, if those who are called philosophers, and especially the Platonists, have said aught that is true and in harmony with our faith, we are not only not to shrink from it, but to claim it for our own use from those who have unlawful possession of it. For, as the Egyptians had not only the idols and heavy burdens which the people of Israel hated and fled from, but also vessels and ornaments of gold and silver, and garments, which the same people when going out of Egypt appropriated to themselves, designing them for a better use, not doing this on their own authority, but by the command of God, the Egyptians themselves, in their ignorance, providing them with things which they themselves were not making a good use of; in the same way all branches of heathen learning have not only false and superstitious fancies and heavy burdens of unnecessary toil, which every one of us, when going out under the leadership of Christ from the fellowship of the heathen, ought to abhor and avoid; but they contain also liberal instruction which is better adapted to the use of the truth, and some most excellent precepts of morality; and some truths in regard even to the worship of the One God are found among them. Now these are, so to speak, their gold and silver, which they did not create themselves, but dug out of the mines of God's providence which are everywhere scattered abroad, and are perversely and unlawfully prostituting to the worship of devils. These, therefore, the Christian, when he separates himself in spirit from the miserable fellowship of these men, ought to take away from them, and to devote to their proper use in preaching the gospel. Their garments, also,—that is, human institutions such as are adapted to that intercourse with men which is indispensable in this life—we must take and turn to a Christian use.

And what else have many good and faithful men among our brethren done? Do we not see with what a quantity of gold and silver and garments Cyprian, that most persuasive teacher and most blessed martyr, was loaded when he came out of Egypt? How much Lactantius brought with him! And Victorinus, and Optatus, and Hilary, not to speak of living men! How much Greeks out of number have borrowed! And prior to all these, that most faithful servant of God, Moses, had done the same thing; for of him it is written that he was learned in all the wisdom of the Egyptians. And to none of all these would heathen superstition (especially in those times when, kicking against the yoke of Christ, it was persecuting the Christians) have ever furnished branches of knowledge it held useful, if it had suspected they were about to turn them to the use of worshipping the One God, and thereby overturning the vain worship of idols. But they gave their gold and their silver and their garments to the people of God as they were going out of Egypt, not knowing how the things they gave would be turned to the service of Christ. For what was done at the time of the exodus was no doubt a type prefiguring what happens now. And this I say without prejudice to any other interpretation that may be as good, or better.

What kind of spirit is required for the study of Holy Scripture.

But when the student of the Holy Scriptures, prepared in the way I have indicated, shall enter upon his investigations, let him constantly meditate upon that saying of the apostle's, "Knowledge puffeth up, but charity edifieth." For so he will feel that, whatever may be the riches he brings with him out of Egypt, yet unless he has kept the passover, he cannot be safe. Now Christ is our passover sacrificed for us, and there is nothing the sacrifice of Christ more clearly teaches us than the call which He himself addresses to those whom He sees toiling in Egypt under Pharaoh: "Come unto me, all ye that labour and are heavy laden, and I will give you rest. Take my yoke upon you, and learn of me; for I am meek and lowly in heart: and ye shall find rest unto your souls. For my yoke is easy, and my burden is light." To whom is it light but to the meek and lowly in heart, whom knowledge doth not puff up, but charity edifieth? Let them remember, then, that those who celebrated the passover at that time in type and shadow, when they were ordered to mark their door-posts with the blood of the lamb, used hyssop to mark them with. Now this is a meek and lowly herb, and yet nothing is stronger and more penetrating than its roots; that being rooted and grounded in love, we may be able to comprehend with all saints what is the breadth, and length, and depth, and height,—that is, to comprehend the cross of our Lord, the breadth of which is indicated by the transverse wood on which the hands are stretched, its length by the part from the ground up to the cross-bar on which the whole body from the head downwards is fixed, its height by the part from the cross-bar to the top on which the head lies, and its depth by the part which is hidden, being fixed in the earth. And by this sign of the cross all Christian action is symbolized, viz. to do good works in Christ, to cling with constancy to Him, to hope for heaven, and not to desecrate the sacraments. And purified by this Christian action, we shall be able to know even "the love of Christ which passeth knowledge," who is equal to the Father, by whom all things were made, "that we may be filled with all the fulness of God." There is besides in hyssop a purgative virtue, that the breast may not be swollen with that knowledge which puffeth up, nor boast vainly of the riches brought out from Egypt. "Purge me with hyssop," the psalmist says, "and I shall be clean; wash me, and I shall be whiter than snow. Make me to hear joy and gladness." Then he immediately adds, to show that it is purifying from pride that is indicated by hyssop, "that the bones which Thou hast broken may rejoice."

Sacred Scripture compared with profane authors.

But just as poor as the store of gold and silver and garments which the people of Israel brought with them out of Egypt was in comparison with the riches which they afterwards attained at Jerusalem, and which reached their height in the reign of King Solomon, so poor is all the useful knowledge which is gathered from the books of the heathen when compared with the knowledge of Holy Scripture. For whatever man may have learnt from other sources, if it is hurtful, it is there condemned; if it is useful, it is therein contained. And while every man may find there all that he has learnt of useful elsewhere, he will find there in much greater abundance things that are to be found nowhere else, but can be learnt only in the wonderful sublimity and wonderful simplicity of the Scriptures.

When, then, the reader is possessed of the instruction here pointed out, so that unknown signs have ceased to be a hindrance to him; when he is meek and lowly of heart, subject to the easy yoke of Christ, and loaded with His light burden, rooted and grounded and built up in faith, so that knowledge cannot puff him up, let him then approach the consideration and discussion of ambiguous signs in Scripture. And about these I shall now, in a third book, endeavour to say what the Lord shall be pleased to vouchsafe.

The Nature of Sin and Evil

Your law, O Lord, punishes theft; and this law is so written in the hearts of men that not even the breaking of it blots it out: for no thief

---

SOURCE: *The Confessions of Saint Augustine*, translated by F. J. Sheed (New York: Sheed and Ward, 1943), pp. 24–29, 101–107, 113–117. Reprinted with permission of the publishers.

bears calmly being stolen from—not even if he is rich and the other
steals through want. Yet I chose to steal, and not because want
drove me to it—unless a want of justice and contempt for it and an
excess for iniquity. For I stole things which I already had in plenty
and of better quality. Nor had I any desire to enjoy the things I stole,
but only the stealing of them and the sin. There was a pear tree near
our vineyard, heavy with fruit, but fruit that was not particularly
tempting either to look at or to taste. A group of young blackguards,
and I among them, went out to knock down the pears and carry them
off late one night, for it was our bad habit to carry on our games in
the streets till very late. We carried off an immense load of pears,
not to eat—for we barely tasted them before throwing them to the
hogs. Our only pleasure in doing it was that it was forbidden. Such
was my heart, O God, such was my heart: yet in the depth of the abyss
You had pity on it. Let that heart now tell You what it sought when
I was thus evil for no object, having no cause for wrong-doing save
my wrongness. The malice of the act was base and I loved it—that
is to say I loved my own undoing, I loved the evil in me—not the
thing for which I did the evil, simply the evil: my soul was depraved,
and hurled itself down from security in You into utter destruction,
seeking no profit from wickedness but only to be wicked.

There is an appeal to the eye in beautiful things, in gold and silver
and all such; the sense of touch has its own powerful pleasures; and
the other senses find qualities in things suited to them. Worldly success
has its glory, and the power to command and to overcome: and from
this springs the thirst for revenge. But in our quest of all these things,
we must not depart from You, Lord, or deviate from Your Law. This
life we live here below has its own attractiveness, grounded in the
measure of beauty it has and its harmony with the beauty of all lesser
things. The bond of human friendship is admirable, holding many
souls as one. Yet in the enjoyment of all such things we commit sin
if through immoderate inclination to them—for though they are
good, they are of the lowest order of good—things higher and better
are forgotten, even You, O Lord our God, and Your Truth and
Your Law. These lower things have their delights but not such as my
God has, for He made them all: *and in Him doth the righteous delight, and
He is the joy of the upright of heart.*

Now when we ask why this or that particular evil act was done, it is
normal to assume that it could not have been done save through the
desire of gaining or the fear of losing some one of these lower goods.
For they have their own charm and their own beauty, though compared
with the higher values of heaven they are poor and mean enough.
Such a man has committed a murder. Why? He wanted the other
man's wife or his property; or he had chosen robbery as a means of

livelihood; or he feared to lose this or that through his victim's act; or he had been wronged and was aflame for vengeance. Would any man commit a murder for no cause, for the sheer delight of murdering? The thing would be incredible. There is of course the case of the man [Catiline] who was said to be so stupidly and savagely cruel that he practised cruelty and evil even when he had nothing to gain by them. But even there a cause was stated—he did it, he said, lest through idleness his hand or his resolution should grow slack. And why did he want to prevent that? So that one day by the multiplication of his crimes the city should be his, and he would have gained honours and authority and riches, and would no longer be in fear of the law or in the difficulties that want of money and the awareness of his crimes had brought him. So that not even Catiline loved his crimes as crimes: he loved some other thing which was his reason for committing them.

What was it then that in my wretched folly I loved in you, O theft of mine, deed wrought in that dark night when I was sixteen? For you were not lovely: you were a theft. Or are you anything at all, that I should talk with you? The pears that we stole were beautiful for they were created by Thee, Thou most Beautiful of all, Creator of all, Thou good God, my Sovereign and true Good. The pears were beautiful but it was not pears that my empty soul desired. For I had any number of better pears of my own, and plucked those only that I might steal. For once I had gathered them I threw them away, tasting only my own sin and savouring that with delight; for if I took so much as a bite of any one of those pears, it was the sin that sweetened it. And now, Lord my God, I ask what was it that attracted me in that theft, for there was no beauty in it to attract. I do not mean merely that it lacked the beauty that there is in justice and prudence, or in the mind of man or his senses and vegetative life: or even so much as the beauty and glory of the stars in the heavens, or of earth and sea with their oncoming of new life to replace the generations that pass. It had not even that false show or shadow of beauty by which sin tempts us.

[For there *is* a certain show of beauty in sin.] Thus pride wears the mask of loftiness of spirit, although You alone, O God, are high over all. Ambition seeks honour and glory, although You alone are to be honoured before all and glorious forever. By cruelty the great seek to be feared, yet who is to be feared but God alone: from His power what can be wrested away, or when or where or how or by whom? The caresses by which the lustful seduce are a seeking for love: but nothing is more caressing than Your charity, nor is anything more healthfully loved than Your supremely lovely, supremely luminous Truth. Curiosity may be regarded as a desire for knowledge, whereas You supremely know all things. Ignorance and sheer stupidity hide under the names of simplicity and innocence: yet no being has simplicity like to Yours: and none is more innocent than You, for it is their own deeds that harm the wicked. Sloth pretends that it wants quietude: but what sure rest is there save the Lord? Luxuriousness would be called abundance and completeness; but You are the fullness and inexhaustible abundance of incorruptible delight. Wastefulness is a parody of generosity: but You are the infinitely generous giver of all good. Avarice wants to possess overmuch: but You possess all. Enviousness claims that it strives to excel: but what can excel before You? Anger clamours for just vengeance: but whose vengeance is so just as Yours? Fear is the recoil from a new and sudden threat to something one holds dear, and a cautious regard for one's own safety: but nothing new or sudden can happen to You, nothing can threaten Your hold upon things loved, and where is safety secure save in You? Grief pines at the loss of things in which desire delighted: for it wills to be like to You from whom nothing can be taken away.

Thus the soul is guilty of fornication when she turns from You and seeks from any other source what she will nowhere find pure and without taint unless she returns to You. Thus even those who go from You and stand up against You are still perversely imitating You. But by the mere fact of their imitation, they declare that You are the creator of all that is, and that there is nowhere for them to go where You are not.

So once again what did I enjoy in that theft of mine? Of what excellence of my Lord was I making perverse and vicious imitation? Perhaps it was the thrill of acting against Your law—at least in appearance, since I had no power to do so in fact, the delight a prisoner might have in making some small gesture of liberty—getting a deceptive sense of omnipotence from doing something forbidden without immediate punishment. I was that slave, who fled from his Lord and pursued his Lord's shadow. O rottenness, O monstrousness of life and abyss of death! Could you find pleasure only in what was forbidden, and only because it was forbidden?

What shall I render unto the Lord, that I can recall these things and yet not be afraid! *I shall love thee, Lord, and shall give thanks to Thee and confess Thy name*, because Thou hast forgiven me such great sins and evil deeds. I know that it is only by Thy grace and mercy that Thou hast melted away the ice of my sins. And the evil I have not done, that also I know is by Thy grace: for what might I not have done, seeing that I loved evil solely because it was evil? I confess that Thou hast forgiven all alike—the sins I committed of my own motion, the sins I would have committed but for Thy grace.

Would any man, considering his own weakness, dare to attribute his chastity or his innocence to his own powers and so love Thee less—

as if he did not need the same mercy as those who return to Thee after sin. If any man has heard Thy voice and followed it and done none of the things he finds me here recording and confessing, still he must not scorn me: for I am healed by the same doctor who preserved him from falling into sickness, or at least into such grievous sickness. But let him love Thee even more: seeing me rescued out of such sickness of sin, and himself saved from falling into such sickness of sin, by the one same Saviour.

What fruit therefore had I (in my vileness) *in those things of which I am now ashamed?* Especially in that piece of thieving, in which I loved nothing except the thievery—though that in itself was no *thing* and I only the more wretched for it. Now—as I think back on the state of my mind then—I am altogether certain that I would not have done it alone. Perhaps then what I really loved was the companionship of those with whom I did it. If so, can I still say that I loved nothing over and above the thievery? Surely I can; that companionship was nothing over and above, because it was nothing. What is the truth of it? Who shall show me, unless He that illumines my heart and brings light into its dark places? What is the thing that I am trying to get at in all this discussion? If I had liked the pears that I stole and wanted to enjoy eating them, I might have committed the offence alone, if that had been sufficient, to get me the pleasure I wanted; I should not have needed to inflame the itch of my desires by rubbing against accomplices. But since the pleasure I got was not in the pears, it must have been in the crime itself, and put there by the companionship of others sinning with me.

What was my feeling in all this? Depraved, undoubtedly, and woe is me that I had it. But what exactly was it? *Who can understand sins?* We laughed together as if our hearts were tickled to be playing a trick upon the owners, who had no notion of what we were doing and should very strongly have objected. But what delight did I find in that, which I would not equally have found if I had done it alone? Because we are not much given to laughing when we are alone? Not much given, perhaps, but laughter does sometimes overcome a man when no one else is about, if something especially ridiculous is seen or heard or floats into the mind. Yet I would not have done this by myself: quite definitely I would not have done it by myself.

Here, then, O God, is the memory still vivid in my mind. I would not have committed that theft alone: my pleasure in it was not what I stole but that I stole: yet I would not have enjoyed doing it, I would not have done it, alone. O friendship unfriendly, unanalysable attraction for the mind, greediness to do damage for the mere sport and jest of it, desire for another's loss with no gain to oneself or vengeance to be satisfied! Someone cries "Come on, let's do it"—and we should be ashamed to be ashamed!

Who can unravel that complex twisted knottedness? It is unclean, I hate to think of it or look at it. I long for Thee, O Justice and Innocence, Joy and Beauty of the clear of sight, I long for Thee with unquenchable longing. There is sure repose in Thee and life untroubled. He that enters into Thee, enters into the joy of his Lord and will not fear and shall be well in Him who is the Best. I went away from Thee, my God, in my youth I strayed too far from Thy sustaining power, and I became to myself a barren land.

. . . .

Now my evil sinful youth was over and I had come on into young manhood; but the older in years, the baser was my vanity, in that I could not conceive any other kind of substance than what these eyes are accustomed to see. I did not indeed, O God, think of You under the figure of a human body. From the moment I began to know anything of philosophy, I had rejected the idea; and I rejoiced to find the same rejection in the faith of our spiritual mother, Your Catholic Church. But what else to think You I did not know.

As a man, though so poor a man, I set myself to think of You as the supreme and sole and true God; and with all my heart I believed You incorruptible and inviolable and immutable, for though I did not see whence or how, yet I saw with utter certainty that what can be corrupted is lower than what cannot be corrupted, that the inviolable is beyond question better than the violable, and that what can suffer no change is better than what can be changed. My heart cried out passionately against all my imaginings; and I tried with this one truth to beat away all that circling host of uncleannesses from the eyes of my mind. But they were scarce gone for the space of a single glance. They came again close packed upon me, pressed upon my gaze and so clouded it that though I did not even then think of You under the shape of a human body, yet I could not but think of You as some corporeal substance, occupying all space, whether infused in the world, or else diffused through infinite space beyond the world. Yet even at this I thought of You as incorruptible and inviolable and immutable, and I still saw those as better than corruptible and violable and mutable. But whatever I tried to see as not in space seemed to me to be nothing, absolutely nothing, not even a void: for if a body were taken out of its place and the place remained without any body, whether of earth or water or air or sky, it would still be an empty place, a space-occupying nothingness.

Thus I was so gross of mind—not seeing even myself clearly—that whatever was not extended in space, either diffused or massed together or swollen out or having some such qualities or at least capable of having them, I thought must be nothing whatsoever. My mind was in search of such images as the forms my eye was accustomed to see; and I did not realize that the mental act by which I formed these images, was not itself a bodily image: yet it could not have formed them, unless it were something and something great. I conceived of You, Life of my life, as mighty everywhere and throughout infinite space, piercing through the whole mass of the world, and spread measureless and limitless every way beyond the world, so that the earth should have You and the sky should have You and all things should have You, and that they should be bounded in You but You nowhere bounded. For as the body of the air, which is above the earth, does not hinder the sun's light from passing through it, and that light penetrates it yet does not break it or cut it but fills it wholly: so I thought that the body not only of the sky and air and sea but of the earth also was penetrable by You and easily to be pierced in all its parts, great and small, for the receiving of Your presence, while Your secret inspiration governed inwardly and outwardly all the things You had created.

This I held because I could think of nothing else. But it was false. For if it were so, a greater part of the earth would have contained a greater part of You, and a lesser a lesser; and all things should be filled with You in such a way that the body of an elephant should contain more of You than the body of a sparrow simply because it is larger and takes up so much more room; and so You would make Your parts present in the parts of the world piece by piece, little pieces in the little pieces, great masses in the great masses. That of course is not the truth of it. But You had not as yet enlightened my darkness.

But against the Manichees who deceived others because they were deceived themselves, and whose speech was dumbness because Your word did not sound from them, that argument was sufficient which long before, as far back as our Carthage days, had been proposed by Nebridius. I remember that when we heard it we were all powerfully struck by it. What would that imaginary brood of Darkness, which the Manichees were wont to set up as an opposing substance, have done against You if You had refused to fight with it. For if the answer was that it would have done You some damage, that would have been to make You violable and subject to corruption. But if the answer was that it could in no way have harmed You, then they would show no reason for Your fighting with it. But it was precisely the result of Your fighting that some part or member of You, some offspring of Your substance, was mingled with those contrary powers, those natures not created by You; and was so far corrupted by them and changed for the worse as to be turned from beatitude into misery and to need assistance to deliver it and make it clean. This was the human soul. It was enslaved, contaminated and corrupted; and to its aid came Your word in its freedom and purity and integrity. But that Word was itself corruptible, because it was from one and the same substance [as the soul]. Thus if they affirmed You, whatever You are—that is Your substance by which You are—to be incorruptible, all these ideas of theirs must be false and execrable; but if they affirm You corruptible, that would on the face of it be false and to be abominated. Therefore this argument of Nebridius was sufficient against these men, and I should utterly have vomited them up from my overcharged breast, because they had no way of escape, without horrible sacrilege of heart and tongue, from what they held and said of You.

But though I said and firmly held that the Lord God was incorruptible and unalterable and in no way changeable, the true God who made not only our souls but our bodies also, and not only our souls and bodies but all things whatsoever, as yet I did not see, clear and unravelled, what was the cause of Evil. Whatever that cause might be, I saw that no explanation would do which would force me to believe the immutable God mutable; for if I did that I should have been the very thing I was trying to find [namely a cause of evil]. From now it was with no anxiety that I sought it, for I was sure that what the Manichees said was not true. With all my heart I rejected them, because I saw that while they inquired as to the source of evil, they were full of evil themselves, in that they preferred rather to hold that Your substance suffered evil than that their own substance committed it.

So I set myself to examine an idea I had heard—namely that our free-will is the cause of our doing evil, and Your just judgment the cause of our suffering evil. I could not clearly discern this. I endeavoured to draw the eye of my mind from the pit, but I was again plunged into it; and as often as I tried, so often was I plunged back. But it raised me a little towards Your light that I now was as much aware that I had a will as that I had a life. And when I willed to do or not do anything, I was quite certain that it was myself and no other who willed, and I came to see that the cause of my sin lay there.

But what I did unwillingly, it still seemed to me that I rather suffered than did, and I judged it to be not my fault but my punishment: though as I held You most just, I was quite ready to admit that I was being justly punished.

But I asked further: "Who made me? Was it not my God, who is not only Good but Goodness itself? What root reason is there for my willing evil and failing to will good, which would make it just for me to be punished? Who was it that set and ingrafted in me this root of bitterness, since I was wholly made by my most loving God? If the devil is the author, where does the devil come from? And if by his own perverse will he was turned from a good angel into a devil, what was the origin in him of the perverse will by which he became a devil, since by the all-good Creator he was made wholly angel?" By such thoughts I was cast down again and almost stifled; yet I was not brought down so far as the hell of that error where no man confesses unto you, the error which holds rather that You suffer evil than that man does it.

I now tried to discover other truths, as I had already come to realise that incorruptible is better than corruptible, so that You must be incorruptible, whatever might be Your nature. For no soul ever has been able to conceive or ever will be able to conceive anything better than You, the supreme and perfect Good. Therefore since the incorruptible is unquestionably to be held greater than the corruptible —and I so held it—I could now draw the conclusion that unless You were incorruptible there was something better than my God. But seeing the superiority of the incorruptible, I should have looked for You in that truth and have learned from it where evil is—that is learned the origin of the corruption by which Your substance cannot be violated. For there is no way in which corruption can affect our God, whether by His will or by necessity or by accident: for He is God, and what He wills is good, and Himself is Goodness; whereas to be corrupted is not good. Nor are You against Your will constrained to anything, for Your will is not greater than Your power. It would be greater, only if You were greater than Yourself: for God's will and God's power are alike God Himself. And what unlooked for accident can befall You, since You know all things? No nature exists save because You know it. Why indeed should I multiply reasons to show that the substance which is God is not corruptible, since if it were, it would not be God?

I sought for the origin of evil, but I sought in an evil manner, and failed to see the evil that there was in my manner of enquiry. I ranged before the eyes of my mind the whole creation, both what we are able to see—earth and sea and air and stars and trees and mortal creatures; and what we cannot see—like the firmament of the Heaven above, and all its angels and spiritual powers: though even these I imagined as if they were bodies disposed each in its own place. And I made one great mass of God's Creation, distinguished according to the kinds of bodies in it, whether they really were bodies, or only such bodies as I imagined spirits to be. I made it huge, not as huge as it is, which I had no means of knowing, but as huge as might be necessary, though in every direction finite. And I saw You, Lord, in every part containing and penetrating it, Yourself altogether infinite: as if Your Being were a sea, infinite and immeasurable everywhere, though still only a sea: and within it there were some mighty but not infinite sponge, and that sponge filled in every part with the immeasurable sea. Thus I conceived Your Creation as finite, and filled utterly by Yourself, and You were Infinite. And I said: "Here is God, and here is what God has created; and God is good, mightily and incomparably better than all these; but of His goodness He created them good: and see how He contains and fills them.

"Where then is evil, and what is its source, and how has it crept into the Creation? What is its root, what is its seed? Can it be that it is wholly without being? But why should we fear and be on guard against what is not? Or if our fear of it is groundless, then our very fear is itself an evil thing. For by it the heart is driven and tormented for no cause; and that evil is all the worse, if there is nothing to fear yet we do fear. Thus either there is evil which we fear, or the fact that we fear is evil.

"Whence then is evil, since God who is good made all things good? It was the greater and supreme Good who made these lesser goods, but Creator and Creation are alike good. Whence then comes evil? Was there perhaps some evil matter of which He made this creation, matter which He formed and ordered, while yet leaving in it some element which He did not convert into good? But why? Could He who was omnipotent be unable to change matter wholly so that no evil might remain in it? Indeed why did He choose to make anything of it and not rather by the same omnipotence cause it wholly not to be? Could it possibly have existed against His will? And if it had so existed from eternity, why did He allow it so long to continue through the infinite spaces of time past, and then after so long a while choose to make something of it? If He did suddenly decide to act, surely the Omnipotent should rather have caused it to cease to be, that He Himself, the true and supreme and infinite Good, alone should be. Or, since it was not good that He who was good should frame and create something not good, could He not have taken away and reduced to nothing that matter which was evil, and provided good matter of which to create all things? For He would not be omnipotent if He could not create something good without the aid of matter which He had not created."

Such thoughts I revolved in my unhappy heart, which was further burdened and gnawed at by the fear that I should die without having found the truth. But at least the faith of Your Christ, Our Lord and Saviour, taught by the Catholic Church, stood firm in my heart, though on many points I was still uncertain and swerving from the norm of doctrine. Yet my mind did not forsake it, but drank of it more deeply with every day that passed. . . .

Being admonished by all this to return to myself, I entered into my own depths, with You as guide; and I was able to do it because You were my helper. I entered, and with the eye of my soul, such as it was, I saw Your unchangeable Light shining over that same eye of my soul, over my mind. It was not the light of every day that the eye of flesh can see, nor some greater light of the same order, such as might be if the brightness of our daily light should be seen shining with a more intense brightness and filling all things with its greatness. Your Light was not that, but other, altogether other, than all such lights. Nor was it above my mind as oil above the water it floats on, nor as the sky is above the earth; it was above because it made me, and I was below because made by it. He who knows the truth knows that Light, and he that knows the Light knows eternity. Charity knows it. O eternal truth and true love and beloved eternity! Thou art my God, I sigh to Thee by day and by night. When first I knew Thee, Thou didst lift me up so that I might see that there was something to see, but that I was not yet the man to see it. And Thou didst beat back the weakness of my gaze, blazing upon me too strongly, and I was shaken with love and with dread. And I knew that I was far from Thee in the region of unlikeness, as if I heard Thy voice from on high: "I am the food of grown men: grow and you shall eat Me. And you shall not change Me into yourself as bodily food, but into Me you shall be changed." And I learned that *Thou hast corrected man for iniquity and Thou didst make my soul shrivel up like a moth.* And I said "Is truth then nothing at all, since it is not extended either through finite spaces or infinite?" And Thou didst cry to me from afar, "I am who am." And I heard Thee, as one hears in the heart; and there was from that moment no ground of doubt in me: I would more easily have doubted my own life than have doubted that truth is: which is *clearly seen, being understood by the things that are made.*

Then I thought upon those other things that are less than You, and I saw that they neither absolutely are nor yet totally are not: they are, in as much as they are from You: they are not, in as much as they are not what You are. For that truly is, which abides unchangeably. But *it is good for me to adhere to my God,* for if I abide not in Him, I cannot abide in myself. But He, abiding in Himself, renews all things; and *Thou art my God for Thou hast no need of my goods.*

And it became clear to me that corruptible things are good: if they were supremely good they could not be corrupted, but also if they were not good at all they could not be corrupted: if they were supremely good they would be incorruptible, if they were in no way good there would be nothing in them that might corrupt. For corruption damages; and unless it diminished goodness, it would not damage. Thus either corruption does no damage, which is impossible or—and this is the certain proof of it—all things that are corrupted are deprived of some goodness. But if they were deprived of all goodness, they would be totally without being. For if they might still be and yet could no longer be corrupted, they would be better than in their first state, because they would abide henceforth incorruptibly. What could be more monstrous than to say that things could be made better by losing all their goodness? If they were deprived of all goodness, they would be altogether nothing: therefore as long as they are, they are good. Thus whatsoever things are, are good; and that evil whose origin I sought is not a substance, because if it were a substance it would be good. For either it would be an incorruptible substance, that is to say, the highest goodness; or it would be a corruptible substance, which would not be corruptible unless it were good. Thus I saw and clearly realized that You have made all things good, and that there are no substances not made by You. And because all the things You have made are not equal, they have a goodness [over and above] as a totality: because they are good individually, and they are very good altogether, for our God has made all things very good.

To You, then, evil utterly is not—and not only to You, but to Your whole creation likewise, evil is not: because there is nothing over and above Your creation that could break in or derange the order that You imposed upon it. But in certain of its parts there are some things which we call evil because they do not harmonize with other things; yet these same things do harmonize with still others and thus are good; and in themselves they are good. All these things which do not harmonize with one another, do suit well with that lower part of creation which we call the earth, which has its cloudy and windy sky in some way apt to it. God forbid that I should say: "I wish that these things were not"; because even if I saw only them, though I should want better things, yet even for them alone I should praise You: for that You are to be praised, *things of earth show—dragons, and all deeps, fire, hail, snow, ice, and stormy winds, which fulfill Thy word; mountains and all hills, fruitful trees and all cedars; beasts and all cattle, serpents and feathered fowl; kings of the earth and all people, princes and all judges of the earth; young men and maidens, old men and young, praise Thy name.* And since from the heavens, O our God, *all Thy angels praise Thee in the high places, and all Thy hosts, sun and moon, all the stars and lights, the heavens of heavens, and the waters that are above the heavens, praise thy name* —I no longer desired better, because I had thought upon them all and with clearer judgment I realized that while certain higher things are better than lower things, yet all things together are better than the higher alone.

There is no sanity in those whom anything in creation displeases, any more than there was in me when I was displeased with many things that You had made. Because my soul did not dare to be displeased with my God, it would not allow that what displeased it was Yours. Thus it strayed off into the error of holding two substances, and it found no rest but talked wildly. Turning from that error it had made for itself a god occupying the infinite measures of all space, and had thought this god to be You, and had placed it in its heart, and thus had once again become the temple of its own idol, a temple abominable to You. But You caressed my head, though I knew it not, and closed my eyes that they should not see vanity; and I ceased from myself a little and found sleep from my madness. And from that sleep I awakened in You, and I saw You infinite in a different way; but that sight was not with the eyes of flesh.

And I looked upon other things, and I saw that they owed their being to You, and that all finite things are in You: but in a different manner, being in You not as in a place, but because You are and hold all things in the hand of Your truth, and all things are true inasmuch as they are: nor is falsehood anything, save that something is thought to be which is not. And I observed that all things harmonized not only with their places but also with their times; and that You, who alone are eternal, did not begin to work after innumerable spaces of time had gone by: since all the spaces of time, spaces past, spaces to come, could neither go nor come if You did not operate and abide.

My own experience had shown me that there was nothing extraordinary in the same bread being loathsome to a sick palate and agreeable to a healthy, and in light being painful to sore eyes which is a joy to clear. Your justice displeases the wicked: but so do the viper and the smaller worms: yet these You have created good, and suited to the lower parts of Your creation—to which lower parts indeed the wicked themselves are well suited, insofar as they are unlike You, though they become suited to the higher parts as they grow more like You. So that when I now asked what is iniquity, I realized that it was not a substance but a swerving of the will which is turned towards lower things and away from You, O God, who are the supreme substance: so that it casts away what is most inward to it and swells greedily for outward things.

Free Will and God's Foreknowledge

Concerning the foreknowledge of God and the free will of man, in opposition to the definition of Cicero.

The manner in which Cicero addresses himself to the task of refuting the Stoics, shows that he did not think he could effect anything against them in argument unless he had first demolished divination. And this he attempts to accomplish by denying that there is any knowledge of future things, and maintains with all his might that there is no such knowledge either in God or man, and that there is no prediction of events. Thus he both denies the foreknowledge of God, and attempts

SOURCE: *City of God*, translated by Marcus Dods (Edinburgh: T. & T. Clark, 1872), *1*, pp. 190–192.

by vain arguments, and by opposing to himself certain oracles very easy to be refuted, to overthrow all prophecy, even such as is clearer than the light (though even these oracles are not refuted by him).

But, in refuting these conjectures of the mathematicians, his argument is triumphant, because truly these are such as destroy and refute themselves. Nevertheless, they are far more tolerable who assert the fatal influence of the stars than they who deny the foreknowledge of future events. For, to confess that God exists, and at the same time to deny that He has foreknowledge of future things, is the most manifest folly. This Cicero himself saw, and therefore attempted to assert the doctrine embodied in the words of Scripture, "The fool hath said in his heart, There is no God." That, however, he did not do in his own person, for he saw how odious and offensive such an opinion would be; and therefore in his book on the nature of the gods, he makes Cotta dispute concerning this against the Stoics, and preferred to give his own opinion in favour of Lucilius Balbus, to whom he assigned the defence of the Stoical position, rather than in favour of Cotta, who maintained that no divinity exists. However, in his book on divination, he in his own person most openly opposes the doctrine of the prescience of future things. But all this he seems to do in order that he may not grant the doctrine of fate, and by so doing destroy free will. For he thinks that, the knowledge of future things being once conceded, fate follows as so necessary a consequence that it cannot be denied.

But, let these perplexing debatings and disputations of the philosophers go on as they may, we, in order that we may confess the most high and true God Himself, do confess His will, supreme power, and prescience. Neither let us be afraid lest, after all, we do not do by will that which we do by will, because He, whose foreknowledge is infallible, foreknew that we would do it. It was this which Cicero was afraid of, and therefore opposed foreknowledge. The Stoics also maintained that all things do not come to pass by necessity, although they contended that all things happen according to destiny. What is it, then, that Cicero feared in the prescience of future things? Doubtless it was this,—that if all future things have been foreknown, they will happen in the order in which they have been foreknown; and if they come to pass in this order, there is a certain order of things foreknown by God; and if a certain order of things, then a certain order of causes, for nothing can happen which is not preceded by some efficient cause. But if there is a certain order of causes according to which everything happens which does happen, then by fate, says he, all things happen which do happen. But if this be so, then is there nothing in our own power, and there is no such thing as freedom of will; and if we grant that, says he, the whole economy of human life is subverted. In vain are laws enacted. In vain are reproaches, praises, chidings, exhortations had recourse to; and there is no justice whatever in the appointment of rewards for the good, and punishments for the wicked. And that consequences so disgraceful, and absurd, and pernicious to humanity may not follow, Cicero chooses to reject the foreknowledge of future things, and shuts up the religious mind to this alternative, to make choice between two things, either that something is in our own power, or that there is foreknowledge—both of which cannot be true; but if the one is affirmed, the other is thereby denied. He therefore, like a truly great and wise man, and one who consulted very much and very skilfully for the good of humanity, of those two chose the freedom of the will, to confirm which he denied the foreknowledge of future things; and thus, wishing to make men free, he makes them sacrilegious. But the religious mind chooses both, confesses both, and maintains both by the faith of piety. But how so? says Cicero; for the knowledge of future things being granted, there follows a chain of consequences which ends in this, that there can be nothing depending on our own free wills. And further, if there is anything depending on our wills, we must go backwards by the same steps of reasoning till we arrive at the conclusion that there is no foreknowledge of future things. For we go backwards through all the steps in the following order:— If there is free will, all things do not happen according to fate; if all things do not happen according to fate, there is not a certain order of causes; and if there is not a certain order of causes, neither is there a certain order of things foreknown by God—for things cannot come to pass except they are preceded by efficient causes,—but, if there is no fixed and certain order of causes foreknown by God, all things cannot be said to happen according as He foreknew that they would happen. And further, if it is not true that all things happen just as they have been foreknown by Him, there is not, says he, in God any foreknowledge of future events.

Now, against the sacrilegious and impious darings of reason, we assert both that God knows all things before they come to pass, and that we do by our free will whatsoever we know and feel to be done by us only because we will it. But that all things come to pass by fate, we do not say; nay we affirm that nothing comes to pass by fate; for we demonstrate that the name of fate, as it is wont to be used by those who speak of fate, meaning thereby the position of the stars at the time of each one's conception or birth, is an unmeaning word, for astrology itself is a delusion. But an order of causes in which the highest efficiency is attributed to the will of God, we neither deny nor do we designate it by the name of fate, unless, perhaps, we may understand fate to mean that which is spoken, deriving it from *fari*, to speak; for we cannot deny that it is written in the sacred Scriptures, "God hath spoken once; these two things have I heard, that power belongeth unto God. Also unto Thee, O God, belongeth mercy: for Thou wilt render unto every man according to his works." Now the expression, "Once hath He spoken," is to be understood as meaning "*immovably*," that is, unchangeably hath He spoken, inasmuch as He knows unchangeably all things which shall be, and all things which He will do. We might, then, use the word fate in the sense it bears when derived from *fari*, to speak, had it not already come to be understood in another sense, into which I am unwilling that the hearts of men should unconsciously slide. But it does not follow that, though there is for God a certain order of all causes, there must therefore be nothing depending on the free exercise of our own wills, for our wills themselves are included in that order of causes which is certain to God, and is embraced by His foreknowledge, for human wills are also causes of human actions; and He who foreknew all the causes of things would certainly among those causes not have been ignorant of our wills. For even that very concession which Cicero himself makes is enough to refute him in this argument. For what does it help him to say that nothing takes place without a cause, but that every cause is not fatal, there being a fortuitous cause, a natural cause, and a voluntary cause? It is sufficient that he confesses that whatever happens must be preceded by a cause. For we say that those causes which are called fortuitous are not a mere name for the absence of causes, but are only latent, and we attribute them either to the will of the true God, or to that of spirits of some kind or other. And as to natural causes, we by no means separate them from the will of Him who is the author and framer of all nature. But now as to voluntary causes. They are referable either to God, or to angels, or to men, or to animals of whatever description, if indeed those instinctive movements of animals devoid of reason, by which, in accordance with their own nature, they seek or shun various things, are to be called wills. And when I speak of the wills of angels, I mean either the wills of good angels, whom we call the angels of God, or of the wicked angels, whom we call the angels of the devil, or demons. Also by the wills of men I mean the wills either of the good or of the wicked. And from this we conclude that there are no efficient causes of all things which come to pass unless voluntary causes, that is, such as belong to that nature which is the spirit of life. For the air or wind is called spirit, but, inasmuch as it is a body, it is not the spirit of life. The spirit of life, therefore, which quickens all things, and is the creator of every body, and of every created spirit, is God Himself, the uncreated spirit. In His supreme will resides the power which acts on the wills of all created spirits, helping the good, judging the evil, controlling all, granting power to some, not granting it to others. For, as He is the creator of all natures, so also is He the bestower of all powers, not of all wills; for wicked wills are not from Him, being contrary to nature, which is from Him. As to bodies, they are more subject to wills: some to our wills, by which I mean the wills of all living mortal creatures, but more to the wills of men than of beasts. But all of them are most of all subject to the will of God, to whom all wills also are subject, since they have no power except what He has bestowed upon them. The cause of things, therefore, which makes but is not made, is God; but all other causes both make and are made. Such are all created spirits, and especially the rational. Material causes, therefore, which may rather be said to be made than to make, are not to be reckoned among efficient causes, because they can only do what the wills of spirits do by them. How, then, does an order of causes which is certain to the foreknowledge of God necessitate that there should be nothing which is dependent on our wills, when our wills themselves have a very important place in the order of causes? Cicero, then, contends with those who call this order of causes fatal, or rather designate this order itself by the name of fate; to which we have an abhorrence, especially on account of the word, which men have become accustomed to understand as meaning what is not true. But, whereas he denies that the order of all causes is most certain, and perfectly clear to the prescience of God, we detest his opinion more than the Stoics do. For he either denies that God exists,—which, indeed, in an assumed personage, he has laboured to do, in his book *De Natura Deorum*,— or if he confesses that He exists, but denies that He is prescient of future things, what is that but just "the fool saying in his heart there is no God?" For one who is not prescient of all future things is not God. Wherefore our wills also have just so much power as God willed and foreknew that they should have; and therefore whatever power they have, they have it within most certain limits; and whatever they are to do, they are most assuredly to do, for He whose foreknowledge is infallible foreknew that they would have the power to do it, and would do it. Wherefore, if I should choose to apply the name of fate to anything at all, I should rather say that fate belongs to the weaker of two parties, will to the stronger, who has the other in his power, than that the freedom of our will is excluded by that order of causes, which, by an unusual application of the word peculiar to themselves, the Stoics call *Fate*.

Whether our wills are ruled by necessity.

Wherefore, neither is that necessity to be feared, for dread of which the Stoics laboured to make such distinctions among the causes of things as should enable them to rescue certain things from the dominion of necessity, and to subject others to it. Among those things which they wished not to be subject to necessity they placed our wills, knowing that they would not be free if subjected to necessity. For if that is to be called *our necessity* which is not in our power, but even though we be unwilling, effects what it can effect,—as, for instance, the necessity of death,—it is manifest that our wills by which we live uprightly or wickedly are not under such a necessity; for we do many things which, if we were not willing, we should certainly not do. This is primarily true of the act of willing itself,—for if we will, it *is;* if we will not, it *is* not—for we should not will if we were unwilling. But if we define necessity to be that according to which we say that it is necessary that anything be of such or such a nature, or be done in such and such a manner, I know not why we should have any dread of that necessity taking away the freedom of our will. For we do not put the life of God or the foreknowledge of God under necessity if we should say that it is necessary that God should live for ever, and foreknow all things; as neither is His power diminished when we say that He cannot die or fall into error,—for this is in such a way impossible to Him, that if it were possible for Him, He would be of less power. But assuredly He is rightly called omnipotent, though He can neither die nor fall into error. For He is called omnipotent on account of His doing what He wills, not on account of His suffering what He wills not; for if that should befall Him, He would by no means be omnipotent. Wherefore, He cannot do some things for the very reason that He is omnipotent. So also, when we say that it is necessary that, when we will, we will by free choice, in so saying we both affirm what is true beyond doubt, and do not still subject our wills thereby to a necessity which destroys liberty. Our wills, therefore, *exist* as *wills*, and do themselves whatever we do by willing, and which would not be done if we were unwilling. But when any one suffers anything, being unwilling, by the will of another, even in that case will retains its essential validity, —we do not mean the will of the party who inflicts the suffering, for we resolve it into the power of God. For if a will should simply exist, but not be able to do what it wills, it would be overborne by a more powerful will. Nor would this be the case unless there had existed will, and that not the will of the other party, but the will of him who willed, but was not able to accomplish what he willed. Therefore, whatsoever a man suffers contrary to his own will, he ought not to attribute to the will of men, or of angels, or of any created spirit, but rather to His will who gives power to wills. It is not the case, therefore, that because God foreknew what would be in the power of our wills, there is for that reason nothing in the power of our wills. For he who foreknew this did not foreknow nothing. Moreover, if He who foreknew what would be in the power of our wills did not foreknow nothing, but something, assuredly, even though He did foreknow, there is something in the power of our wills. Therefore we are by no means compelled, either, retaining the prescience of God, to take away the freedom of the will, or, retaining the freedom of the will, to deny that He is prescient of future things, which is impious. But we embrace both.

We faithfully and sincerely confess both. The former, that we may believe well; the latter, that we may live well. For he lives ill who does not believe well concerning God. Wherefore, be it far from us, in order to maintain our freedom, to deny the prescience of Him by whose help we are or shall be free. Consequently, it is not in vain that laws are enacted, and that reproaches, exhortations, praises, and vituperations are had recourse to; for these also He foreknew, and they are of great avail, even as great as He foreknew that they would be of. Prayers, also, are of avail to procure those things which He foreknew that He would grant to those who offered them; and with justice have rewards been appointed for good deeds, and punishments for sins. For a man does not therefore sin because God foreknew that he would sin. Nay, it cannot be doubted but that it is the man himself who sins when he does sin, because He, whose foreknowledge is infallible, foreknew not that fate, or fortune, or something else would sin, but that the man himself would sin, who, if he wills not, sins not. But if he shall not will to sin, even this did God foreknow.

Time

This then, O God, was the Beginning in which You created Heaven and Earth: marvellously speaking and marvellously creating in Your Word, who is Your Son and Your Strength and Your Wisdom and Your Truth. Who shall understand this? Who shall relate it? What is that light which shines upon me but not continuously, and strikes upon my heart with no wounding? I draw back in terror: I am on fire with longing: terror in so far as I am different from it, longing in the degree of my likeness to it. It is Wisdom, Wisdom Itself, which in those moments shines upon me, cleaving through my cloud. And the cloud returns to wrap me round once more as my strength is beaten down under its darkness and the weight of my sins: for *my strength is weakened through poverty*, so that I can no longer support my good, until Thou, Lord who art merciful to my iniquities, shalt likewise heal my weakness: redeeming my life from corruption and crowning me with pity and compassion, and filling my desire with good things: *my youth shall be renewed like the eagle's. For we are saved by hope and we wait with patience for Thy promises.*

Let him who can hear Thy voice speaking within him; I, relying upon Thy inspired word, shall cry aloud: *How great are Thy works, O Lord! Thou hast made all things in wisdom.* Wisdom is "the Beginning"; and it is in that Beginning that You made heaven and earth.

SOURCE: *The Confessions of Saint Augustine*, translated by F. J. Sheed (New York: Sheed and Ward, 1943), pp. 214–220, 222–223, 226–230. Reprinted with permission of the publishers.

Surely those are still in their ancient error who say to us: "What was God doing before He made heaven and earth?" If, they say, He was at rest and doing nothing, why did He not continue to do nothing for ever after as for ever before? If it was a new movement and a new will in God to create something He had never created before, how could that be a true eternity in which a will should arise which did not exist before? For the will of God is not a creature: it is prior to every creature, since nothing would be created unless the will of the Creator first so willed. The will of God belongs to the very substance of God. Now if something arose in the substance of God which was not there before, that substance could not rightly be called eternal; but if God's will that creatures should be is from eternity, why are creatures not from eternity?

Those who speak thus do not yet understand You, O Wisdom of God, Light of minds: they do not yet understand how the things are made that are made by You and in You. They strive for the savour of eternity, but their mind is still tossing about in the past and future movements of things, and is still vain.

Who shall lay hold upon their mind and hold it still, that it may stand a little while, and a little while glimpse the splendour of eternity which stands for ever: and compare it with time whose moments never stand, and see that it is not comparable. Then indeed it would see that a long time is long only from the multitude of movements that pass away in succession, because they cannot co-exist: that in eternity nothing passes but all is present, whereas time cannot be present all at once. It would see that all the past is thrust out by the future, and all the future follows upon the past, and past and future alike are wholly created and upheld in their passage by that which is always present? Who shall lay hold upon the mind of man, that it may stand and see that time with its past and future must be determined by eternity, which stands and does not pass, which has in itself no past or future. Could my hand have the strength [so to lay hold upon the mind of man] or could my mouth by its speaking accomplish so great a thing?

I come now to answer the man who says: "What was God doing before He made Heaven and earth?" I do not give the jesting answer—said to have been given by one who sought to evade the force of the question—"He was getting Hell ready for people who pry too deep." To poke fun at a questioner is not to see the answer. My reply will be different. I would much rather say "I don't know," when I don't, than hold one up to ridicule who had asked a profound question, and win applause for a worthless answer.

But, O my God, I say that You are the Creator of all creation, and if by the phrase heaven and earth we mean all creation, then I make bold to reply: Before God made heaven and earth, He did not make anything. For if He had made something, what would it have been but a creature? And I wish I knew all that it would be profitable for me to know, as well as I know that no creature was made before any creature was made.

But a lighter mind, adrift among images of time and its passing, might wonder that You, O God almighty and all-creating and all-conserving, Maker of heaven and earth, should have abstained from so vast a work for the countless ages that passed before You actually wrought it. Such a mind should awaken and realize how ill-grounded is his wonder.

How could countless ages pass when You, the Author and Creator of all ages, had not yet made them? What time could there be that You had not created? or how could ages pass, if they never were?

Thus, since You are the Maker of all times, if there actually was any time before You made heaven and earth, how can it be said that You were not at work? If there was time, You made it, for time could not pass before You made time. On the other hand, if before heaven and earth were made there was no time, then what is meant by the question "What were You doing *then?*" If there was not any time, there was not any "then."

It is not in time that You are before all time: otherwise You would not be before all time. You are before all the past by the eminence of Your ever-present eternity: and You dominate all the future in as much as it is still to be: and once it has come it will be past: but *Thou art always the self-same, and Thy years shall not fail.* Your years neither go nor come: but our years come and go, that all may come. Your years abide all in one act of abiding: for they abide and the years that go are not thrust out by those that come, for none pass: whereas our years shall not all be, till all are no more. Your years are as a single day; and Your day comes not daily but is today, a today which does not yield place to any tomorrow or follow upon any yesterday. In You today is eternity: thus it is that You begot one co-eternal with Yourself to whom you said: *Today have I begotten Thee.* You are the Maker of all time, and before all time You are, nor was there ever a time when there was no time!

At no time then had You not made anything, for time itself You made. And no time is co-eternal with You, for You stand changeless; whereas if time stood changeless, it would not be time. What then is time? Is there any short and easy answer to that? Who can put the answer into words or even see in it his mind? Yet what commoner or more familiar word do we use in speech than time? Obviously when we use it, we know what we mean, just as when we hear another use it, we know what he means.

What then *is* time? If no one asks me, I know; if I want to explain it to a questioner, I do not know. But at any rate this much I dare affirm I know: that if nothing passed there would be no past time; if nothing were approaching, there would be no future time; if nothing were, there would be no present time.

But the two times, past and future, how can they *be*, since the past is no more and the future is not yet? On the other hand, if the present were always present and never flowed away into the past, it would not be time at all, but eternity. But if the present is only time, because it flows away into the past, how can we say that it *is?* For it is, only because it will cease to be. Thus we can affirm that time *is* only in that it tends towards not-being.

Yet we speak of a long time or a short time, applying these phrases only to past or future. Thus for example we call a hundred years ago a long time past, and a hundred years hence a long time ahead, and ten days ago a short time past, ten days hence a short time ahead. But in what sense can that which does not exist be long or short? The past no longer is, the future is not yet. Does this mean that we must not say: "It is long," but of the past "It was long," of the future "It will be long?"

O, my Lord, my Light, here too man is surely mocked by your truth! If we say the past was long, was it long when it was already past or while it was still present? It could be long only while it was in existence to *be* long. But the past no longer exists; it cannot be long, because it is not at all.

Thus we must not say that the past was long: for we shall find nothing in it capable of being long, since, precisely because it is past, it is not at all. Let us say then that a particular time was long while it was present, because in so far as it was present, it was long. For it had not yet passed away and so become non-existent; therefore it still was something, and therefore capable of being long: though once it passed away, it ceased to be long by ceasing to be.

Let us consider, then, O human soul, whether present time can be long: for it has been given you to feel and measure time's spaces. What will you answer me?

Are the present hundred years a long time? But first see whether a hundred years *can* be present. If it is the first year of the hundred, then that year is present, but the other ninety-nine are still in the future, and so as yet are not: if we are in the second year, then one year is past, one year is present, the rest future. Thus whichever year of our hundred-year period we choose as present, those before it have passed away, those after it are still to come. Thus a hundred years cannot be present.

But now let us see if the chosen year is itself present. If we are in the first month, the others are still to come, if in the second, the first has passed away and the rest are not yet. Thus a year is not wholly present while it runs, and if the whole of it is not present, then the year is not present. For a year is twelve months, and the month that happens to be running its course is the only one present, the others either are no longer or as yet are not. Even the current month is not present, but only one day of it: if that day is the first, the rest are still to come; if the last, the rest are passed away; if somewhere between, it has days past on one side and days still to come on the other.

Thus the present, which we have found to be the only time capable of being long, is cut down to the space of scarcely one day. But if we examine this one day, even it is not wholly present. A day is composed of twenty-four hours—day-hours, night-hours: the first hour finds the rest still to come, the last hour finds the rest passed away, any hour between has hours passed before it, hours to come after it. And that one hour is made of fleeing moments: so much of the hour as has fled away is past, what still remains is future. If we conceive of some point of time which cannot be divided into even the minutest parts of moments, that is the only point that can be called present: and that point flees at such lightning speed from being future to being past, that it has no extent of duration at all. For if it were so extended it would be divisible into past and future: the present has no length.

Where, then, is there a time that can be called long? Is it the future? But we cannot say of the future "It is long" because as yet it is not at all and therefore is not long. We say "It will be long." But when will it be long? While it is still in the future, it will not be long, because it does not yet exist and so cannot be long. Suppose we say, then, that it is to be long only when, coming out of the future [which is not yet], it begins to be and is now present—and thus something, and thus capable of being long. But the present cries aloud, as we have just heard, that it cannot have length.

Yet, Lord, we are aware of periods of time; we compare one period with another and say that some are longer, some shorter. We measure how much one is longer than another and say that it is double, or triple, or single, or simply that one is as long as the other. But it is time actually passing that we measure by our awareness; who can measure times past which are now no more or times to come which are not yet, unless you are prepared to say that that which does not exist can be measured? Thus while time is passing, it can be perceived and measured; but when it has passed it cannot, for it *is* not.

. . . .

At any rate it is now quite clear that neither future nor past actually exists. Nor is it right to say there are three times, past, present and future. Perhaps it would be more correct to say: there are three times, a present of things past, a present of things present, a present of things future. For these three exist in the mind, and I find them nowhere else: the present of things past is memory, the present of things present is sight, the present of things future is expectation. If we are allowed to speak thus, I see and admit that there are three times, that three times truly are.

By all means continue to say that there are three times, past, present and future; for, though it is incorrect, custom allows it. By all means say it. I do not mind, I neither argue nor object: provided that you understand what you are saying and do not think future or past now exists. There are few things that we phrase properly; most things we phrase badly: but what we are trying to say is understood.

I said a little while ago that we measure time in its passing, so that we are able to say that this period of time is to that as two to one, or that this is of the same duration as that, and can measure and describe any other proportions of time's parts.

Thus, as I said, we measure time *'in its passing.* If you ask me how I know this, my answer is that I know it because we measure time, and we cannot measure what does not exist, and past and future do not exist. But how do we measure time present, since it has no extent? It is measured while it is passing; once it has passed, it cannot be measured, for then nothing exists to measure.

But where does time come from, and by what way does it pass, and where does it go, while we are measuring it? Where is it from?—obviously from the future. By what way does it pass?—by the present. Where does it go?—into the past. In other words it passes from that which does not yet exist, by way of that which lacks extension, into that which is no longer.

But how are we measuring time unless in terms of some kind of duration? We cannot say single or double or triple or equal or proportioned in any other way, save of the duration of periods of time. But in what duration do we measure time while it is actually passing? In the future, from which it comes? But what does not yet exist cannot be measured. In the present, then, by which it passes? But that which has no space cannot be measured. In the past, to which it passes? But what no longer exists cannot be measured.

. . . .

Does not my soul speak truly to You when I say that I can measure time? For so it is, O Lord my God, I measure it and I do not know what it is that I am measuring. I measure the movement of a body, using time to measure it by. Do I not then measure time itself? Could I measure the movement of a body—its duration and how long it takes to move from place to place—if I could not measure the time in which it moves?

But if so, what do I use to measure time with? Do we measure a longer time by a shorter one, as we measure a beam in terms of cubits? Thus we say that the duration of a long syllable is measured by the space of a short syllable and is said to be double. Thus we measure the length of poems by the lengths of the lines, and the lengths of the lines by the lengths of the feet, and the lengths of the feet by the lengths of the syllables, and the lengths of long syllables by the lengths of short. We do not measure poems by pages, for that would be to measure space not time; we measure by the way the voice moves in uttering the poem, and we say: "It is a long poem, for it consists of so many lines; the lines are long for they are composed of so many feet; the feet are long for they include so many syllables; this syllable is long for it is the double of a short syllable."

But not by all this do we arrive at an exact measure of time. It may well happen that a shorter line may take longer if it is recited slowly than a longer line hurried through. And the same is true of a poem or a foot or a syllable.

Thus it seems to me that time is certainly extendedness—but I do not know what it is extendedness of: probably of the mind itself. Tell me, O my God, what am I measuring, when I say either, with no aim at precision, that one period is longer than the other, or, precisely, that one is double the other? That I measure time, I know. But I do not measure the future, for it is not yet; nor the present, for it is not extended in space; nor the past, which no longer exists. So what do I measure? Is it time in passage but not past? So I have already said.

Persevere, O my soul, fix all the power of your gaze. *God is our helper. He made us, and not we ourselves.* Fix your gaze where truth is whitening toward the dawn.

Consider the example of a bodily voice. It begins to sound, it sounds and goes on sounding, then it ceases: and now there is silence, the sound has passed, the sound no longer is. It was future before it began to sound, and so could not be measured, for as yet it did not exist; and now it cannot be measured because now it exists no longer. Only while sounding could it be measured for then it was, and so was measurable. But even then it was not standing still; it was moving, and moving out of existence. Did this make it more measurable? Only in the sense that by its passing it was spread over a certain space of time which made it measurable: for the present occupies no space.

At any rate, let us grant that it could be measured. And now again imagine a voice. It begins to sound and goes on sounding continuously without anything to break its even flow. Let us measure it, while it is sounding. For when it has ceased to sound, it will be past and will no longer be measurable. Let us measure it then and say how long it is. But it is still sounding and can be measured only from its beginning when it began to sound to its end, when it ceased. For what we measure is the interval between some starting point and some conclusion. This means that a sound which is not yet over cannot be measured so that we may say how long or short it is, nor can it be said either to be equal to some other sound or single or double or any other proportion in relation to it. But when it *is* over, it will no longer be. Then how will it be possible to measure it? Yet we do measure time—not that which is not yet, nor that which is no longer, nor that which has no duration, nor that which lacks beginning and end. Thus it seems that we measure neither time future nor time past nor time present nor time passing: and yet we measure time.

Deus creator omnium: This line is composed of eight syllables, short and long alternately: the four short syllables, the first, third, fifth, seventh are single in relation to the four long syllables, the second, fourth, sixth, eighth. Each long syllable has double the time of each short syllable. I pronounce them and I say that it is so, and so it is, as is quite obvious to the ear. As my ear distinguishes I measure a long syllable by a short and I perceive that it contains it twice. But since I hear a syllable only when the one before it has ceased—the one before being short and the one following long—how am I to keep hold of the short syllable, and how shall I set it against the long one to measure it and find that the long one is twice its length—given that the long syllable does not begin to sound until the short one has ceased? And again can I measure the long one while it is present, since I cannot measure it until it is completed? And its completion is its passing out of existence.

What then is it that I measure? Where is the short syllable by which I measure? Where is the long syllable which I measure? Both have sounded, have fled away, have gone into the past, are now no more: yet I do measure, and I affirm with confidence, in so far as a practised sense can be trusted, that one is single, the other double, in the length of time it occupies. And I could not do this unless they had both passed away and ended. Thus it is not the syllables themselves that I measure, for they are now no more, but something which remains engraved in my memory.

It is in you, O my mind, that I measure time. Do not bring against me, do not bring against yourself the disorderly throng of your impressions. In you, I say, I measure time. What I measure is the impress produced in you by things as they pass and abiding in you when they have passed: and it is present. I do not measure the things themselves whose passage produced the impress; it is the impress that I measure when I measure time. Thus either that is what time is, or I am not measuring time at all.

But when we measure silences, and say that some particular silence lasted as long as some particular phrase, do we not stretch our mind to measure the phrase as though it were actually sounded, so as to be able to form a judgment of the relation between the space of the silence and that space of time? For without voice or lips we can go through poems and verses and speeches in our minds, and we can allow for the time it takes for their movement, one part in relation to another, exactly as if we were reciting them aloud. If a man decides to utter a longish sound and settles in his mind how long the sound is to be, he goes through that space of time in silence, entrusts it to his memory, then begins to utter the sound, and it sounds until it reaches the length he had fixed for it. Or rather I should say [not that it sounds but] that it has sounded and will sound: for as much of it as has been uttered at a given moment has obviously sounded, and what remains will sound: and so he completes the sound: at every moment his attention, which is present, causes the future to make its way into the past, the future diminishing and the past growing, until the future is exhausted and everything is past.

But how is the future diminished or exhausted, since the future does not yet exist: or how does the past grow, since it no longer is? Only because, in the mind which does all this, there are three acts. For the mind expects, attends and remembers: what it expects passes, by way of what it attends to, into what it remembers. Would anyone deny that the future is as yet not existent? But in the mind there is already an expectation of the future. Would anyone deny that the past no longer exists? Yet still there is in the mind a memory of the past. Would anyone deny that the present time lacks extension, since it is but a point that passes on? Yet the attention endures, and by it that which is to be passes on its way to being no more. Thus it is not the future that is long, for the future does not exist: a long future is merely a long expectation of the future; nor is the past long since the past does not exist: a long past is merely a long memory of the past.

Suppose that I am about to recite a psalm that I know. Before I begin, my expectation is directed to the whole of it; but when I have begun, so much of it as I pluck off and drop away into the past becomes matter for my memory; and the whole energy of the action is divided between my memory, in regard to what I have said, and my expectation, in regard to what I am still to say. But there is a present act of attention, by which what was future passes on its way to becoming past. The further I go in my recitation, the more my expectation is diminished and my memory lengthened, until the whole of my expectation is used up when the action is completed and has passed wholly into my memory. And what is true of the whole psalm, is true for each part of the whole, and for each syllable: and likewise for any longer action, of which the canticle may be only a part: indeed it is the same for the whole life of man, of which all a man's actions are parts: and likewise for the whole history of the human race, of which all the lives of all men are parts.

Against the Cyclical View of History

Of the revolution of the ages, which some philosophers
believe will bring all things round again, after a certain
fixed cycle, to the same order and form as at first.

This controversy some philosophers have seen no other approved means of solving than by introducing cycles of time, in which there should be a constant renewal and repetition of the order of nature; and they have therefore asserted that these cycles will ceaselessly recur, one passing away and another coming, though they are not agreed as to whether one permanent world shall pass through all these cycles, or whether the world shall at fixed intervals die out, and be renewed so as to exhibit a recurrence of the same phenomena—the things which have been, and those which are to be, coinciding. And from this fantastic vicissitude they exempt not even the immortal soul that has attained wisdom, consigning it to a ceaseless transmigration between delusive blessedness and real misery. For how can that be truly called blessed which has no assurance of being so eternally, and is either in ignorance of the truth, and blind to the misery that is approaching, or, knowing it, is in misery and fear? Or if it passes to bliss, and leaves miseries for ever, then there happens in time a new thing which time shall not end. Why not, then, the world also? Why may not man, too, be a similar thing? So that, by following the straight path of sound doctrine, we escape, I know not what circuitous paths, discovered by deceiving and deceived sages.

Some, too, in advocating these recurring cycles that restore all things to their original, cite in favour of their supposition what Solomon says in the book of Ecclesiastes: "What is that which hath been? It is that which shall be. And what is that which is done? It is that which shall be done: and there is no new thing under the sun. Who can speak and say, See, this is new? It hath been already of old time, which was before us." This he said either of those things of which he had just been speaking—the succession of generations, the orbit of the sun, the course of rivers,—or else of all kinds of creatures that are born and die. For men were before us, are with us, and shall be after us; and so all living things and all plants. Even monstrous and irregular productions, though differing from one another, and though some are reported as solitary instances, yet resemble one another generally, in

SOURCE: *City of God*, translated by Marcus Dods (Edinburgh: T. & T. Clark, 1872), *2*, pp. 498–507, 509–514.

so far as they are miraculous and monstrous, and, in this sense, have been, and shall be, and are no new and recent things under the sun. However, some would understand these words as meaning that in the predestination of God all things have already existed, and that thus there is no new thing under the sun. At all events, far be it from any true believer to suppose that by these words of Solomon those cycles are meant, in which, according to those philosophers, the same periods and events of time are repeated; as if, for example, the philosopher Plato, having taught in the school at Athens which is called the Academy, so, numberless ages before, at long but certain intervals, this same Plato, and the same school, and the same disciples existed, and so also are to be repeated during the countless cycles that are yet be be,— far be it, I say, from us to believe this. For once Christ died for our sins; and, rising from the dead, He dieth no more. "Death hath no more dominion over Him;" and we ourselves after the resurrection shall be "ever with the Lord," to whom we now say, as the sacred Psalmist dictates, "Thou shalt keep us, O Lord, Thou shalt preserve us from this generation." And that too which follows, is, I think, appropriate enough: "The wicked walk *in a circle;*" not because their life is to recur by means of these circles, which these philosophers imagine, but because the path in which their false doctrine now runs is circuitous.

Of the creation of the human race in time, and how this was effected without any new design or change of purpose on God's part.

What wonder is it if, entangled in these circles, they find neither entrance nor egress? For they know not how the human race, and this mortal condition of ours, took its origin, nor how it will be brought to an end, since they cannot penetrate the inscrutable wisdom of God. For, though Himself eternal, and without beginning, yet He caused time to have a beginning; and man, whom He had not previously made, He made in time, not from a new and sudden resolution, but by His unchangeable and eternal design. Who can search out the unsearchable depth of this purpose, who can scrutinize the inscrutable wisdom, wherewith God, without change of will, created man, who had never before been, and gave him an existence in time, and increased the human race from one individual? For the Psalmist himself, when he had first said, "Thou shalt keep us, O Lord, Thou shalt preserve us from this generation for ever," and had then rebuked those whose foolish and impious doctrine preserves for the soul no eternal deliverance and blessedness, adds immediately, "The wicked walk in a circle." Then, as if it were said to him, "What then do you believe, feel, know? Are we to believe that it suddenly occurred to God to create man, whom He had never before made in a past eternity,—God, to whom nothing new can occur, and in whom is no changeableness?" the Psalmist goes on to reply, as if addressing God Himself, "According to the depth of Thy wisdom Thou hast multiplied the children of men." Let men, he seems to say, fancy what they please, let them conjecture and dispute as seems good to them, but Thou hast multiplied the children of men according to the depth of thy wisdom, which no man can comprehend. For this is a depth indeed, that God always has been, and that man, whom He had never made before, He willed to make in time, and this without changing His design and will.

Whether we are to believe that God, as He has always been sovereign Lord, has always had creatures over whom He exercised His sovereignty; and In what sense we can say that the creature has always been, and yet cannot say it is co-eternal.

For my own part, indeed, as I dare not say that there ever was a time when the Lord God was not Lord, so I ought not to doubt that man had no existence before time, and was first created in time. But when I consider what God could be the Lord of, if there was not always some creature, I shrink from making any assertion, remembering my own insignificance, and that it is written, "What man is he that can know the counsel of God? or who can think what the will of the Lord is? For the thoughts of mortal men are timid, and our devices are but uncertain. For the corruptible body presseth down the soul, and the earthly tabernacle weigheth down the mind that museth upon many things." Many things certainly do I muse upon in this earthly tabernacle, because the one thing which is true among the many, or beyond the many, I cannot find. If, then, among these many thoughts, I say that there have always been creatures for Him to be Lord of, who is always and ever has been Lord, but that these creatures have not always been the same, but succeeded one another (for we would not seem to say that any is co-eternal with the Creator, an assertion condemned equally by faith and sound reason), I must take care lest I fall into the absurd and ignorant error of maintaining that by these successions and changes mortal creatures have always existed, whereas the immortal creatures had not begun to exist until the date of our own world, when the angels were created; if at least the angels are intended by that light which was first made, or, rather, by that heaven of which it is said, "In the beginning God created the heavens and the earth." The angels at least did not exist before they were created; for if we say that they have always existed, we shall seem to make them co-eternal with the Creator. Again, if I say that the angels were not created in time, but existed before all times, as those over whom God, who has ever been Sovereign, exercised His sovereignty, then I shall be asked whether, if they were created before all time, they, being creatures, could possibly always exist. It may perhaps be replied, Why not *always*, since that which is in all time may very properly be said to be "always?" Now, so true is it that these angels have existed in all time, that even before time was, they were created; if at least time began with the heavens, and the angels existed before the heavens. And if time was even before the heavenly bodies, not indeed marked by hours, days, months, and years,—for these measures of time's periods which are commonly and properly called times, did manifestly begin with the motion of the heavenly bodies, and so God said, when He appointed them, "Let them be for signs, and for seasons, and for days, and for years,"—if, I say, time was before these heavenly bodies by some changing movement, whose parts succeeded one another and could not exist simultaneously, and if there was some such movement among the angels which necessitated the existence of time, and that they from their very creation should be subject to these temporal changes, then they have existed in all time, for time came into being along with them. And who will say that what was in all time, was not always?

But if I make such a reply, it will be said to me, How, then, are they not co-eternal with the Creator, if He and they always have been? How even can they be said to have been created, if we are to understand that they have always existed? What shall we reply to this? Shall we say that both statements are true? that they always have been, since they have been in all time, they being created along with time, or time along with them, and yet that also they were created? For, similarly, we will not deny that time itself was created, though no one doubts that time has been in all time; for if it has not been in all time, then there was a time when there was no time. But the most foolish person could not make such an assertion. For we can reasonably say there was a time when Rome was not; there was a time when Jerusalem was not; there was a time when Abraham was not; there was a time when man was not, and so on: in fine, if the world was not made at the commencement of time, but after some time had elapsed, we can say there was a time when the world was not. But to say there was a time when time was not, is as absurd as to say there was a man when there was no man; or, this world was when this world was not. For if we are not referring to the same object, the form of expression may be used, as, there was another man when this man was not. Thus we can reasonably say there was another time when this time was not; but not the merest simpleton could say there was a time when there

was no time. As, then, we say that time was created, though we also
say that it always has been, since in all time time has been, so it does
not follow that if the angels have always been, they were therefore not
created. For we say that they have always been, because they have
been in all time; and we say they have been in all time, because time
itself could no wise be without them. For where there is no creature
whose changing movements admit of succession, there cannot be
time at all. And consequently, even if they have always existed, they
were created; neither, if they have always existed, are they therefore
co-eternal with the Creator. For He has always existed in unchangeable
eternity; while they were created, and are said to have been always,
because they have been in all time, time being impossible without the
creature. But time passing away by its changefulness, cannot be co-
eternal with changeless eternity. And consequently, though the
immortality of the angels does not pass in time, does not become past as
if now it were not, nor has a future as if it were not yet, still their
movements, which are the basis of time, do pass from future to past; and
therefore they cannot be co-eternal with the Creator, in whose movement we cannot say that there has been that which now is not, or shall
be that which is not yet. Wherefore, if God always has been Lord,
He has always had creatures under His dominion,—creatures, however, not begotten of Him, but created by Him out of nothing; nor
co-eternal with Him, for He was before them, though at no time
without them, because He preceded them, not by the lapse of time,
but by His abiding eternity. But if I make this reply to those who
demand how He was always Creator, always Lord, if there were not
always a subject creation; or how this was created, and not rather
co-eternal with its Creator, if it always was, I fear I may be accused
of recklessly affirming what I know not, instead of teaching what I
know. I return, therefore, to that which our Creator has seen fit that
we should know; and those things which He has allowed the abler
men to know in this life, or has reserved to be known in the next by
the perfected saints, I acknowledge to be beyond my capacity. But I
have thought it right to discuss these matters without making positive
assertions, that they who read may be warned to abstain from hazardous
questions, and may not deem themselves fit for everything. Let them
rather endeavour to obey the wholesome injunction of the apostle,
when he says, "For I say, through the grace given unto me, to every
man that is among you, not to think of himself more highly than he
ought to think; but to think soberly, according as God hath dealt to
every man the measure of faith." For if an infant receive nourishment
suited to its strength, it becomes capable, as it grows, of taking more;
but if its strength and capacity be overtaxed, it dwines away in place
of growing.

How we are to understand God's promise of life eternal,
which was uttered before the "eternal times."

I own that I do not know what ages passed before the human race was
created, yet I have no doubt that no created thing is co-eternal with
the Creator. But even the apostle speaks of time as eternal, and this
with reference, not to the future, but, which is more surprising, to the
past. For he says, "In hope of eternal life, which God that cannot lie
promised before the eternal times, but hath in due times manifested
His word." You see he says that in the past there have been eternal
times, which, however, were not co-eternal with God. And since God
before these eternal times not only existed, but also "promised" life
eternal, which He manifested in its own times (that is to say, in due
times), what else is this than His word? For this is life eternal. But
then, how did He promise; for the promise was made to men, and
yet they had no existence before eternal times? Does this not mean
that, in His own eternity, and in His co-eternal word, that which was
to be in its own time was already predestined and fixed?

What defence is made by sound faith regarding God's
unchangeable counsel and will, against the reasonings of
those who hold that the works of God are eternally repeated
in revolving cycles that restore all things as they were.

Of this, too, I have no doubt, that before the first man was created,
there never had been a man at all, neither this same man himself
recurring by I know not what cycles, and having made I know not
how many revolutions, nor any other of similar nature. From this
belief I am not frightened by philosophical arguments, among which
that is reckoned the most acute which is founded on the assertion
that the infinite cannot be comprehended by any mode of knowledge.
Consequently, they argue, God has in His own mind finite conceptions
of all finite things which He makes. Now it cannot be supposed that
His goodness was ever idle; for if it were, there should be ascribed to
Him an awakening to activity in time, from a past eternity of inactivity
as if He repented of an idleness that had no beginning, and proceeded,
therefore, to make a beginning of work. This being the case, they say
it must be that the same things are always repeated, and that as they
pass, so they are destined always to return, whether amidst all these
changes the world remains the same,—the world which has always
been, and yet was created,—or that the world in these revolutions is
perpetually dying out and being renewed; otherwise, if we point to a
time when the works of God were begun, it would be believed that He
considered His past eternal leisure to be inert and indolent, and
therefore condemned and altered it as displeasing to Himself. Now
if God is supposed to have been indeed always making temporal
things, but different from one another, and one after the other, so

that He thus came at last to make man, whom He had never made before, then it may seem that He made man not with knowledge (for they suppose no knowledge can comprehend the infinite succession of creatures), but at the dictate of the hour, as it struck Him at the moment, with a sudden and accidental change of mind. On the other hand, say they, if those cycles be admitted, and if we suppose that the same temporal things are repeated, while the world either remains identical through all these rotations, or else dies away and is renewed, then there is ascribed to God neither the slothful ease of a past eternity, nor a rash and unforeseen creation. And if the same things be not thus repeated in cycles, then they cannot by any science or prescience be comprehended in their endless diversity. Even though reason could not refute, faith would smile at these argumentations, with which the godless endeavour to turn our simple piety from the right way, that we may walk with them "in a circle." But by the help of the Lord our God, even reason, and that readily enough, shatters these revolving circles which conjecture frames. For that which specially leads these men astray to prefer their own circles to the straight path of truth, is, that they measure by their own human, changeable, and narrow intellect the divine mind, which is absolutely unchangeable, infinitely capacious, and, without succession of thought, counting all things without number. So that saying of the apostle comes true of them, for, "comparing themselves with themselves, they do not understand." For because they do, in virtue of a new purpose, whatever new thing has occurred to them to be done (their minds being changeable), they conclude it is so with God; and thus compare, not God,—for they cannot conceive God, but think of one like themselves when they think of Him,—not God, but themselves, and not with Him, but with themselves. For our part, we dare not believe that God is affected in one way when He works, in another when He rests. Indeed, to say that He is affected at all, is an abuse of language, since it implies that there comes to be something in His nature which was not there before. For he who is affected is acted upon, and whatever is acted upon is changeable. In His leisure, therefore, is no laziness, indolence, inactivity; as in His work is no labour, effort, industry. He can act while He reposes, and repose while He acts. He can begin a new work with (not a new, but) an eternal design; and what He has not made before, He does not now begin to make because He repents of His former repose. But when one speaks of His former repose and subsequent operation (and I know not how men can understand these things), this "former" and "subsequent" are applied only to the things created, which formerly did not exist, and subsequently came into existence. But in God the former purpose is not altered and obliterated by the subsequent and different purpose, but by one and the same eternal and unchangeable will He effected regarding the things He created, both that formerly, so long as they were not, they should not be, and that subsequently, when they began to be, they should come into existence. And thus, perhaps, He would show in a very striking way, to those who have eyes for such things, how independent He is of what He makes, and how it is of His own gratuitous goodness He creates, since from eternity He dwelt without creatures in no less perfect a blessedness.

. . . .

Of the impiety of those who assert that the souls which enjoy true and perfect blessedness, must yet again in these periodic revolutions return to labour and misery.

What pious ears could bear to hear that after a life spent in so many and severe distresses (if, indeed, that should be called a life at all which is rather a death, so utter that the love of this present death makes us fear that death which delivers us from it), that after evils so disastrous, and miseries of all kinds have at length been expiated and finished by the help of true religion and wisdom, and when we have thus attained to the vision of God, and have entered into bliss by the contemplation of spiritual light and participation in His unchangeable immortality, which we burn to attain,—that we must at some time lose all this, and that they who do lose it are cast down from that eternity, truth, and felicity to infernal mortality and shameful foolishness, and are involved in accursed woes, in which God is lost, truth held in detestation, and happiness sought in iniquitous impurities? and that this will happen endlessly again and again, recurring at fixed intervals, and in regularly returning periods? and that this everlasting and ceaseless revolution of definite cycles, which remove and restore true misery and deceitful bliss in turn, is contrived in order that God may be able to know His own works, since on the one hand He cannot rest from creating, and on the other, cannot know the infinite number of His creatures, if He always makes creatures? Who, I say, can listen to such things? Who can accept or suffer them to be spoken? Were they true, it were not only more prudent to keep silence regarding them, but even (to express myself as best I can) it were the part of wisdom not to know them. For if in the future world we shall not remember these things, and by this oblivion be blessed, why should we now increase our misery, already burdensome enough, by the knowledge of them? If, on the other hand, the knowledge of them will be forced upon us hereafter, now at least let us remain in ignorance, that in the present expectation we may enjoy a blessedness which the future reality is not to bestow; since in this life we are expecting to obtain life everlasting, but in the world to come are to discover it to be blessed, but not everlasting.

And if they maintain that no one can attain to the blessedness of the world to come, unless in this life he has been indoctrinated in those cycles in which bliss and misery relieve one another, how do they avow that the more a man loves God, the more readily he attains to blessedness,—they who teach what paralyzes love itself? For who would not be more remiss and lukewarm in his love for a person whom he thinks he shall be forced to abandon, and whose truth and wisdom he shall come to hate; and this, too, after he has quite attained to the utmost and most blissful knowledge of Him that he is capable of? Can any one be faithful in his love, even to a human friend, if he knows that he is destined to become his enemy? God forbid that there be any truth in an opinion which threatens us with a real misery that is never to end, but is often and endlessly to be interrupted by intervals of fallacious happiness. For what happiness can be more fallacious and false than that in whose blaze of truth we yet remain ignorant that we shall be miserable, or in whose most secure citadel we yet fear that we shall be so? For if, on the one hand, we are to be ignorant of coming calamity, then our present misery is not so shortsighted, for it is assured of coming bliss. If, on the other hand, the disaster that threatens is not concealed from us in the world to come, then the time of misery which is to be at last exchanged for a state of blessedness, is spent by the soul more happily than its time of happiness, which is to end in a return to misery. And thus our expectation of unhappiness is happy, but of happiness unhappy. And therefore, as we here suffer present ills, and hereafter fear ills that are imminent, it were truer to say that we shall always be miserable, than that we can some time be happy.

But these things are declared to be false by the loud testimony of religion and truth; for religion truthfully promises a true blessedness, of which we shall be eternally assured, and which cannot be interrupted by any disaster. Let us therefore keep to the straight path, which is Christ, and, with Him as our Guide and Saviour, let us turn away in heart and mind from the unreal and futile cycles of the godless. Porphyry, Platonist though he was, abjured the opinion of his school, that in these cycles souls are ceaselessly passing away and returning, either being struck with the extravagance of the idea, or sobered by his knowledge of Christianity. As I mentioned in the tenth book, he preferred saying that the soul, as it had been sent into the world that it might know evil, and be purged and delivered from it, was never again exposed to such an experience after it had once returned to the Father. And if he abjured the tenets of his school, how much more ought we Christians to abominate and avoid an opinion so unfounded and hostile to our faith? But having disposed of these cycles and escaped out of them, no necessity compels us to suppose that the human race had no beginning in time, on the ground that there is nothing new in nature which, by I know not what cycles, has not at some previous period existed, and is not hereafter to exist again. For if the soul, once delivered, as it never was before, is never to return to misery, then there happens in its experience something which never happened before; and this, indeed, something of the greatest consequence, to wit, the secure entrance into eternal felicity. And if in an immortal nature there can occur a novelty, which never has been, nor ever shall be, reproduced by any cycle, why is it disputed that the same may occur in mortal natures? If they maintain that blessedness is no new experience to the soul, but only a return to that state in which it has been eternally, then at least its deliverance from misery is something new, since, by their own showing, the misery from which it is delivered is itself, too, a new experience. And if this new experience fell out by accident, and was not embraced in the order of things appointed by Divine Providence, then where are those determinate and measured cycles in which no new thing happens, but all things are reproduced as they were before? If, however, this new experience was embraced in that providential order of nature (whether the soul was exposed to the evil of this world for the sake of discipline, or fell into it by sin), then it is possible for new things to happen which never happened before, and which yet are not extraneous to the order of nature. And if the soul is able by its own imprudence to create for itself a new misery, which was not unforeseen by the Divine Providence, but was provided for in the order of nature along with the deliverance from it, how can we, even with all the rashness of human vanity, presume to deny that God can create new things—new to the world, but not to Him—which He never before created, but yet foresaw from all eternity? If they say that it is indeed true that ransomed souls return no more to misery, but that even so no new thing happens, since there always have been, now are, and ever shall be a succession of ransomed souls, they must at least grant that in this case there are new souls to whom the misery and the deliverance from it are new. For if they maintain that those souls out of which new men are daily being made (from whose bodies, if they have lived wisely, they are so delivered that they never return to misery) are not new, but have existed from eternity, they must logically admit that they are infinite. For however great a finite number of souls there were, that would not have sufficed to make perpetually new men from eternity,—men whose souls were to be eternally freed from this mortal state, and never afterwards to return to it. And our philosophers will find it hard to explain how there is an infinite number of souls in an order of nature which they require shall be finite, that it may be known by God.

And now that we have exploded these cycles which were supposed to bring back the soul at fixed periods to the same miseries, what can seem more in accordance with godly reason than to believe that it is possible for God both to create new things never before created, and in doing so, to preserve His will unaltered? But whether the number of eternally redeemed souls can be continually increased or not, let the philosophers themselves decide, who are so subtle in determining where infinity cannot be admitted. For our own part, our reasoning holds in either case. For if the number of souls can be indefinitely increased, what reason is there to deny that what had never before been created, could be created? since the number of ransomed souls never existed before, and has yet not only been once made, but will never cease to be anew coming into being. If, on the other hand, it be more suitable that the number of eternally ransomed souls be definite, and that this number will never be increased, yet this number, whatever it be, did assuredly never exist before, and it cannot increase, and reach the amount it signifies, without having some beginning; and this beginning never before existed. That this beginning, therefore, might be, the first man was created.

That there as created at first but one individual, and that the human race was created in him.

Now that we have solved, as well as we could, this very difficult question about the eternal God creating new things, without any novelty of will, it is easy to see how much better it is that God was pleased to produce the human race from the one individual whom He created, than if He had originated it in several men. For as to the other animals, He created some solitary, and naturally seeking lonely places,—as the eagles, kites, lions, wolves, and such like; others gregarious, which herd together, and prefer to live in company—as pigeons, starlings, stags, and little fallow deer, and the like: but neither class did He cause to be propagated from individuals, but called into being several at once. Man, on the other hand, whose nature was to be a mean between the angelic and bestial, He created in such sort, that if he remained in subjection to His Creator as his rightful Lord, and piously kept His commandments, he should pass into the company of the angels, and obtain, without the intervention of death, a blessed and endless immortality; but if he offended the Lord his God by a proud and disobedient use of his free will, he should become subject to death, and live as the beasts do,—the slave of appetite, and doomed to eternal punishment after death. And therefore God created only one single man, not, certainly, that he might be a solitary bereft of all society, but that by this means the unity of society and the bond of concord might be more effectually commended to him, men being bound together not only by similarity of nature, but by family affection. And indeed He did not even create the woman that was to be given him as his wife, as he created the man, but created her out of the man, that the whole human race might derive from one man.

The Two Cities

That the disobedience of the first man would have plunged
all men into the endless misery of the second death, had
not the grace of God rescued many.

We have already stated in the preceding books that God, desiring not only that the human race might be able by their similarity of nature to associate with one another, but also that they might be bound together in harmony and peace by the ties of relationship, was pleased to derive all men from one individual, and created man with such a nature that the members of the race should not have died, had not the two first (of whom the one was created out of nothing, and the other out of him) merited this by their disobedience; for by them so great a sin was committed, that by it the human nature was altered for the worse, and was transmitted also to their posterity, liable to sin and subject to death. And the kingdom of death so reigned over men, that the deserved penalty of sin would have hurled all headlong even into the second death, of which there is no end, had not the undeserved grace of God saved some therefrom. And thus it has come to pass, that though there are very many and great nations all over the earth, whose rites and customs, speech, arms, and dress, are distinguished by marked differences, yet there are no more than two kinds of human society, which we may justly call two cities, according to the language of our Scriptures. The one consists of those who wish to live after the flesh, the other of those who wish to live after the spirit; and when they severally achieve what they wish, they live in peace, each after their kind.

. . . .

What it is to live according to man, and what to live
according to God.

When, therefore, man lives according to man, not according to God, he is like the devil. Because not even an angel might live according to an angel, but only according to God, if he was to abide in the truth, and speak God's truth and not his own lie. And of man, too, the same apostle says in another place, "If the truth of God hath more abounded through my lie;"—"my lie," he said, and "God's truth." When, then, a man lives according to the truth, he lives not according to himself, but according to God; for He was God who said, "I am the

---

SOURCE: *City of God*, translated by Marcus Dods (Edinburgh: T. & T. Clark, 1872), 2, pp. 1–2, 6–8, 9–12, 15–29.

truth." When, therefore, man lives according to himself,—that is, according to man, not according to God,—assuredly he lives according to a lie; not that man himself is a lie, for God is his author and creator, who is certainly not the author and creator of a lie, but because man was made upright, that he might not live according to himself, but according to Him that made him,—in other words, that he might do IIis will and not his own; and not to live as he was made to live, that is a lie. For he certainly desires to be blessed even by not living so that he may be blessed. And what is a lie if this desire be not? Wherefore it is not without meaning said that all sin is a lie. For no sin is committed save by that desire or will by which we desire that it be well with us, and shrink from it being ill with us. That, therefore, is a lie which we do in order that it may be well with us, but which makes us more miserable than we were. And why is this, but because the source of man's happiness lies only in God, whom he abandons when he sins, and not in himself, by living according to whom he sins?

In enunciating this proposition of ours, then, that because some live according to the flesh and others according to the spirit there have arisen two diverse and conflicting cities, we might equally well have said, "because some live according to man, others according to God." For Paul says very plainly to the Corinthians, "For whereas there is among you envying and strife, are ye not carnal, and walk according to man?" So that to walk according to man and to be carnal are the same; for by *flesh*, that is, by a part of man, man is meant. For before he said that those same persons were animal whom afterwards he calls carnal, saying, "For what man knoweth the things of a man, save the spirit of man which is in him? even so the things of God knoweth no man, but the Spirit of God. Now we have received not the spirit of this world, but the Spirit which is of God; that we might know the things which are freely given to us of God. Which things also we speak, not in the words which man's wisdom teacheth, but which the Holy Ghost teacheth; comparing spiritual things with spiritual. But the animal man perceiveth not the things of the Spirit of God; for they are foolishness unto him." It is to men of this kind, then, that is, to animal men, he shortly after says, "And I, brethren, could not speak unto you as unto spiritual, but as unto carnal." And this is to be interpreted by the same usage, a part being taken for the whole. For both the soul and the flesh, the component parts of man, can be used to signify the whole man; and so the animal man and the carnal man are not two different things, but one and the same thing, viz. man living according to man. In the same way it is nothing else than men that are meant either in the words, "By the deeds of the law there shall no *flesh* be justified;" or in the words, "Seventy-five *souls* went down into Egypt with Jacob." In the one passage, "no flesh" signifies "no man;" and in the other, by "seventy-five souls" seventy-five men are meant. And the expression, "not in words which man's wisdom teacheth," might equally be "not in words which fleshly wisdom teacheth;" and the expression, "ye walk according to man," might be "according to the flesh." And this is still more apparent in the words which followed: "For while one saith, I am of Paul, and another, I am of Apollos, are ye not men?" The same thing which he had before expressed by "ye are animal," "ye are carnal," he now expresses by "ye are men;" that is, ye live according to man, not according to God, for if you lived according to Him, you should be gods.

. . . .

Of the character of the human will which makes the affections of the soul right or wrong.

But the character of the human will is of moment; because, if it is wrong, these motions of the soul will be wrong, but if it is right, they will be not merely blameless, but even praiseworthy. For the will is in them all; yea, none of them is anything else than will. For what are desire and joy but a volition of consent to the things we wish? And what are fear and sadness but a volition of aversion from the things which we do not wish? But when consent takes the form of seeking to possess the things we wish, this is called desire; and when consent takes the form of enjoying the things we wish, this is called joy. In like manner, when we turn with aversion from that which we do not wish to happen, this volition is termed fear; and when we turn away from that which has happened against our will, this act of will is called sorrow. And generally in respect of all that we seek or shun, as a man's will is attracted or repelled, so it is changed and turned into these different affections. Wherefore the man who lives according to God, and not according to man, ought to be a lover of good, and therefore a hater of evil. And since no one is evil by nature, but whoever is evil is evil by vice, he who lives according to God ought to cherish towards evil men a perfect hatred, so that he shall neither hate the man because of his vice, nor love the vice because of the man, but hate the vice and love the man. For the vice being cursed, all that ought to be loved, and nothing that ought to be hated, will remain.

That the words love and regard (*amor* and *dilectio*) are in Scripture used indifferently of good and evil affection.

He who resolves to love God, and to love his neighbour as himself, not according to man but according to God, is on account of this love said to be of a good will; and this is in Scripture more commonly called charity, but it is also, even in the same books, called love. For the apostle says that the man to be elected as a ruler of the people must be a lover of good. And when the Lord Himself had asked Peter, "Hast thou a regard for me (*diligis*) more than these?" Peter replied, "Lord, Thou knowest that I love (*amo*) Thee." And again a second time the Lord asked not whether Peter loved (*amaret*) Him, but whether he had a regard (*diligeret*) for Him, and he again answered, "Lord, Thou knowest that I love (*amo*) Thee." But on the third interrogation the Lord Himself no longer says, "Hast thou a regard (*diligis*) for me," but "Lovest thou (*amas*) me?" And then the evangelist adds, "Peter was grieved because He said unto him the third time, Lovest thou (*amas*) me?" though the Lord had not said three times but only once, "Lovest thou (*amas*) me?" and twice "*Diligis me?*" from which we gather that, even when the Lord said "*diligis*," He used an equivalent for "amas." Peter, too, throughout used one word for the one thing, and the third time also replied, "Lord, Thou knowest all things, Thou knowest that I love (*amo*) Thee."

I have judged it right to mention this, because some are of opinion that charity or regard (*dilectio*) is one thing, love (*amor*) another. They say that *dilectio* is used of a good affection, *amor* of an evil love. But it is very certain that even secular literature knows no such distinction. However, it is for the philosophers to determine whether and how they differ, though their own writings sufficiently testify that they make great account of love (*amor*) placed on good objects, and even on God Himself. But we wished to show that the Scriptures of our religion, whose authority we prefer to all writings whatsoever, make no distinction between *amor*, *dilectio*, and *caritas;* and we have already shown that *amor* is used in a good connection. And if any one fancy that *amor* is no doubt used both of good and bad loves, but that *dilectio* is reserved for the good only, let him remember what the psalm says, "He that loveth (*diligit*) iniquity hateth his own soul;" and the words of the Apostle John, "If any man love (*diligere*) the world, the love (*dilectio*) of the Father is not in him." Here you have in one passage *dilectio* used both in a good and a bad sense. And if any one demands an instance of *amor* being used in a bad sense (for we have already shown its use in a good sense), let him read the words, "For men shall be lovers (*amantes*) of their own selves, lovers (*amatores*) of money."

The right will is, therefore, well-directed love, and the wrong will is ill-directed love. Love, then, yearning to have what is loved, is desire; and having and enjoying it, is joy; fleeing what is opposed to it, it is fear; and feeling what is opposed to it, when it has befallen it, it is sadness. Now these motions are evil if the love is evil; good if the love is good. What we assert let us prove from Scripture. The apostle "desires to depart, and to be with Christ." And, "My soul desired to long for Thy judgments;" or if it is more appropriate to say, "My soul longed to desire Thy judgments." And, "The desire of wisdom bringeth to a kingdom." Yet there has always obtained the usage of understanding desire and concupiscence in a bad sense if the object be not defined. But joy is used in a good sense: "Be glad in the Lord, and rejoice, ye righteous." And, "Thou hast put gladness in my heart." And, "Thou wilt fill me with joy with Thy countenance." Fear is used in a good sense by the apostle when he says, "Work out your salvation with fear and trembling." And, "Be not high-minded, but fear." And, "I fear, lest by any means, as the serpent beguiled Eve through his subtilty, so your minds should be corrupted from the simplicity that is in Christ." But with respect to sadness, which Cicero prefers to call sickness (*ægritudo*), and Virgil pain (*dolor*) (as he says, "*Dolent gaudentque*"), but which I prefer to call sorrow, because sickness and pain are more commonly used to express bodily suffering, —with respect to this emotion, I say, the question whether it can be used in a good sense is more difficult.

. . . .

Of the perturbations of the soul which appear as right affections in the life of the righteous.

But so far as regards this question of mental perturbations, we have answered these philosophers in the ninth book of this work, showing that it is rather a verbal than a real dispute, and that they seek contention rather than truth. Among ourselves, according to the sacred Scriptures and sound doctrine, the citizens of the holy city of God, who live according to God in the pilgrimage of this life, both fear and desire, and grieve and rejoice. And because their love is rightly placed, all these affections of theirs are right. They fear eternal punishment, they desire eternal life; they grieve because they themselves groan within themselves, waiting for the adoption, the redemption of their body; they rejoice in hope, because there "shall be brought to pass the saying that is written, Death is swallowed up in victory." In like manner they fear to sin, they desire to persevere; they grieve in sin, they rejoice in good works. They fear to sin, because they hear that "because iniquity shall abound, the love of many shall wax cold." They desire to persevere, because they hear that it is written, "He that endureth to the end shall be saved." They grieve for sin, hearing that "If we say that we have no sin, we deceive ourselves, and the truth is not in us." They rejoice in good works, because they hear that "the Lord loveth a cheerful giver." In like manner, according as they are strong or weak, they fear or desire to be tempted, grieve or rejoice in temptation. They fear to be tempted, because they hear the injunction, "If a man be overtaken in a fault, ye which are spiritual restore such an one in the spirit of meekness; considering thyself, lest thou also be tempted." They desire to be tempted, because they hear one of the heroes of the city of God saying, "Examine me, O Lord, and tempt me; try my reins and my heart." They grieve in temptations, because they see Peter weeping; they rejoice in temptations, because they hear James saying, "My brethren, count it all joy when ye fall into divers temptations."

And not only on their own account do they experience these emotions, but also on account of those whose deliverance they desire and whose perdition they fear, and whose loss or salvation affects them with grief or with joy. For if we who have come into the Church from among the Gentiles may suitably instance that noble and mighty hero who glories in his infirmities, the teacher (*doctor*) of the nations in faith and truth, who also laboured more than all his fellow-apostles, and instructed the tribes of God's people by his epistles, which edified not only those of his own time, but all those who were to be gathered in,—that hero, I say, and athlete of Christ, instructed by Him, anointed of His Spirit, crucified with Him, glorious in Him, lawfully maintaining a great conflict on the theatre of this world, and being made a spectacle to angels and men, and pressing onwards for the prize of his high calling,—very joyfully do we with the eyes of faith behold him rejoicing with them that rejoice, and weeping with them that weep, though hampered by fightings without and fears within; desiring to depart and to be with Christ; longing to see the Romans, that he might have some fruit among them as among other Gentiles; being jealous over the Corinthians, and fearing in that jealousy lest their minds should be corrupted from the chastity that is in Christ; having great heaviness and continual sorrow of heart for the Israelites, because they, being ignorant of God's righteousness, and going about to establish their own righteousness, have not submitted themselves unto the righteousness of God; and expressing not only his sorrow, but bitter lamentation over some who had formally sinned and had not repented of their uncleanness and fornications.

If these emotions and affections, arising as they do from the love of what is good and from a holy charity, are to be called vices, then let us allow these emotions which are truly vices to pass under the name of virtues. But since these affections, when they are exercised in a becoming way, follow the guidance of right reason, who will dare to say that they are diseases or vicious passions? Wherefore even the Lord Himself, when He condescended to lead a human life in the form of a slave, had no sin whatever, and yet exercised these emotions where He judged they should be exercised. For as there was in Him a true human body and a true human soul, so was there also a true human emotion. When, therefore, we read in the Gospel that the hardheartedness of the Jews moved Him to sorrowful indignation, that He said, "I am glad for your sakes, to the intent ye may believe," that when about to raise Lazarus He even shed tears, that He earnestly desired to eat the passover with His disciples, that as His passion drew near His soul was sorrowful, these emotions are certainly not falsely ascribed to Him. But as He became man when it pleased Him, so, in the grace of His definite purpose, when it pleased Him He experienced those emotions in His human soul.

But we must further make the admission, that even when these affections are well regulated, and according to God's will, they are peculiar to this life, not to that future life we look for, and that often we yield to them against our will. And thus sometimes we weep in spite of ourselves, being carried beyond ourselves, not indeed by culpable desire, but by praiseworthy charity. In us, therefore, these affections arise from human infirmity; but it was not so with the Lord Jesus, for even His infirmity was the consequence of His power. But so long as we wear the infirmity of this life, we are rather worse men than better if we have none of these emotions at all. For the apostle vituperated and abominated some who, as he said, were "without natural affection." The sacred Psalmist also found fault with those of whom he said, "I looked for some to lament with me, and there was none." For to be quite free from pain while we are in this place of misery is only purchased, as one of this world's literati perceived and remarked, at the price of blunted sensibilities both of mind and body. And therefore that which the Greeks call $\dot{a}\pi\dot{a}\theta\epsilon\iota a$ and what the Latins would call, if their language would allow them, "impassibilitas," if it be taken to mean an impassibility of spirit and not of body, or, in other words, a freedom from those emotions which are contrary to reason and disturb the mind, then it is obviously a good and most desirable quality, but it is not one which is attainable in this life. For the words of the apostle are the confession, not of the common herd, but of the eminently pious, just, and holy men: "If we say we have no sin, we deceive ourselves, and the truth is not in us." When there shall be no sin in a man, then there shall be this $\dot{a}\pi\dot{a}\theta\epsilon\iota a$. At present it is enough if we live without crime; and he who thinks he lives without sin puts aside not sin, but pardon. And if that is to be called apathy, where the mind is the subject of no emotion, then who would not consider this insensibility to be worse than all vices? It may, indeed, reasonably be maintained that the perfect blessedness we hope for shall be free from all sting of fear or sadness; but who that is not quite lost to truth would say that neither love nor joy shall be experienced there? But if by apathy a condition be meant in which no fear terrifies nor any pain annoys, we must in this life renounce such a state if we would live according to God's will, but may hope to enjoy it in that blessedness which is promised as our eternal condition.

For that fear of which the Apostle John says, "there is no fear in love; but perfect love casteth out fear, because fear hath torment. He that feareth is not made perfect in love,"—that fear is not of the same kind as the Apostle Paul felt lest the Corinthians should be seduced by the subtlety of the serpent; for love is susceptible of this fear, yea, love alone is capable of it. But the fear which is not in love is of that kind of which Paul himself says, "For ye have not received the spirit of bondage again to fear." But as for that "clean fear which endureth for ever," if it is to exist in the world to come (and how else can it be said to endure for ever?), it is not a fear deterring us from evil which may happen, but preserving us in the good which cannot be lost. For where the love of acquired good is unchangeable, there certainly the fear that avoids evil is, if I may say so, free from anxiety. For under the name of "clean fear" David signifies that will by which we shall necessarily shrink from sin, and guard against it, not with the anxiety of weakness, which fears that we may strongly sin, but with the tranquillity of perfect love. Or if no kind of fear at all shall exist in that most imperturbable security of perpetual and blissful delights, then the expression, "The fear of the Lord is clean, enduring for ever," must be taken in the same sense as that other, "The patience of the poor shall not perish for ever." For patience, which is necessary only where ills are to be borne, shall not be eternal, but that which patience leads us to will be eternal. So perhaps this "clean fear" is said to endure for ever, because that to which fear leads shall endure.

And since this is so,—since we must live a good life in order to attain to a blessed life,—a good life has all these affections right, a bad life has them wrong. But in the blessed life eternal there will be love and joy, not only right, but also assured; but fear and grief there will be none. Whence it already appears in some sort what manner of persons the citizens of the city of God must be in this their pilgrimage, who live after the spirit, not after the flesh,—that is to say, according to God, not according to man,—and what manner of persons they shall be also in that immortality whither they are journeying. And the city or society of the wicked, who live not according to God, but according to man, and who accept the doctrines of men or devils in the worship of a false and contempt of the true divinity, is shaken with those wicked emotions as by diseases and disturbances. And if there be some of its citizens who seem to restrain and, as it were, temper those passions, they are so elated with ungodly pride, that their disease is as much greater as their pain is less. And if some, with a vanity monstrous in proportion to its rarity, have become enamoured of themselves because they can be stimulated and excited by no emotion, moved or bent by no affection, such persons rather lose all humanity than obtain true tranquillity. For a thing is not necessarily right because it is inflexible, nor healthy because it is insensible.

Whether it is to be believed that our first parents in Paradise, before they sinned, were free from all perturbation.

But it is a fair question, whether our first parent or first parents (for there was a marriage of two), before they sinned, experienced in their animal body such emotions as we shall not experience in the spiritual body when sin has been purged and finally abolished. For if they did, then how were they blessed in that boasted place of bliss, Paradise? For who that is affected by fear or grief can be called absolutely blessed? And what could those persons fear or suffer in such affluence of blessings, where neither death nor ill-health was feared, and where nothing was wanting which a good will could desire, and nothing present which could interrupt man's mental or bodily enjoyment? Their love to God was unclouded, and their mutual affection was that of faithful and sincere marriage; and from this love flowed a wonderful delight, because they always enjoyed what was loved. Their avoidance of sin was tranquil; and, so long as it was maintained, no other ill at all could invade them and bring sorrow. Or did they perhaps desire to touch and eat the forbidden fruit, yet feared to die; and thus both fear and desire already, even in that blissful place, preyed upon those first of mankind? Away with the thought that such could be the case where there was no sin! And, indeed, this is already sin, to desire those things which the law of God forbids, and to abstain from them through fear of punishment, not through love of righteousness. Away, I say, with the thought, that before there was any sin, there should already have been committed regarding that fruit the very sin which our Lord warns us against regarding a woman: "Whosoever looketh on a woman to lust after her, hath committed adultery with her already in his heart." As happy, then, as were these our first parents, who were agitated by no mental perturbations, and annoyed by no bodily discomforts, so happy should the whole human race have been, had they not introduced that evil which they have transmitted to their posterity, and had none of their descendants committed iniquity worthy of damnation; but this original blessedness continuing until, in virtue of that benediction which said, "Increase and multiply," the number of the predestined saints should have been completed, there would then have been bestowed that higher felicity which is enjoyed by the most blessed angels,—a blessedness in which there should have been a secure assurance that no one would sin, and no one die; and so should the saints have lived, after no taste of labour, pain, or death, as now they shall live in the resurrection, after they have endured all these things.

Of the fall of the first man, in whom nature was created good, and can be restored only by its Author.

But because God foresaw all things, and was therefore not ignorant that man also would fall, we ought to consider this holy city in connection with what God foresaw and ordained, and not according to our own ideas, which do not embrace God's ordination. For man, by his sin, could not disturb the divine counsel, nor compel God to change what He had decreed; for God's foreknowledge had anticipated both,—that is to say, both how evil the man whom He had created good should become, and what good He Himself should even thus derive from him. For though God is said to change His determinations (so that in a tropical sense the Holy Scripture says even that God repented), this is said with reference to man's expectation, or the order of natural causes, and not with reference to that which the Almighty had foreknown that He would do. Accordingly God, as it is written, made man upright, and consequently with a good will. For if he had not had a good will, he could not have been upright. The good will, then, is the work of God; for God created him with it. But the first evil will, which preceded all man's evil acts, was rather a kind of falling away from the work of God to its own works than any positive work. And therefore the acts resulting were evil, not having God, but the will itself for their end; so that the will or the man himself, so far as his will is bad, was as it were the evil tree bringing forth evil fruit. Moreover, the bad will, though it be not in harmony with, but opposed to nature, inasmuch as it is a vice or blemish, yet it is true of it as of all vice, that it cannot exist except in a nature, and only in a nature created out of nothing, and not in that which the Creator has begotten of Himself, as He begot the Word, by whom all things were made. For though God formed man of the dust of the earth, yet the earth itself, and every earthly material, is absolutely created out of nothing; and man's soul, too, God created out of nothing, and joined to the body, when He made man. But evils are so thoroughly overcome by good, that though they are permitted to exist, for the sake of demonstrating how the most righteous foresight of God can make a good use even of them, yet good can exist without evil, as in the true and supreme God Himself, and as in every invisible and visible celestial creature that exists above this murky atmosphere; but evil cannot exist without good, because the natures in which evil exists, in so far as they are natures, are good. And evil is removed, not by removing any nature, or part of a nature, which had been introduced by the evil, but by healing and correcting that which had been vitiated and depraved.

The will, therefore, is then truly free, when it is not the slave of vices and sins. Such was it given us by God; and this being lost by its own fault, can only be restored by Him who was able at first to give it. And therefore the truth says, "If the Son shall make you free, ye shall be free indeed;" which is equivalent to saying, If the Son shall save you, ye shall be saved indeed. For He is our Liberator, inasmuch as He is our Saviour.

Man then lived with God for his rule in a paradise at once physical and spiritual. For neither was it a paradise only physical for the advantage of the body, and not also spiritual for the advantage of the mind; nor was it only spiritual to afford enjoyment to man by his internal sensations, and not also physical to afford him enjoyment through his external senses. But obviously it was both for both ends. But after that proud and therefore envious angel (of whose fall I have said as much as I was able in the eleventh and twelfth books of this work, as well as that of his fellows, who, from being God's angels, became his angels), preferring to rule with a kind of pomp of empire rather than to be another's subject, fell from the spiritual Paradise, and essaying to insinuate his persuasive guile into the mind of man, whose unfallen condition provoked him to envy now that himself was fallen, he chose the serpent as his mouthpiece in that bodily Paradise in which it and all the other earthly animals were living with those two human beings, the man and his wife, subject to them, and harmless; and he chose the serpent because, being slippery, and moving in tortuous windings, it was suitable for his purpose. And this animal being subdued to his wicked ends by the presence and superior force of his angelic nature, he abused as his instrument, and first tried his deceit upon the woman, making his assault upon the weaker part of that human alliance, that he might gradually gain the whole, and not supposing that the man would readily give ear to him, or be deceived, but that he might yield to the error of the woman. For as Aaron was not induced to agree with the people when they blindly wished him to make an idol, and yet yielded to constraint; and as it is not credible that Solomon was so blind as to suppose that idols should be worshipped, but was drawn over to such sacrilege by the blandishments of women; so we cannot believe that Adam was deceived, and supposed the devil's word to be truth, and therefore transgressed God's law, but that he by the drawings of kindred yielded to the woman, the husband to the wife, the one human being to the only other human being. For not without significance did the apostle say, "And Adam was not deceived, but the woman being deceived was in the transgression;" but he speaks thus, because the woman accepted as true what the serpent told her, but the man could not bear to be severed from his only companion, even though this involved a partnership in sin. He was not on this account less culpable, but sinned

with his eyes open. And so the apostle does not say, "He did not sin,"
but "He was not deceived." For he shows that he sinned when he says,
"By one man sin entered into the world," and immediately after more
distinctly, "In the likeness of Adam's transgression." But he meant that
those are deceived who do not judge that which they do to be sin; but
he knew. Otherwise how were it true "Adam was not deceived?" But
having as yet no experience of the divine severity, he was possibly deceived in so far as he thought his sin venial. And consequently he was
not deceived as the woman was deceived, but he was deceived as to the
judgment which would be passed on his apology: "The woman whom
thou gavest to be with me, she gave me, and I did eat." What need of
saying more? Although they were not both deceived by credulity, yet
both were entangled in the snares of the devil, and taken by sin.

Of the nature of man's first sin.

If any one finds a difficulty in understanding why other sins do not alter
human nature as it was altered by the transgression of those first human
beings, so that on account of it this nature is subject to the great corruption we feel and see, and to death, and is distracted and tossed with so
many furious and contending emotions, and is certainly far different
from what it was before sin, even though it were then lodged in an
animal body,—if, I say, any one is moved by this, he ought not to think
that that sin was a small and light one because it was committed about
food, and that not bad nor noxious, except because it was forbidden;
for in that spot of singular felicity God could not have created and
planted any evil thing. But by the precept He gave, God commended
obedience, which is, in a sort, the mother and guardian of all the virtues
in the reasonable creature, which was so created that submission is
advantageous to it, while the fulfilment of its own will in preference to
the Creator's is destruction. And as this commandment enjoining
abstinence from one kind of food in the midst of great abundance of
other kinds was so easy to keep,—so light a burden to the memory,—
and, above all, found no resistance to its observance in lust, which only
afterwards sprung up as the penal consequence of sin, the iniquity of
violating it was all the greater in proportion to the ease with which it
might have been kept.

That in Adam's sin an evil will preceded the evil act.

Our first parents fell into open disobedience because already they were
secretly corrupted; for the evil act had never been done had not an evil
will preceded it. And what is the origin of our evil will but pride? For
"pride is the beginning of sin." And what is pride but the craving for
undue exaltation? And this is undue exaltation, when the soul abandons Him to whom it ought to cleave as its end, and becomes a kind of

end to itself. This happens when it becomes its own satisfaction. And it does so when it falls away from that unchangeable good which ought to satisfy it more than itself. This falling away is spontaneous; for if the will had remained stedfast in the love of that higher and changeless good by which it was illumined to intelligence and kindled into love, it would not have turned away to find satisfaction in itself, and so become frigid and benighted; the woman would not have believed the serpent spoke the truth, nor would the man have preferred the request of his wife to the command of God, nor have supposed that it was a venial transgression to cleave to the partner of his life even in a partnership of sin. The wicked deed, then,—that is to say, the transgression of eating the forbidden fruit,—was committed by persons who were already wicked. That "evil fruit" could be brought forth only by "a corrupt tree." But that the tree was evil was not the result of nature; for certainly it could become so only by the vice of the will, and vice is contrary to nature. Now, nature could not have been depraved by vice had it not been made out of nothing. Consequently, that it is a nature, this is because it is made by God; but that it falls away from Him, this is because it is made out of nothing. But man did not so fall away as to become absolutely nothing; but being turned towards himself, his being became more contracted than it was when he clave to Him who supremely is. Accordingly, to exist in himself, that is, to be his own satisfaction after abandoning God, is not quite to become a nonentity, but to approximate to that. And therefore the holy Scriptures designate the proud by another name, "self-pleasers." For it is good to have the heart lifted up, yet not to one's self, for this is proud, but to the Lord, for this is obedient, and can be the act only of the humble. There is, therefore, something in humility which, strangely enough, exalts the heart, and something in pride which debases it. This seems, indeed, to be contradictory, that loftiness should debase and lowliness exalt. But pious humility enables us to submit to what is above us; and nothing is more exalted above us than God; and therefore humility, by making us subject to God, exalts us. But pride, being a defect of nature, by the very act of refusing subjection and revolting from Him who is supreme, falls to a low condition; and then comes to pass what is written: "Thou castedst them down when they lifted up themselves." For he does not say, "when they had been lifted up," as if first they were exalted, and then afterwards cast down; but "when they lifted up themselves" even then they were cast down,—that is to say, the very lifting up was already a fall. And therefore it is that humility is specially recommended to the city of God as it sojourns in this world, and is specially exhibited in the city of God, and in the person of Christ its King; while the contrary vice of pride, according to the testimony of the sacred writings, specially rules his adversary the devil. And certainly this is the great difference which distinguishes the two cities of which we speak, the one being the society of the godly men, the other of the ungodly, each associated with the angels that adhere to their party, and the one guided and fashioned by love of self, the other by love of God.

The devil, then, would not have ensnared man in the open and manifest sin of doing what God had forbidden, had man not already begun to live for himself. It was this that made him listen with pleasure to the words, "Ye shall be as gods," which they would much more readily have accomplished by obediently adhering to their supreme and true end than by proudly living to themselves. For created gods are gods not by virtue of what is in themselves, but by a participation of the true God. By craving to be more, man becomes less; and by aspiring to be self-sufficing, he fell away from Him who truly suffices him. Accordingly, this wicked desire which prompts man to please himself as if he were himself light, and which thus turns him away from that light by which, had he followed it, he would himself have become light,—this wicked desire, I say, already secretly existed in him, and the open sin was but its consequence. For that is true which is written, "Pride goeth before destruction, and before honour is humility;" that is to say, secret ruin precedes open ruin, while the former is not counted ruin. For who counts exaltation ruin, though no sooner is the Highest forsaken than a fall is begun? But who does not recognise it as ruin, when there occurs an evident and indubitable transgression of the commandment? And consequently, God's prohibition had reference to such an act as, when committed, could not be defended on any pretence of doing what was righteous. And I make bold to say that it is useful for the proud to fall into an open and indisputable transgression, and so displease themselves, as already, by pleasing themselves, they had fallen. For Peter was in a healthier condition when he wept and was dissatisfied with himself, than when he boldly presumed and satisfied himself. And this is averred by the sacred Psalmist when he says, "Fill their faces with shame, that they may seek Thy name, O Lord;" that is, that they who have pleased themselves in seeking their own glory may be pleased and satisfied with Thee in seeking Thy glory.

Of the pride in the sin, which was worse than the sin itself.

But it is a worse and more damnable pride which casts about for the shelter of an excuse even in manifest sins, as these our first parents did, of whom the woman said, "The serpent beguiled me, and I did eat;" and the man said, "The woman whom Thou gavest to be with me, she gave me of the tree, and I did eat." Here there is no word of begging pardon, no word of entreaty for healing. For though they do not, like Cain, deny that they have perpetrated the deed, yet their pride seeks to refer its wickedness to another,—the woman's pride to the serpent, the man's to the woman. But where there is a plain transgression of a divine commandment, this is rather to accuse than to excuse oneself. For the fact that the woman sinned on the serpent's persuasion, and the man at the woman's offer, did not make the transgression less, as if there were any one whom we ought rather to believe or yield to than God.

Of the justice of the punishment with which our first parents were visited for their disobedience.

Therefore, because the sin was a despising of the authority of God,— who had created man; who had made him in His own image; who had set him above the other animals; who had placed him in Paradise; who had enriched him with abundance of every kind and of safety; who had laid upon him neither many, nor great, nor difficult commandments, but, in order to make a wholesome obedience easy to him had given him a single very brief and very light precept by which He reminded that creature whose service was to be free that He was Lord,— it was just that condemnation followed, and condemnation such that man, who by keeping the commandments should have been spiritual even in his flesh, became fleshly even in his spirit; and as in his pride he had sought to be his own satisfaction, God in His justice abandoned him to himself, not to live in the absolute independence he affected, but instead of the liberty he desired, to live dissatisfied with himself in a hard and miserable bondage to him to whom by sinning he had yielded himself, doomed in spite of himself to die in body as he had willingly become dead in spirit, condemned even to eternal death (had not the grace of God delivered him) because he had forsaken eternal life. Whoever thinks such punishment either excessive or unjust shows his inability to measure the great iniquity of sinning where sin might so easily have been avoided. For as Abraham's obedience is with justice pronounced to be great, because the thing commanded, to kill his son, was very difficult, so in Paradise the disobedience was the greater, because the difficulty of that which was commanded was imperceptible. And as the obedience of the second Man was the more laudable because He became obedient even "unto death," so the disobedience of the first man was the more detestable because he became disobedient even unto death. For where the penalty annexed to disobedience is great, and the thing commanded by the Creator is easy, who can sufficiently estimate how great a wickedness it is, in a matter so easy, not to obey the authority of so great a power, even when that power deters with so terrible a penalty?

In short, to say all in a word, what but disobedience was the punishment of disobedience in that sin?

The Theory of the State

Of the universal peace which the law of nature preserves
through all disturbances, and by which every one reaches
his desert in a way regulated by the just Judge.

The peace of the body then consists in the duly proportioned arrangement of its parts. The peace of the irrational soul is the harmonious repose of the appetites, and that of the rational soul the harmony of knowledge and action. The peace of body and soul is the well-ordered and harmonious life and health of the living creature. Peace between man and God is the well-ordered obedience of faith to eternal law. Peace between man and man is well-ordered concord. Domestic peace is the well-ordered concord between those of the family who rule and those who obey. Civil peace is a similar concord among the citizens. The peace of the celestial city is the perfectly ordered and harmonious enjoyment of God, and of one another in God. The peace of all things is the tranquillity of order. Order is the distribution which allots things equal and unequal, each to its own place. And hence, though the miserable, in so far as they are such, do certainly not enjoy peace, but are severed from that tranquillity of order in which there is no disturbance, nevertheless, inasmuch as they are deservedly and justly miserable, they are by their very misery connected with order. They are not, indeed, conjoined with the blessed, but they are disjoined from them by the law of order. And though they are disquieted, their circumstances are notwithstanding adjusted to them, and consequently they have some tranquillity of order, and therefore some peace. But they are wretched because, although not wholly miserable, they are not in that place where any mixture of misery is impossible. They would, however, be more wretched if they had not that peace which arises from being in harmony with the natural order of things. When they suffer, their peace is in so far disturbed; but their peace continues in so far as they do not suffer, and in so far as their nature continues to exist. As, then, there may be life without pain, while there cannot be pain without some kind of life, so there may be peace without war, but there cannot be war without some kind of peace, because war supposes the existence of some natures to wage it, and these natures cannot exist without peace of one kind or other.

And therefore there is a nature in which evil does not or even cannot exist; but there cannot be a nature in which there is no good. Hence not even the nature of the devil himself is evil, in so far as it is nature, but it was made evil by being perverted. Thus he did not abide in the truth, but could not escape the judgment of the Truth; he did not abide in the tranquillity of order, but did not therefore escape the power of the Ordainer. The good imparted by God to his nature did not screen

Source: *City of God*, translated by Marcus Dods (Edinburgh: T. & T. Clark, 1872), 2, pp. 319–328.

him from the justice of God by which order was preserved in his punishment; neither did God punish the good which He had created, but the evil which the devil had committed. God did not take back all He had imparted to his nature, but something He took and something He left, that there might remain enough to be sensible of the loss of what was taken. And this very sensibility to pain is evidence of the good which has been taken away and the good which has been left. For, were nothing good left, there could be no pain on account of the good which had been lost. For he who sins is still worse if he rejoices in his loss of righteousness. But he who is in pain, if he derives no benefit from it, mourns at least the loss of health. And as righteousness and health are both good things, and as the loss of any good thing is matter of grief, not of joy,—if, at least, there is no compensation, as spiritual righteousness may compensate for the loss of bodily health,—certainly it is more suitable for a wicked man to grieve in punishment than to rejoice in his fault. As, then, the joy of a sinner who has abandoned what is good is evidence of a bad will, so his grief for the good he has lost when he is punished is evidence of a good nature. For he who laments the peace his nature has lost is stirred to do so by some relics of peace which make his nature friendly to itself. And it is very just that in the final punishment the wicked and godless should in anguish bewail the loss of the natural advantages they enjoyed, and should perceive that they were most justly taken from them by that God whose benign liberality they had despised. God, then, the most wise Creator and most just Ordainer of all natures, who placed the human race upon earth as its greatest ornament, imparted to men some good things adapted to this life, to wit, temporal peace, such as we can enjoy in this life from health and safety and human fellowship, and all things needful for the preservation and recovery of this peace, such as the objects which are accommodated to our outward senses, light, night, the air, and waters suitable for us, and everything the body requires to sustain, shelter, heal, or beautify it: and all under this most equitable condition, that every man who made a good use of these advantages suited to the peace of this mortal condition, should receive ampler and better blessings, namely, the peace of immortality, accompanied by glory and honour in an endless life made fit for the enjoyment of God and of one another in God; but that he who used the present blessings badly should both lose them and should not receive the others.

Of the order and law which obtain in heaven and earth, whereby it comes to pass that human society is served by those who rule it.

The whole use, then, of things temporal has a reference to this result of earthly peace in the earthly community, while in the city of God it is connected with eternal peace. And therefore, if we were irrational animals, we should desire nothing beyond the proper arrangement of the parts of the body and the satisfaction of the appetites,—nothing, therefore, but bodily comfort and abundance of pleasures, that the peace of the body might contribute to the peace of the soul. For if bodily peace be awanting, a bar is put to the peace even of the irrational soul, since it cannot obtain the gratification of its appetites. And these two together help out the mutual peace of soul and body, the peace of harmonious life and health. For as animals, by shunning pain, show that they love bodily peace, and, by pursuing pleasure to gratify their appetites, show that they love peace of soul, so their shrinking from death is a sufficient indication of their intense love of that peace which binds soul and body in close alliance. But, as man has a rational soul, he subordinates all this which he has in common with the beasts to the peace of his rational soul, that his intellect may have free play and may regulate his actions, and that he may thus enjoy the well-ordered harmony of knowledge and action which constitutes, as we have said, the peace of the rational soul. And for this purpose he must desire to be neither molested by pain, nor disturbed by desire, nor extinguished by death, that he may arrive at some useful knowledge by which he may regulate his life and manners. But, owing to the liability of the human mind to fall into mistakes, this very pursuit of knowledge may be a snare to him unless he has a divine Master, whom he may obey without misgiving, and who may at the same time give him such help as to preserve his own freedom. And because, so long as he is in this mortal body, he is a stranger to God, he walks by faith, not by sight; and he therefore refers all peace, bodily or spiritual or both, to that peace which mortal man has with the immortal God, so that he exhibits the well-ordered obedience of faith to eternal law. But as this divine Master inculcates two precepts,—the love of God and the love of our neighbour, —and as in these precepts a man finds three things he has to love,— God, himself, and his neighbour,—and that he who loves God loves himself thereby, it follows that he must endeavour to get his neighbour to love God, since he is ordered to love his neighbour as himself: He ought to make this endeavour in behalf of his wife, his children, his household, all within his reach, even as he would wish his neighbour to do the same for him if he needed it; and consequently he will be at peace, or in well-ordered concord, with all men, as far as in him lies. And this is the order of this concord, that a man, in the first place, injure no one, and, in the second, do good to every one he can reach. Primarily, therefore, his own household are his care, for the law of nature and of society gives him readier access to them and greater opportunity of serving them. And hence the apostle says, "Now, if any provide not for his own, and specially for those of his own house, he hath denied the faith, and is worse than an infidel." This is the origin of domestic peace,

or the well-ordered concord of those in the family who rule and those
who obey. For they who care for the rest rule,—the husband the wife,
the parents the children, the masters the servants; and they who are
cared for obey,—the women their husbands, the children their parents,
the servants their masters. But in the family of the just man who lives
by faith and is as yet a pilgrim journeying on to the celestial city, even
those who rule serve those whom they seem to command; for they rule
not from a love of power, but from a sense of the duty they owe to others
—not because they are proud of authority, but because they love mercy.

**Of the liberty proper to man's nature, and the servitude
introduced by sin,—a servitude in which the man whose
will is wicked is the slave of his own lust, though he
is free so far as regards other men.**

This is prescribed by the order of nature: it is thus that God has created
man. For "let them," He says, "have dominion over the fish of the
sea, and over the fowl of the air, and over every creeping thing which
creepeth on the earth." He did not intend that His rational creature,
who was made in His image, should have dominion over anything but
the irrational creation,—not man over man, but man over the beasts.
And hence the righteous men in primitive times were made shepherds
of cattle rather than kings of men, God intending thus to teach us what
the relative position of the creatures is, and what the desert of sin; for it
is with justice, we believe, that the condition of slavery is the result of
sin. And this is why we do not find the word "slave" in any part of
Scripture until righteous Noah branded the sin of his son with this
name. It is a name, therefore, introduced by sin and not by nature.
The origin of the Latin word for slave is supposed to be found in the
circumstance that those who by the law of war were liable to be killed
were sometimes preserved by their victors, and were hence called servants. And these circumstances could never have arisen save through
sin. For even when we wage a just war, our adversaries must be sinning;
and every victory, even though gained by wicked men, is a result of the
first judgment of God, who humbles the vanquished either for the sake
of removing or of punishing their sins. Witness that man of God, Daniel,
who, when he was in captivity, confessed to God his own sins and the
sins of his people, and declares with pious grief that these were the
cause of the captivity. The prime cause, then, of slavery is sin, which
brings man under the dominion of his fellow,—that which does not
happen save by the judgment of God, with whom is no unrighteousness,
and who knows how to award fit punishments to every variety of offence.
But our Master in heaven says, "Every one who doeth sin is the servant
of sin." And thus there are many wicked masters who have religious
men as their slaves, and who are yet themselves in bondage; "for of
whom a man is overcome, of the same is he brought in bondage." And

beyond question it is a happier thing to be the slave of a man than of a lust; for even this very lust of ruling, to mention no others, lays waste men's hearts with the most ruthless dominion. Moreover, when men are subjected to one another in a peaceful order, the lowly position does as much good to the servant as the proud position does harm to the master. But by nature, as God first created us, no one is the slave either of man or of sin. This servitude is, however, penal, and is appointed by that law which enjoins the preservation of the natural order and forbids its disturbance; for if nothing had been done in violation of that law, there would have been nothing to restrain by penal servitude. And therefore the apostle admonishes slaves to be subject to their masters, and to serve them heartily and with good-will, so that, if they cannot be freed by their masters, they may themselves make their slavery in some sort free, by serving not in crafty fear, but in faithful love, until all unrighteousness pass away, and all principality and every human power be brought to nothing, and God be all in all.

Of equitable rule.

And therefore, although our righteous fathers had slaves, and administered their domestic affairs so as to distinguish between the condition of slaves and the heirship of sons in regard to the blessings of this life, yet in regard to the worship of God, in whom we hope for eternal blessings, they took an equally loving oversight of all the members of their household. And this is so much in accordance with the natural order, that the head of the household was called *paterfamilias;* and this name has been so generally accepted, that even those whose rule is unrighteous are glad to apply it to themselves. But those who are true fathers of their households desire and endeavour that all the members of their household, equally with their own children, should worship and win God, and should come to that heavenly home in which the duty of ruling men is no longer necessary, because the duty of caring for their everlasting happiness has also ceased; but, until they reach that home, masters ought to feel their position of authority a greater burden than servants their service. And if any member of the family interrupts the domestic peace by disobedience, he is corrected either by word or blow, or some kind of just and legitimate punishment, such as society permits, that he may himself be the better for it, and be readjusted to the family harmony from which he had dislocated himself. For as it is not benevolent to give a man help at the expense of some greater benefit he might receive, so it is not innocent to spare a man at the risk of his falling into graver sin. To be innocent, we must not only do harm to no man, but also restrain him from sin or punish his sin, so that either the man himself who is punished may profit by his experience, or others be warned by his example. Since, then, the house ought to be the beginning or element of the city, and every beginning bears reference to some end of its own kind, and every element to the integrity of the whole of which it is an element, it follows plainly enough that domestic peace has a relation to civic peace,—in other words, that the well-ordered concord of domestic obedience and domestic rule has a relation to the well-ordered concord of civic obedience and civic rule. And therefore it follows, further, that the father of the family ought to frame his domestic rule in accordance with the law of the city, so that the household may be in harmony with the civic order.

What produces peace, and what discord, between the heavenly and earthly cities.

But the families which do not live by faith seek their peace in the earthly advantages of this life; while the families which live by faith look for those eternal blessings which are promised, and use as pilgrims such advantages of time and of earth as do not fascinate and divert them from God, but rather aid them to endure with greater ease, and to keep down the number of those burdens of the corruptible body which weigh upon the soul. Thus the things necessary for this mortal life are used by both kinds of men and families alike, but each has its own peculiar and widely different aim in using them. The earthly city, which does not live by faith, seeks an earthly peace, and the end it proposes, in the well-ordered concord of civic obedience and rule, is the combination of men's wills to attain the things which are helpful to this life. The heavenly city, or rather the part of it which sojourns on earth and lives by faith, makes use of this peace only because it must, until this mortal condition which necessitates it shall pass away. Consequently, so long as it lives like a captive and a stranger in the earthly city, though it has already received the promise of redemption, and the gift of the Spirit as the earnest of it, it makes no scruple to obey the laws of the earthly city, whereby the things necessary for the maintenance of this mortal life are administered; and thus, as this life is common to both cities, so there is a harmony between them in regard to what belongs to it. But, as the earthly city has had some philosophers whose doctrine is condemned by the divine teaching, and who, being deceived either by their own conjectures or by demons, supposed that many gods must be invited to take an interest in human affairs, and assigned to each a separate function and a separate department,—to one the body, to another the soul; and in the body itself, to one the head, to another the neck, and each of the other members to one of the gods; and in like manner, in the soul, to one god the natural capacity was assigned, to another education, to another anger, to another lust; and so the various affairs of life were assigned,— cattle to one, corn to another, wine to another, oil to another, the woods to another, money to another, navigation to another, wars and victories to another, marriages to another, births and fecundity to another, and other things to other gods: and as the celestial city, on the other hand, knew that one God only was to be worshipped, and that to Him alone was due that service which the Greeks call λατρεία and which can be given only to a god, it has come to pass that the two cities could not have common laws of religion, and that the heavenly city has been compelled in this matter to dissent, and to become obnoxious to those who think differently, and to stand the brunt of their anger and hatred and persecutions, except in so far as the minds of their enemies have been alarmed by the multitude of the Christians and quelled by the manifest protection of God accorded to them. This heavenly city, then, while it sojourns on earth, calls citizens out of all nations, and gathers together a society of pilgrims of all languages, not scrupling about diversities in the manners, laws, and institutions whereby earthly peace is secured and maintained, but recognising that, however various these are, they all tend to one and the same end of earthly peace. It therefore is so far from rescinding and abolishing these diversities, that it even preserves and adopts them, so long only as no hindrance to the worship of the one supreme and true God is thus introduced. Even the heavenly city, therefore, while in its state of pilgrimage, avails itself of the peace of earth, and, so far as it can without injuring faith and godliness, desires and maintains a common agreement among men regarding the acquisition of the necessaries of life, and makes this earthly peace bear upon the peace of heaven; for this alone can be truly called and esteemed the peace of the reasonable creatures, consisting as it does in the perfectly ordered and harmonious enjoyment of God and of one another in God. When we shall have reached that peace, this mortal life shall give place to one that is eternal, and our body shall be no more this animal body which by its corruption weighs down the soul, but a spiritual body feeling no want, and in all its members subjected to the will. In its pilgrim state the heavenly city possesses this peace by faith; and by this faith it lives righteously when it refers to the attainment of that peace every good action towards God and man; for the life of the city is a social life.

A STUDY GUIDE TO AUGUSTINE'S THOUGHT

1. Why does Augustine begin the *Confessions* with a long praise of God? What purpose does it serve?

2. What were the circumstances under which Augustine finally converted? What was the meaning and significance of the passage, Romans 13:13, which he read in the garden?

3. When Augustine speaks of the love of God, how is the word "love" used? What is the difference between the love of man and the

love of God? Can you compare the Augustinian, Christian notion of love with the Greek notion (see Plato's *Symposium* or *Phaedrus*)? How do they differ?

4.   What is Augustine's position on the use of pagan literature? What does the parable "plundering the Egyptians" mean? What are some of the pitfalls in interpreting the Scriptures, and what are some useful principles for understanding them? Do you agree with Augustine's method of interpreting the Bible?

5.   Why did the young Augustine steal the pears? What was the theological purpose of the story? In the *Confessions* God and goodness are treated in three different ways, according to different ways of viewing substance. What are they? What was the point of the "sparrow and the elephant" argument? Why did Augustine reject the Manichee position? the Platonic position? What is the nature of sin according to Augustine? How can there be evil in the world if evil does not exist?

6.   How is it possible for man to have free choice of his actions if God has predetermined them? What is the difference between the human and the divine perspective?

7.   What is the difference between psychological time and real time? Why does Augustine devote so much interest to the question of time in his *Confessions*?

8.   What is the cyclical view of history? What are Augustine's arguments against it?

9.   What are the two cities? What is the relationship of the struggle of the two cities to the individual in history? How does Augustine's dualism differ from Manichaeism? Why is man born in sin? What was his sin?

10.   What is the function and role of the state? What is the function of the church?

4

SELECTIONS FROM THOMAS AQUINAS' WORK

The Existence of God

Whether the existence of God is self-evident?

Objection 1. It seems that the Existence of God is self-evident. Those things are said to be self-evident to us the knowledge of which is naturally implanted in us, as we can see in regard to first principles. But the Damascene says that, *the knowledge of God is naturally implanted in all.* Therefore the Existence of God is self-evident.

Obj. 2. Further, those things are said to be self-evident which are known as soon as the terms are known, which the Philosopher says is true of the first principles of demonstration. Thus, when the nature of a whole and of a part is known, it is at once recognized that every whole is greater than its part. But as soon as the signification of the word "God" is understood, it is at once seen that God exists. For by this word is signified that thing than which nothing greater can exist. But that which exists actually and mentally is greater than that which exists only mentally. Therefore, because as soon as the word "God" is understood it exists mentally, it also follows that it exists actually. Therefore the proposition that God exists is self-evident.

Obj. 3. Further, the existence of Truth is self-evident; for whoever denies the existence of Truth concedes that Truth does not exist. Now, if Truth does not exist, then the proposition "Truth does not exist" is true. But if there is anything true, there must be Truth. God is Truth itself: *I am the way, the truth, and the life* (John xiv. 6). Therefore the proposition that God exists is self-evident.

On the contrary, No one can mentally admit the opposite of what is self-evident; as is clear from the Philosopher, concerning the first

SOURCE: *Summa Theologica,* translated by Fathers of English Dominican Province (New York: Benziger Brothers, 1911), *1,* pp. 19–27. Reprinted with permission of Benziger Brothers and Burns & Oates, Ltd., London.

principles of demonstration. The opposite of the proposition "God is" can be mentally admitted: *The fool hath said in his heart, There is no God* (Ps. lii. 1). Therefore, that God exists is not self-evident.

I answer that, A thing can be self-evident in either of two ways; on the one hand, self-evident in itself, though not to us; on the other, self-evident in itself, and to us. A proposition is self-evident because the predicate is included in the notion of the subject, as "Man is an animal," for animal is contained in the formal idea of man. If, therefore, the essence of the predicate and subject be known to all, the proposition will be self-evident to all; as is clear with regard to the first principles of demonstration, the terms of which are common things that no one is ignorant of, such as being and non-being, whole and part, and such like. If there are some to whom the essence of the predicate and subject are unknown, the proposition will be self-evident in itself, but not to those who do not know the meaning of the predicate and subject of the proposition. Therefore, it happens, as Boethius says, that there are some mental concepts self-evident only to the learned, as that incorporeal substances are not in space. Therefore I say that this proposition, "God exists," of itself is self-evident, for the predicate is the same as the subject; because God is His Own Existence. Forasmuch as we do not know the Essence of God, the proposition is not self-evident to us; but needs to be proved by such things as are more evident to us, though less evident in their nature—namely, by effects.

Reply Obj. 1. To know that God exists in a general and indefinite way is implanted in us by nature, inasmuch as God is man's beatitude. For man naturally desires happiness, and what is naturally desired by a man must be naturally known to him. This, however, is not to know absolutely that God exists; as to know that someone is approaching is not the same as to know that Peter is approaching, even though it is Peter who is approaching; for many there are who imagine that man's perfect good (which is happiness) consists in riches, and others in pleasures, and others in something else.

Reply Obj. 2. Perhaps not everyone who hears of this word "God" may understand it to signify something than which nothing better can be imagined, seeing that some have believed God to be a body. Yet, granted that everyone understands that by this word "God" is signified something than which nothing greater can be imagined, nevertheless, it does not therefore follow that he understands that what the word signifies exists actually, but only that it exists mentally. Nor can it be argued logically that it actually exists, unless it be admitted that there exists something than which nothing greater can be imagined; and this precisely is not admitted by those who hold that God does not exist.

Reply Obj. 3. The existence of truth in a general way is self-evident, but the existence of a Primal Truth is not self-evident to us.

Whether it can be demonstrated that God exists?

Objection 1. It seems that the existence of God cannot be demonstrated; for it is an article of Faith that God exists. But what is of Faith cannot be demonstrated, because a demonstration produces knowledge; whereas Faith is of the unseen (Heb. xi. 1). Therefore it cannot be demonstrated that God exists.

Obj. 2. Further, the essence is the middle term of demonstration. But we cannot know in what God's essence consists, but solely in what it does not consist; as the Damascene says. Therefore we cannot demonstrate that God exists.

Obj. 3. Further, if the existence of God were demonstrated, this could only be from His effects. But the effects are not proportionate to Him, since He is infinite and His effects are finite; and between the finite and infinite there is no proportion. Therefore, since a cause cannot be demonstrated by an effect not proportionate to it, it seems that the existence of God cannot be demonstrated.

On the contrary, The Apostle says: *The invisible things of God are clearly seen, being understood by the things that are made* (Rom. i. 20). But this would not be unless the existence of God could be demonstrated through the things that are made; for the first thing we must know of anything is, whether it exists.

I answer that, Demonstration can be made in two ways: One is through the cause, and is called *a priori*, and this is to argue from what is prior absolutely. The other is through the effect, and is called a demonstration *a posteriori;* this is to argue from what is prior relatively only to us. When an effect is better known to us than its cause, from the effect we proceed to the knowledge of the cause. From every effect the existence of a proportionate cause can be demonstrated, so long as its effects are better known to us. Since every effect depends upon its cause, if the effect exists, the cause must have pre-existed. Hence the existence of God, in so far as it is not self-evident to us, can be demonstrated from those of His effects which are known to us.

Reply Obj. 1. The existence of God and other like truths about God, which can be known by natural reason, are not articles of Faith, but are preambles to the articles; for Faith presupposes natural knowledge, even as grace presupposes nature, and perfection supposes something that can be perfected. Nevertheless, there is nothing to prevent a man, who cannot grasp its proof, accepting, as a matter of Faith, something in itself capable of being known and demonstrated.

Reply Obj. 2. When the existence of a cause is demonstrated from an effect, this effect takes the place of the definition of the cause in proof of the cause's existence. This is especially the case in regard to God, because, in order to prove the existence of anything, it is necessary to accept as a middle term the meaning of the word, and not its essence, for the question of its essence follows on the question of its existence. The names given to God are derived from His effects; consequently, in demonstrating the existence of God from His effects, we may take for the middle term the meaning of the word "God."

Reply Obj. 3. From effects not proportionate to the cause, no perfect knowledge of that cause can be obtained. Yet from every effect the existence of the cause can be demonstrated, and so we can demonstrate the existence of God from His effects; though from them we cannot perfectly know God as He is in His own Essence.

Whether God exists?

Objection 1. It seems that God does not exist; because if one of two contraries be infinite, the other would be altogether destroyed. But the word "God" means that He is infinite goodness. If, therefore, God existed, there would be no evil discoverable; but there is evil in the world. Therefore God does not exist.

Obj. 2. Further, it is superfluous to suppose that, what can be accounted for by a few principles has been produced by many. But it seems that everything that appears in the world can be accounted for by other principles, supposing God did not exist. For all natural things can be reduced to one principle, which is nature; and all things that happen intentionally can be reduced to one principle, which is human reason, or will. Therefore there is no need to suppose God's existence.

On the contrary, It is said in the person of God: *I am Who am* (Exod. iii. 14).

I answer that, The existence of God can be proved in five ways.

The first and more manifest way is the argument from motion. It is certain and evident to our senses that some things are in motion. Whatever is in motion is moved by another, for nothing can be in motion except it have a potentiality for that towards which it is being moved; whereas a thing moves inasmuch as it is in act. By "motion" we mean nothing else than the reduction of something from a state of potentiality into a state of actuality. Nothing, however, can be reduced from a state of potentiality into a state of actuality unless by something already in a state of actuality. Thus, that which is actually hot as fire, makes wood, which is potentially hot, to be actually hot, and thereby moves and changes it. It is not possible that the same thing should be at once in a state of actuality and potentiality from the same point of view, but only from different points of view. What is actually hot cannot simultaneously be only potentially hot; still, it is simultaneously potentially cold. It is therefore impossible that from the same point of view and in the same way anything should be both moved and mover, or that it should move itself. Therefore, whatever is in motion must be put in motion by another. If that by which it is put in motion be itself put in motion, then this also must needs be put in motion by another, and that by another again. This cannot go on to infinity, because then there would be no first mover, and, consequently, no other mover—seeing that subsequent movers only move inasmuch as they are put in motion by the first mover; as the staff only moves because it is put in motion by the hand. Therefore it is necessary to arrive at a First Mover, put in motion by no other; and this everyone under-' stands to be God.

The second way is from the formality of efficient causation. In the world of sense we find there is an order of efficient causation. There is no case known (neither is it, indeed, possible) in which a thing is found to be the efficient cause of itself; for so it would be prior to itself, which is impossible. In efficient causes it is not possible to go on to infinity, because in all efficient causes following in order the first is the cause of the intermediate cause, and the intermediate is the cause of the ultimate cause, whether the intermediate cause be several, or one only. To take away the cause is to take away the effect. Therefore, if there be no first cause among efficient causes, there will be no ultimate cause, nor any intermediate. If in efficient causes it is possible to go on to infinity, there will be no first efficient cause, neither will there be an ultimate effect, nor any intermediate efficient causes; all of which is plainly false. Therefore it is necessary to put forward a First Efficient Cause, to which everyone gives the name of God.

The third way is taken from possibility and necessity, and runs thus: We find in nature things that could either exist or not exist, since they are found to be generated, and then to corrupt; and, consequently, they can exist, and then not exist. It is impossible for these always to exist, for that which can one day cease to exist must at some time have not existed. Therefore, if everything could cease to exist, then at one time there could have been nothing in existence. If this were true, even now there would be nothing in existence, because that which does not exist only begins to exist by something already existing. Therefore, if at one time nothing was in existence, it would have been impossible for anything to have begun to exist; and thus even now nothing would be in existence—which is absurd. Therefore, not all beings are merely possible, but there must exist something the existence of which is necessary. Every necessary thing either has its necessity caused by another, or not. It is impossible to go on to infinity in necessary things which have their necessity caused by another, as has been already proved in regard to efficient causes. Therefore we cannot but postulate the existence of some being having of itself its own necessity, and not receiving it from another, but rather causing in others their necessity. This all men speak of as God.

The fourth way is taken from the gradation to be found in things. Among beings there are some more and some less good, true, noble, and the like. But "more" and "less" are predicated of different things, according as they resemble in their different ways something which is in the degree of "most," as a thing is said to be hotter according as it more nearly resembles that which is hottest; so that there is something which is truest, something best, something noblest, and, consequently, something which is uttermost being; for the truer things are, the more truly they exist. What is most complete in any genus is the cause of all in that genus; as fire, which is the most complete form of heat, is the cause whereby all things are made hot. Therefore there must also be something which is to all beings the cause of their being, goodness, and every other perfection; and this we call God.

The fifth way is taken from the governance of the world; for we see that things which lack intelligence, such as natural bodies, act for some purpose, which fact is evident from their acting always, or nearly always, in the same way, so as to obtain the best result. Hence it is plain that not fortuitously, but designedly, do they achieve their purpose. Whatever lacks intelligence cannot fulfil some purpose, unless it be directed by some being endowed with intelligence and knowledge; as the arrow is shot to its mark by the archer. Therefore some intelligent being exists by whom all natural things are ordained towards a definite purpose; and this being we call God.

Reply Obj. 1. As Augustine says: *Since God is wholly good, He would not allow any evil to exist in His works, unless His omnipotence and goodness were such as to bring good even out of evil.* This is part of the infinite goodness of God, that He should allow evil to exist, and out of it produce good.

Reply Obj. 2. Since nature works out its determinate end under the direction of a higher agent, whatever is done by nature must needs be traced back to God, as to its first cause. So also whatever is done designedly must also be traced back to some higher cause other than human reason or will, for these can suffer change and are defective; whereas things capable of motion and of defect must be traced back to an immovable and self-necessary first principle.

Man: His Existence and Knowledge

Whether the intellectual principle is united to the body as its form?

Objection 1. It seems that the intellectual principle is not united to the body as its form. For the Philosopher says (*De Anima* iii.) that the intellect is separate, and that it is not the act of any body. Therefore it is not united to the body as its form.

SOURCE: *Summa Theologica*, translated by Fathers of English Dominican Province (New York: Benziger Brothers, 1911), *3*, pp. 20–27, 88–92, 169–173, 178–183. Reprinted with permission of Benziger Brothers and Burns & Oates, Ltd., London.

Obj. 2. Further, every form is determined according to the nature of the matter of which it is the form; otherwise no proportion would be required between matter and form. Therefore if the intellect were united to the body as its form, since every body has a determinate nature, it would follow that the intellect has a determinate nature; thus, it would not be capable of knowledge of all things, as is clear from what has been said . . . ; which is contrary to the nature of the intellect. Therefore the intellect is not united to the body as its form.

Obj. 3. Further, whatever receptive power is an act of a body, receives a form materially and individually; for what is received must be received according to the condition of the receiver. But the form of the thing understood is not received into the intellect materially and individually, but rather immaterially and universally: otherwise the intellect would not be capable of the knowledge of immaterial and universal objects, but only of individuals, like the senses. Therefore the intellect is not united to the body as its form.

Obj. 4. Further, power and action have the same subject; for the same subject is what can, and does, act. But the intellectual action is not the action of a body, as appears from above. . . . Therefore neither is the intellectual faculty a power of the body. But virtue or power cannot be more abstract or more simple than the essence from which the faculty or power is derived. Therefore neither is the substance of the intellect the form of a body.

Obj. 5. Further, whatever has existence of itself is not united to the body as its form; because a form is that by which a thing exists. Thus the very existence of a form does not belong to the form of itself. But the intellectual principle has existence of itself and is subsistent, as was said above. . . . Therefore it is not united to the body as its form.

Obj. 6. Further, whatever exists in a thing by reason of its nature exists in it always. But to be united to matter belongs to the form by reason of its nature; because form is the act of matter, not by any accidental quality, but by its own essence; otherwise matter and form would not make a thing substantially one, but only accidentally one. Therefore a form cannot be without its own proper matter. But the intellectual principle, since it is incorruptible, as was shown above . . . , remains separate from the body, after the dissolution of the body. Therefore the intellectual principle is not united to the body as its form.

On the contrary, According to the Philosopher, *difference* is derived from the *form.* But the difference which constitutes man is *rational,* which is applied to man on account of his intellectual principle. Therefore the intellectual principle is the form of man.

I answer that, We must assert that the intellect which is the principle of intellectual operation is the form of the human body. For that whereby primarily anything acts is a form of the thing to which the act is to be attributed: for instance, that whereby a body is primarily healed is health, and that whereby the soul knows primarily is knowledge; hence health is a form of the body, and knowledge is a form of the soul. The reason is because nothing acts except so far as it is in act; so a thing acts by that whereby it is in act. Now it is clear that the first thing by which the body lives is the soul. And as life appears through various operations in different degrees of living things, that whereby we primarily perform each of all these vital actions is the soul. For the soul is the primary principle of our nourishment, feeling, and local movement; and likewise the primary principle whereby we understand. Therefore this principle by which we primarily understand, whether it be called the intellect or the intellectual soul, is the form of the body. This is the demonstration used by Aristotle (*De Anima* ii.). But if anyone say that the intellectual soul is not the form of the body he must first explain how it is that this action of understanding is the action of this particular man; for each one is conscious that it is himself who understands. Now an action may be attributed to anyone in three ways, as is clear from the Philosopher (*Phys.* v.); for a thing is said to move or act, either by virtue of its whole self, for instance, as a physician heals; or by virtue of a part, as a man sees by his eye; or through an accidental quality, as when we say that something that is white builds, because it is accidental to the builder to be white. So when we say that Socrates or Plato understands, it is clear that this is not attributed by any accidental quality, but by virtue of his being a man, which is predicated of him essentially. So we must say either that Socrates understands by virtue of his whole self, as Plato maintained, holding that man is an intellectual soul; or we must say that intelligence is a part of Socrates. The first cannot stand, as was shown above . . . , for this reason, that it is one and the same man who is conscious both that he understands, and that he feels. But one cannot feel without a body: therefore the body must be some part of man. It follows that the intellect by which Socrates understands is a part of Socrates, so that in some way it is united to the body of Socrates.

The Commentator held that this union is through the intelligible species, as having a double subject, in the passive intellect, and in the phantasms which are in the corporeal organs. Thus through the intelligible species the passive intellect is linked to the body of this or that particular man. But this link or union does not sufficiently explain the fact, that the act of the intellect is the act of Socrates. This can be clearly seen from comparison with the sensitive faculty, from which Aristotle proceeds to consider things relating to the intellect. For the relation of phantasms to the intellect is like the relation of colours to the sense of sight, as he says *De Anima* iii. Therefore, as the species of colours are in the sight, so are the species of phantasms in the passive intellect. But it is clear that because the colours, the images of which are in the sight, are on a wall, the action of seeing is not attributed to the wall: for we do not say that the wall sees, but rather that it is seen. Therefore, from the fact that the species of phantasms are in the passive intellect, it does not follow that Socrates, in whom are the phantasms, understands, but that he or his phantasms are understood.

Some, however, tried to maintain that the intellect is united to the body as its motor; and hence that the intellect and body form one thing so that the act of the intellect could be attributed to the whole. This is, however, absurd for many reasons. Firstly, because the intellect does not move the body except through the appetite, the movement of which presupposes the operation of the intellect. The reason therefore why Socrates understands is not because he is moved by his intellect, but rather, contrariwise, he is moved by his intellect because he understands. Secondly, because, since Socrates is an individual in a nature of one essence composed of matter and form, if the intellect be not the form, it follows that it must be outside the essence, and then the intellect is to the whole Socrates, as a motor to the thing moved. Whereas the act of intellect remains in the agent, and does not pass into something else, as does the action of heating. Therefore the action of understanding cannot be attributed to Socrates for the reason that he is moved by his intellect. Thirdly, because the action of a motor is never attributed to the thing moved, except as to an instrument; as the action of a carpenter to a saw. Therefore if understanding is attributed to Socrates, as the action of what moves him, it follows that it is attributed to him as to an instrument. This is contrary to the teaching of the Philosopher, who holds that understanding is not possible through a corporeal instrument (*De Anima* iii.). Fourthly, because, although the action of a part be attributed to the whole, as the action of the eye is attributed to a man; yet it is never attributed to another part, except perhaps indirectly; for we do not say that the hand sees, because the eye sees. Therefore if the intellect and Socrates are united in the above manner, the action of the intellect cannot be attributed to Socrates. If, however, Socrates be a whole composed of a union of the intellect with whatever else belongs to Socrates, and still the intellect be united to those other things only as a motor, it follows that Socrates is not one absolutely, and consequently neither a being absolutely, for a thing is a being according as it is one.

There remains, therefore, no other explanation than that given by Aristotle—namely, that this particular man understands, because the intellectual principle is his form. So from the very operation of the intellect it is made clear that the intellectual principle is united to the body as its form.

The same can be clearly shown from the nature of the human species. For the nature of each thing is shown by its operation. Now the proper operation of man as man is to understand; because he thereby surpasses all other animals. Whence Aristotle concludes (*Ethic.* x.) that the ultimate happiness of man must consist in this operation as properly belonging to him. Man must therefore derive his species from that which is the principle of this operation. But the species of anything is derived from its form. It follows therefore that the intellectual principle is the proper form of man.

But we must observe that the nobler a form is, the more it rules over corporeal matter, the less it is merged in matter, and the more it excels matter by its power and its operation; hence we find that the form of a mixed body has another operation not caused by its elemental qualities. And the higher we advance in the nobility of forms, the more we find that the power of the form excels the elementary matter; as the vegetable soul excels the form of the metal, and the sensitive soul excels the vegetable soul. Now the human soul is the highest and noblest of forms. Wherefore it excels corporeal matter in its power by the fact that it has an operation and a power in which corporeal matter has no share whatever. This power is called *the intellect.*

It is well to remark that if anyone holds that the soul is composed of matter and form, it would follow that in no way could the soul be the form of the body. For since the form is an act, and matter is only in potentiality, that which is composed of matter and form cannot be the form of another by virtue of itself as a whole. But if it is a form by virtue of some part of itself, then that part which is the form we call the soul, and that of which it is the form we call the *primary animate*, as was said above. . . .

Reply Obj. 1. As the Philosopher says (*Phys.* ii.), the ultimate natural form to which the consideration of the natural philosopher is directed is indeed separate; yet it exists in matter. He proves this from the fact that man and the sun generate man from matter. It is separate indeed according to its intellectual power, because the intellectual power does not belong to a corporeal organ, as the power of seeing is the act of the eye; for understanding is an act which cannot be performed by a corporeal organ, like the act of seeing. But it exists in matter so far as the soul itself, to which this power belongs, is the form of the body, and the term of human generation. And so the Philosopher says (*De Anima* iii.) that the intellect is separate, because it is not the faculty of a corporeal organ.

From this it is clear how to answer the Second and Third objections: since, in order that man may be able to understand all things by means of his intellect, and that his intellect may understand immaterial things and universals, it is sufficient that the intellectual power be not the act of the body.

Reply Obj. 4. The human soul, by reason of its perfection, is not a form merged in matter, or entirely embraced by matter. Therefore there is nothing to prevent some power thereof not being the act of the body, although the soul is essentially the form of the body.

Reply Obj. 5. The soul communicates that existence in which it subsists to the corporeal matter, out of which and the intellectual soul there results unity of existence; so that the existence of the whole composite is also the existence of the soul. This is not the case with other non-subsistent forms. For this reason the human soul retains its own existence after the dissolution of the body; but it is not so with other forms.

Reply Obj. 6. To be united to the body belongs to the soul by reason of itself, as it belongs to a light body by reason of itself to be raised up. And as a light body remains light, when removed from its own proper place, retaining meanwhile an aptitude and an inclination for its proper place: so the human soul retains its own proper existence when separated from the body, having an aptitude and a natural inclination to be united to the body.

. . . .

Whether the intellect is a power of the soul?

Objection 1. It seems that the intellect is not a power of the soul, but the essence of the soul. For the intellect seems to be the same as the mind. Now the mind is not a power of the soul, but the essence: for Augustine says (*De Trin.* ix.), *Mind and spirit are not relative, but denominate the essence.* Therefore the intellect is the essence of the soul.

Obj. 2. Further, different genera of the soul's powers are not united in some one power, but only in the essence of the soul. Now the appetitive and the intellectual are different genera of the soul's powers as the Philosopher says (*De Anima* ii.), but they are united in the mind, for Augustine (*De Trin.* x.) places the intelligence and will in the mind. Therefore the mind and intellect of man is the very essence of the soul and not a power thereof.

Obj. 3. Further, according to Gregory, in a homily for the Ascension, *man understands with the angels.* But angels are called *minds* and *intellects.* Therefore the mind and intellect of man are not a power of the soul, but the soul itself.

Obj. 4. Further, a substance is intellectual by the fact that it is immaterial. But the soul is immaterial through its essence. Therefore it seems that the soul must be intellectual through its essence.

On the contrary, The Philosopher assigns the intellectual faculty as a power of the soul (*De Anima* ii.).

I answer that, In accordance with what has been already shown . . . it is necessary to say that the intellect is a power of the soul, and not the very essence of the soul. For then alone the essence of that which operates is the immediate principle of operation, when operation itself is its being: for as power is to operation as its act, so is the essence to being. But in God alone His action of understanding is His very Being. Wherefore in God alone is His intellect His essence: while in other intellectual creatures, the intellect is a power.

Reply Obj. 1. Sense is sometimes taken for the power, and sometimes for the sensitive soul; for the sensitive soul takes its name from its chief power, which is sense. And in like manner the intellectual soul is sometimes called intellect, as from its chief power; and thus we read (*De Anima* i.), that the *intellect is a substance.* And in this sense also Augustine says that the mind is spirit and essence (*De Trin.* ix., xiv.).

Reply Obj. 2. The appetitive and intellectual powers are different genera of powers in the soul, by reason of the different formalities of their objects. But the appetitive power agrees partly with the intellectual power and partly with the sensitive in its mode of operation either through a corporeal organ or without it: for appetite follows apprehension. And in this way Augustine puts the will in the mind; and the Philosopher, in the reason (*De Anima* iii.).

Reply Obj. 3. In the angels there is no other power besides the intellect, and the will, which follows the intellect. And for this reason an angel is called a *mind* or an *intellect;* because his whole power consists in this. But the soul has many other powers, such as the sensitive and nutritive powers, and therefore there is no likeness between the two orders.

Reply Obj. 4. The immateriality of the created intelligent substance is not its intellect; but its immateriality gives its power of intelligence. Wherefore it does not follow that the intellect is the substance of the soul, but its virtue and power.

Whether the intellect is a passive power?

Objection 1. It seems that the intellect is not a passive power. For everything is passive by its matter, and acts by its form. But the intellectual power results from the immateriality of the intelligent substance. Therefore it seems that the intellect is not a passive power.

Obj. 2. Further, the intellectual power is incorruptible, as we have said above. . . . But *if the intellect is passive, it is corruptible* (*De Anima* iii.). Therefore the intellectual power is not passive.

Obj. 3. Further, the *agent is nobler than the patient,* as Augustine (*Gen. ad lit.* xii.) and Aristotle (*De Anima* iii.) say. But all the powers of the vegetative part are active; yet they are the lowest among the powers of the soul. Much more, therefore, all the intellectual powers, which are the highest, are active.

On the contrary, The Philosopher says that *to understand is in a way to be passive* (*De Anima* iii.).

I answer that, To be passive may be taken in three ways. Firstly, in its most strict sense, when from a thing is taken something which belongs to it by virtue either of its nature, or of its proper inclination: as when water loses coolness by heating, and as when a man becomes ill or sad. Secondly, less strictly, a thing is said to be passive, when something, whether suitable or unsuitable, is taken away from it. And in this way not only he who is ill is said to be passive, but also he who is healed; not only he that is sad, but also he that is joyful; or whatever way he be altered or moved. Thirdly, in a wide sense a thing is said to be passive, from the very fact that what is in potentiality to something receives that to which it was in potentiality, without being deprived of anything. And accordingly, whatever passes from potentiality to act, may be said to be passive, even when it is perfected. And thus with us to understand is to be passive. This is clear from the following reason. For the intellect, as we have seen above . . . , has an operation extending to universal being. We may therefore see whether the intellect be in act or potentiality by observing first of all the nature of the relation of the intellect to universal being. For we find an intellect whose relation to universal being is that of the act of all being: and such is the Divine intellect, which is the Essence of God, in which virtually and as in its origin, all being preexists as in its first cause. And therefore the Divine intellect is not in potentiality, but is pure act. But no created intellect can be an act in relation to the whole universal being; otherwise it would needs be an infinite being. Wherefore every created intellect is not the act of all things intelligible, by reason of its very existence; but is compared to these intelligible things as a potentiality to act.

Now, potentiality has a double relation to act. There is a potentiality which is always perfected by its act: as the matter of the heavenly bodies. . . . And here is another potentiality which is not always in act, but proceeds from potentiality to act; as we observe in things that are corrupted and generated. Wherefore the angelic intellect is always in act as regards those things which we understand, by reason of its proximity to the first intellect which is pure act, as we have said above. But the human intellect, which is the lowest in the order of intelligence and most remote from the perfection of the Divine intellect is in potentiality with regard to things intelligible, and is at first *like a clean tablet on which nothing is written*, as the Philosopher says (*De Anima* iii.). This is made clear from the fact, that at first we are only in potentiality to understand, and afterwards we are made to understand actually. And so it is evident that with us to understand is *in a way to be passive;* taking passion in the third sense. And consequently the intellect is a passive power.

Obj. 1. This objection is verified of passion in the first and second senses, which belong to primary matter. But in the third sense passion is in anything which is reduced from potentiality to act.

Obj. 2. *Passive intellect* is the name given by some to the sensitive appetite, in which are the passions of the soul; which appetite is also called *rational by participation*, because it *obeys the reason* (*Ethic.* i.). Others give the name of passive intellect to the cogitative power, which is called the *particular reason*. And in each case *passive* may be taken in the two first senses; forasmuch as this so-called intellect is the act of a corporeal organ. But the intellect which is in potentiality to things intelligible, and which for this reason Aristotle calls the *possible* intellect (*De Anima* iii.), is not passive except in the third sense: for it is not an act of a corporeal organ. And hence it is incorruptible.

Reply Obj. 3. The agent is nobler than the patient, if the action and the passion are referred to the same thing: but not always, if they refer to different things. Now the intellect is a passive power in regard to the whole universal being: while the vegetative power is active in regard to some particular thing, namely, the body as united to the soul. Wherefore nothing prevents such a passive force being nobler than such an active one.

. . . .

Whether intellectual knowledge is derived from sensible things?

Objection 1. It seems that intellectual knowledge is not derived from sensible things. For Augustine says (*lib.* 83 *qqu.*) *that we cannot expect to learn the fulness of truth from the senses of the body.* This he proves in two ways. Firstly, because *whatever we perceive through the body, is continually being changed; and what is never the same cannot be perceived.* Secondly, because, *whatever we perceive by the body, even when not present to the senses, may be present to the imagination, as we see in those who are asleep or beside themselves with anger; but we cannot discern by the senses, whether what we perceive be the sensible object, or the deceptive images thereof. Now nothing can be perceived which cannot be distinguished from its counterfeit.* And so he concludes that we cannot expect to learn the truth from the senses. But intellectual knowledge apprehends the truth. Therefore intellectual knowledge cannot be conveyed by the senses.

Obj. 2. Further, Augustine says (*Gen. ad lit.* xii.), *We must not think that the body can make any impression on the spirit, as though the spirit were to supply the place of matter in regard to the body's action; for that which acts is in every way more excellent than that which it acts on.* Whence he concludes that *the body does not cause its image in the spirit, but the spirit causes it in itself.* Therefore intellectual knowledge is not derived from sensible things.

Obj. 3. Further, an effect does not surpass the power of its cause. But intellectual knowledge extends beyond sensible things: for we understand some things which cannot be perceived by the senses. Therefore intellectual knowledge is not derived from sensible things.

On the contrary, The Philosopher says (*Metaph.* i.; *Poster.* ii.) that the principle of knowledge is in the senses.

I answer that, On this point the philosophers held three opinions. For Democritus held that *all knowledge is caused by images issuing from the bodies we think of and entering into our souls*, as Augustine says in his letter to Dioscorus. And Aristotle says (*De Somn. et Vigil.*) that Democritus held that knowledge is caused by a *discharge of images*. And the reason for this opinion was that both Democritus and the other early philosophers did not distinguish between intellect and sense, as Aristotle relates (*De Anima*). Consequently, since the sense is affected by the sensible they thought that all our knowledge is effected by this mere impression brought about by sensible things. Which impression Democritus held to be caused by a discharge of images.

Plato, on the other hand, held that the intellect is distinct from the senses; and that it is an immaterial power not making use of a corporeal organ for its action. And since the incorporeal cannot be affected by the corporeal, he held that intellectual knowledge is not brought about by sensible things affecting the intellect, but by separate intelligible forms being participated by the intellect, as we have said above. . . . Moreover he held that sense is a power operating of itself. Consequently neither is sense, since it is a spiritual power, affected by the sensible: but the sensible organs are affected by the sensible, the result being that the soul is in a way roused to form within itself the species of the sensible. Augustine seems to touch on this opinion (*Gen. ad lit.* xii.) where he says that the *body feels not, but the soul through the body, which it makes use of as a kind of messenger, for reproducing within itself what is announced from without*. Thus according to Plato, neither does intellectual knowledge proceed from sensible knowledge, nor sensible knowledge exclusively from sensible things; but these rouse the sensible soul to the sentient act, while the senses rouse the intellect to the act of understanding.

But Aristotle chose a middle course. For with Plato he agreed that intellect and sense are different. But he held that the sense has not its proper operation without the co-operation of the body; so that to feel is not an act of the soul alone, but of the *composite*. And he held the same in regard to all the operations of the sensitive part. Since, therefore, it is not unreasonable that the sensible objects which are outside the soul should produce some effect in the *composite*, Aristotle agreed with Democritus in this, that the operations of the sensitive part are caused by the impression of the sensible on the sense: there is a discharge, as Democritus said, but by some kind of operation. For Democritus maintained that every operation is by way of a discharge of atoms, as we gather from *De Gener.* i. But Aristotle held that the intellect has an operation which is independent of the body's co-operation. Now nothing corporeal can make an impression on the incorporeal. And therefore in order to cause the intellectual operation, according to Aristotle, the impression caused by the sensible does not suffice, but something more noble is required, for *the agent is more noble than the patient*, as he says himself (*ibid.*). Not, indeed, in the sense that the intellectual operation is effected in us by the mere impression of some superior beings, as Plato held; but that the higher and more noble agent which he calls the active intellect, of which we have spoken above . . . , causes the phantasms received from the senses to be actually intelligible, by a process of abstraction.

According to this opinion, then, on the part of the phantasms, intellectual knowledge is caused by the senses. But since the phantasms cannot of themselves affect the passive intellect, and require to be made actually intelligible by the active intellect, it cannot be said that sensible knowledge is the total and perfect cause of intellectual knowledge, but rather that it is in a way the material cause.

Reply Obj. 1. Those words of Augustine mean that we must not expect the entire truth from the senses. For the light of the active intellect is needed, through which we achieve the unchangeable truth of changeable things, and discern things themselves from their likeness.

Reply Obj. 2. In this passage Augustine speaks not of intellectual but of imaginary knowledge. And since, according to the opinion of Plato, the imagination has an operation which belongs to the soul only, Augustine, in order to show that corporeal images are impressed on the imagination, not by bodies but by the soul, uses the same argument as Aristotle does in proving that the active intellect must be separate, namely, because *the agent is more noble than the patient*. And without doubt, according to the above opinion, in the imagination there must needs be not only a passive but also an active power. But if we hold, according to the opinion of Aristotle, that the action of the imagination is an action of the *composite*, there is no difficulty; because the sensible body is more noble than the organ of the animal, in as far as it is compared to it as a being in act to a being in potentiality, as the object actually coloured, to the pupil which is potentially coloured. It may, however, be said, although the first impression of the imagination is through the agency of the sensible, since *fancy is movement produced in accordance with sensation* (*De Anima* iii.), that nevertheless there is in man an operation which by synthesis and analysis forms images of various things, even of things not perceived by the senses. And Augustine's words may be taken in this sense.

Reply Obj. 3. Sensitive knowledge is not the entire cause of intellectual knowledge. And therefore it is not strange that intellectual knowledge should extend further than sensitive knowledge.

. . . .

Whether our intellect understands corporeal and material things by abstraction from phantasms?

Objection 1. It seems that our intellect does not understand corporeal and material things by abstraction from the phantasms. For the intellect is false if it understands an object otherwise than as it really is.

Now the forms of material things do not exist as abstracted from the particular things represented by the phantasms. Therefore, if we understand material things by abstraction of the species from the phantasm, there will be error in the intellect.

Obj. 2. Further, material things are those natural things which include matter in their definition. But nothing can be understood apart from that which enters into its definition. Therefore material things cannot be understood apart from matter. Now matter is the principle of individualization. Therefore material things cannot be understood by abstraction of the universal from the particular, which is the process whereby the intelligible species is abstracted from the phantasm.

Obj. 3. Further, the Philosopher says (*De Anima* iii.) that the phantasm is to the intellectual soul, what colour is to the sight. But seeing is not caused by abstraction of species from colour, but by colour impressing itself on the sight. Therefore neither does the act of understanding take place by abstraction of something from the phantasm, but by the phantasm impressing itself on the intellect.

Obj. 4. Further, the Philosopher says (*De Anima* iii.) there are two things in the intellectual soul—the passive intellect and the active intellect. But it does not belong to the passive intellect to abstract the intelligible species from the phantasm, but to receive them when abstracted. Neither does it seem to be the function of the active intellect, which is related to the phantasm, as light is to colour; since light does not abstract anything from colour, but rather streams on to it. Therefore in no way do we understand by abstraction from phantasms.

Obj. 5. Further, the Philosopher (*De Anima* iii.) says that *the intellect understands the species in the phantasm;* and not, therefore, by abstraction.

On the contrary, The Philosopher says (*De Anima* iii.) that *things are intelligible in proportion as they are separable from matter*. Therefore material things must needs be understood according as they are abstracted from matter and from material images, namely, phantasms.

I answer that, As stated above . . . , the object of knowledge is proportionate to the power of knowledge. Now there are three grades of the cognitive powers. For one cognitive power is the act of a corporeal organ, namely, the sense. And therefore the object of every sensitive power is a form as existing in corporeal matter. And since such matter is the principle of individuality, therefore every power of the sensitive part can only have knowledge of the individual. There is another grade of cognitive power which is neither the act of a corporeal organ, nor in any way connected with corporeal matter; such is the angelic intellect, the object of whose cognitive power is therefore a form existing apart from matter: for though angels know material things, yet they do not know them save in something immaterial, namely, either in themselves or in God. But the human intellect holds a middle place: for it is not the act of an organ; yet it is a power of the soul which is the form of the body, as is clear from what we have said above . . . . And therefore it is proper to it to know a form existing individually in corporeal matter, but not as existing in this individual matter. But to know what is in individual matter, not as existing in such matter, is to abstract the form from individual matter which is represented by the phantasms. Therefore we must needs say that our intellect understands material things by abstracting from the phantasms; and through material things thus considered we acquire some knowledge of immaterial things, just as, on the contrary, angels know material things through the immaterial.

But Plato, considering only the immateriality of the human intellect, and not its being in a way united to the body, held that the objects of the intellect are separate ideas; and that we understand not by abstraction, but by participating in things abstract, as stated above . . . .

Reply Obj. 1. Abstraction may occur in two ways: Firstly, by way of composition and division; thus we may understand that one thing does not exist in some other, or that it is separate therefrom. Secondly, by way of simple and absolute consideration; thus we understand one thing without considering the other. Thus for the intellect to abstract from one another things which are not really abstract from one another, does, in the first mode of abstraction, imply falsehood. But, in the second mode of abstraction, for the intellect to abstract things which are not really abstract from one another, does not involve falsehood, as clearly appears in the case of the senses. For if we understand or say that colour does not exist in a coloured body, or is separate from it, there would be error in this opinion or assertion. But if we consider colour and its properties, without reference to the apple which is coloured; or if we express in word what we thus understand, there is no error in such an opinion or assertion, because an apple is not essential to colour, and therefore colour can be understood independently of the apple. Likewise, the things which belong to the sepcies of a material thing, such as a stone, or a man, or a horse, can be thought of apart from the individualizing principles which do not belong to the notion of the species. This is what we mean by abstracting the universal from the particular, or the intelligible species from the phantasm; that is, by considering the nature of the species apart from its individual qualities represented by the phantasms. If, therefore, the intellect is said to be false when it understands a thing otherwise than as it is, that is so, if the word *otherwise* refers to the thing understood; for the intellect is false when it understands a thing otherwise than as it is; and so the intellect would be false if it abstracted the species of a stone from its matter in such a way as to regard the species as not existing in matter, as Plato held. But it is not so, if the word *otherwise* be taken as referring to the one who understands. For it is quite true that the mode of understanding, in one who understands, is not the same as the mode of a thing in existing: since the thing understood is immaterially in the one who understands, according to the mode of the intellect, and not materially, according to the mode of a material thing.

Reply Obj. 2. Some have thought that the species of a natural thing is a form only, and that matter is not part of the species. If that were so, matter would not enter into the definition of natural things. Therefore it must be said otherwise, that matter is twofold, common, and general or individual; common, such as flesh and bone; and individual, as this flesh and these bones. The intellect therefore abstracts the species of a natural thing from the individual sensible matter, but not from the common sensible matter; for example, it abstracts the species of man from *this flesh and these bones*, which do not belong to the species as such, but to the individual (*Metaph.* vii.), and need not be considered in the species: whereas the species of man cannot be abstracted by the intellect from *flesh and bones*. But mathematical species can be abstracted by the intellect from sensible matter, not only from individual, but also from common matter; not from common intelligible matter, but only from individual matter. For sensible matter is corporeal matter as subject to sensible qualities, such as being cold or hot, hard or soft, and the like. But intelligible matter is substance as subject to quantity. Now it is manifest that quantity is in substance before other sensible qualities are. Hence quantities, such as number dimension, and figures, which are the terminations of quantity, can be considered apart from sensible qualities; and this is to abstract them from sensible matter; but they cannot be considered without understanding the substance which is subject to the quantity; for that would be to abstract them from common intelligible matter. But they can be considered apart from this or that substance; for that is to abstract them from individual intelligible matter. But some things can be abstracted from common intelligible matter, such as *being, unity, power, act,* and the like; all these can exist without matter, as is plain regarding immaterial things. Because Plato failed to consider the two-fold kind of abstraction, as above explained, he held that all those things which we have stated to be abstracted by the intellect, are abstract in reality.

Reply Obj. 3. Colours, as being in individual corporeal matter, have the same mode of existence as the power of sight: and therefore they can impress their own image on the eye. But phantasms, since they are images of individuals, and exist in corporeal organs, have not the same mode of existence as the human intellect, and therefore have not the power of themselves to make an impression on the passive intellect. This is done by the power of the active intellect which by turning towards the phantasm produces in the passive intellect a certain likeness which represents, as to its specific conditions only, the thing reflected in the phantasm. It is thus that the intelligible species is said to be abstracted from the phantasm; not that the identical form which previously was in the phantasm is subsequently in the passive intellect, as a body transferred from one place to another.

Reply Obj. 4. Not only does the active intellect throw light on the phantasm; it does more; by its own power it abstracts the intelligible species from the phantasm. It throws light on the phantasm, because, just as the sensitive part acquires a greater power by its conjunction with the intellectual part, so by the power of the active intellect the phantasms are made more fit for the abstraction therefrom of intelligible intentions. Furthermore, the active intellect abstracts the intelligible species from the phantasm, forasmuch as by the power of the active intellect we are able to disregard the conditions of individuality, and to take into our consideration the specific nature, the image of which informs the passive intellect.

Reply Obj. 5. Our intellect both abstracts the intelligible species from the phantasms, inasmuch as it considers the natures of things in universal, and, nevertheless, understands these natures in the phantasms, since it cannot understand even the things of which it abstracts the species, without turning to the phantasms, as we have said above . . . .

Human Happiness

That man's ultimate happiness consists in
contemplating God.

Accordingly if man's ultimate happiness consists not in external things, which are called goods of chance; nor in goods of the body; nor in goods of the soul, as regards the sensitive faculty; nor as regards the intellective faculty, in the practice of moral virtue; nor as regards intellectual virtue in those which are concerned about action, namely art and prudence; it remains for us to conclude that man's ultimate happiness consists in the contemplation of the truth.

For this operation alone is proper to man, and none of the other animals communicates with him therein.

Again. This is not directed to anything further as its end: since the contemplation of the truth is sought for its own sake.

Again. By this operation man is united to things above him, by becoming like them: because of all human actions this alone is both in God and in separate substances. Also, by this operation man comes into contact with those higher beings, through knowing them in any way whatever.

SOURCE: *Summa Contra Gentiles*, translated by the English Dominican Fathers (London: Burns, Oates and Nashbourne, 1928), vol. 3, part 1, pp. 78–84, 111–116. Reprinted with permission of Benziger Brothers, New York, and Burns & Oates, Ltd., London.

Besides, man is more self-sufficing for this operation, seeing that he stands in little need of the help of external things in order to perform it.

Further. All other human operations seem to be directed to this as their end. Because perfect contemplation requires that the body should be disencumbered, and to this effect are directed all the products of art that are necessary for life. Moreover, it requires freedom from the disturbance caused by the passions, which is achieved by means of the moral virtues and prudence; and freedom from external disturbance, to which all the regulations of the civil life are directed. So that, if we consider the matter rightly, we shall see that all human occupations are brought into the service of those who contemplate the truth. Now, it is not possible that man's ultimate happiness consist in contemplation based on the understanding of first principles: for this is most imperfect, as being universal and containing potential knowledge of things. Moreover, it is the beginning and not the end of human study, and comes to us from nature, and not through the study of the truth. Nor does it consist in contemplation based on the sciences that have the lowest things for their object: since happiness must consist in an operation of the intellect in relation to the highest objects of intelligence. It follows then that man's ultimate happiness consists in wisdom, based on the consideration of divine things. It is therefore evident by way of induction that man's ultimate happiness consists solely in the contemplation of God, which conclusion was proved above by arguments.

That human happiness does not consist in the knowledge of God which is possessed generally by the majority.

It remains for us to inquire in what kind of knowledge of God the ultimate happiness of the intellectual substance consists. For there is a certain general and confused knowledge of God, which is in almost all men, whether from the fact that, as some think, the existence of God, like other principles of demonstration, is self-evident, as we have stated in the First Book: or, as seems nearer to the truth, because by his natural reason, man is able at once to arrive at some knowledge of God. For seeing that natural things are arranged in a certain order,—since there cannot be order without a cause of order—men, for the most part, perceive that there is one who arranges in order the things that we see. But who or of what kind this cause of order may be, or whether there be but one, cannot be gathered from this general consideration: even so, when we see a man in motion, and performing other works, we perceive that in him there is a cause of these operations, which is not in other things, and we give this cause the name of *soul*, but without knowing yet what the soul is, whether it be a body, or how it brings about operations in question.

Now, this knowledge of God cannot possibly suffice for happiness.

For the operation of the happy must be without any defect: and this knowledge is subject to an admixture of many errors. Some believed that there is no other ordainer of mundane things than the heavenly bodies; wherefore they said that the heavenly bodies are gods.—Some ascribed this order to the elements and to the things generated from them; as though they deemed the movements and natural operations thereof, not to be due to another ordainer, and the order in other things to be caused by them.—Some, deeming human acts not to be subject to any but a human ordinance, declared that men who cause order in other men are gods.—Accordingly this knowledge of God is not sufficient for happiness.

Moreover. Happiness is the end of human acts. But human acts are not directed to the aforesaid knowledge as their end: indeed, it is in everyone almost from the very beginning. Therefore happiness does not consist in this kind of knowledge of God.

Again. No one appears to be blamed for lacking happiness: nay, those who have it not and seek it are praised. Whereas he who lacks the aforesaid knowledge of God, is seemingly very much to be blamed: since it is a very clear sign of a man's dullness of perception, if he fail to perceive such evident signs of God's existence: even as a man would be deemed dull who, seeing man, understood not that he has a soul. Hence it is said in the Psalm (xiii. 1: lii. 1): *The fool hath said in his heart: There is no God.*

Further. Knowledge of a thing in general only, and not in respect of a property thereof, is most imperfect; for instance knowledge of man from the fact that he is moved, for this is a knowledge whereby a thing is known only potentially: because the proper is only potentially contained in the common. Now happiness is a perfect operation: and man's supreme good must needs be in respect of what he is actually, and not in respect of what he is only potentially: since potentiality perfected by act has the aspect of a good. Therefore the aforesaid knowledge of God is not sufficient for our happiness.

That man's happiness does not consist in the knowledge of God acquired by demonstration.

There is also another knowledge of God, higher than the one just mentioned, which is acquired by means of a demonstration, and which approaches nearer to a proper knowledge of him: since by means of a demonstration many things are removed from him, so that in consequence we understand him as something apart from other things. For demonstration proves that God is immovable, eternal, incorporeal, utterly simple, one, and the like, as we have shown in the First Book. Now we arrive at the proper knowledge of a thing not only by affirmation, but also by negation: for just as it is proper to man to be a rational animal, so is it proper to him not to be inanimate or irrational. Yet there is this difference between these two modes of knowledge, that when we have proper knowledge of a thing by affirmation, we know what that thing is, and how it is distinguished from others: whereas when we have proper knowledge of a thing by negations, we know that it is distinct from others, but remain ignorant of what it is. Such is the proper knowledge of God, that can be obtained by demonstrations. But neither does this suffice for man's ultimate happiness. For things belonging to one species for the most part attain to the end of that species, because nature achieves its purpose always or nearly always, and fails in a few instances on account of some corruption. Now happiness is the end of the human species; since all men naturally desire it. Therefore happiness is a common good that can be attained by all men, unless some obstacle occur to some whereby they be debarred from it. Few, however, attain to the possession of the aforesaid knowledge of God by way of demonstration, on account of the obstacles to this knowledge, mentioned at the beginning of this work. Therefore this knowledge is not essentially man's happiness.

Again. Actual existence is the end of that which exists potentially, as was made clear above. Wherefore happiness that is the last end, is an act free of any potentiality to a further act. Now this knowledge of God that is acquired by way of demonstration is still in potentiality to a further knowledge of God, or to the same knowledge, but by a better way: because those who came afterwards endeavoured to add something to the knowledge of God besides that which they found handed down to them by those who preceded them. Therefore such knowledge is not man's ultimate happiness.

Further. Happiness excludes all unhappiness: for no man can be at the same time happy and unhappy. Now deception and error have a large place in unhappiness, since all naturally avoid them. But the aforesaid knowledge of God is subject to the admixture of many errors: as evidenced by many who knew some truths about God through demonstration, yet, following their own opinions, when they lacked proof, fell into many errors. And if some there were who by the way of demonstration discovered the truth about divine things, without any admixture of error in their opinions, it is evident that they were very few: which is inconsistent with happiness which should be the common end. Therefore man's ultimate happiness is not seated in such knowledge as this.

Moreover. Happiness consists in a perfect operation. Now perfect knowledge requires certitude: hence we cannot be said to know, unless we be certain that it cannot be otherwise, as stated in 1 *Poster*. ii. But the aforesaid knowledge is beset with uncertainty: as evidenced by the diversity of sciences about divine things, elaborated by those who endeavoured to discover something about them by the way of demonstration. Therefore ultimate happiness does not consist in suchlike knowledge.

Besides. When the will has obtained its last end, its desire is at rest. Now the ultimate end of all human knowledge is happiness. Therefore happiness is essentially that knowledge of God the possession of which leaves no knowledge to be desired of anything knowable. Such, however, is not the knowledge which philosophers were able to have about God by the way of demonstration: because even when we have that knowledge we still desire to know something more;—things that we know not by means of the aforesaid knowledge. Therefore happiness does not consist in suchlike knowledge of God.

Furthermore. The end of everything that is in potentiality is that it be brought to actuality: for to this does it tend by means of the movement with which it is moved to its end. Now everything that is in potentiality tends to be actualized as far as possible. For there are things in potentiality in that their whole potentiality is reducible to act: so that the end of such a thing is that its whole potentiality be actualized: thus a heavy body, that is outside its medium, is in potentiality to its proper place. There are also things whose potentiality cannot be actualized all at once—for instance primary matter: so that by its movement it is appetent of actualization by various forms in succession, which cannot be in matter at the same time on account of their diversity. Now our intellect is in potentiality to all things intelligible, as stated in the Second Book. And it is possible for two intelligible objects to be in the possible intellect at the same time in respect of the first act which is *science*: although perhaps not in respect of the second act which is *consideration*. Accordingly it is clear that the whole potentiality of the possible intellect can be actualized at one time: and consequently this is required for its ultimate end which is happiness. But the aforesaid knowledge which can be acquired about God by the way of demonstration, does not effect this: since when we have it we still are ignorant of many things. Therefore suchlike knowledge of God does not suffice for ultimate happiness.

That man's happiness does not consist in the knowledge of God by faith.

There is yet another knowledge of God, in one respect superior to the knowledge we have been discussing, namely that whereby God is known by men through faith. In this respect it surpasses the knowledge of God through demonstration, because by faith we know certain things about God, which are so sublime that reason cannot reach them by means of demonstration, as we have stated at the beginning of this work. But not even in this knowledge of God can man's ultimate happiness consist.

For happiness is the intellect's perfect operation, as already declared. But in knowledge by faith the operation of the intellect is found to be most imperfect as regards that which is on the part of the intellect:—although it is most perfect on the part of the object:—for the intellect in believing does not grasp the object of its assent. Therefore neither does man's happiness consist in this knowledge of God.

Again. It has been shown that ultimate happiness does not consist chiefly in an act of the will. Now in knowledge by faith the will has the leading place: for the intellect assents by faith to things proposed to it, because it wills, and not through being constrained by the evidence of their truth. Therefore man's final happiness does not consist in this knowledge.

Besides. The believer assents to things proposed to him by another, but not seen by himself: so that the knowledge of faith resembles hearing rather than seeing. Now a man does not believe in what is unseen by him, and proposed to him by another, unless he thinks this other to have a more perfect knowledge of the things proposed, than he himself has who sees not. Either therefore the believer thinks wrong: or the proposer must have more perfect knowledge of the things proposed. And if the latter also knows these things only through hearing them from another, we cannot proceed thus indefinitely: for then the assent of faith would be without foundation or certitude; since we should not come to some first principle certain in itself, to give certitude to the faith of believers. But it is not possible that the assent of faith be false and without foundation, as is clear from what we have said at the beginning of this work: and yet if it were false and baseless, happiness could not consist in suchlike knowledge. There is therefore some knowledge of God that is higher than the knowledge of faith: whether he who proposes faith sees the truth immediately, as when we believe Christ: or receive the truth from him who sees it immediately, as when, we believe the Apostles and prophets. Since then man's happiness consists in the highest knowledge of God, it cannot consist in the knowledge of faith.

Moreover. Since happiness is the last end, the natural desire is set at rest thereby. But the knowledge of faith does not set the desire at rest, but inflames it: because everyone desires to see what he believes. Therefore man's ultimate happiness does not consist in the knowledge of faith.

Further. Knowledge of God has been declared to be the end, inasmuch as it unites us to the last end of all, namely God. Now the knowledge of faith does not make the thing believed to be perfectly present to the mind: since faith is of distant, and not present things. Wherefore the Apostle says (2 Cor. v. 6, 7) that *so long as we walk by faith, we are pilgrims from the Lord.* Yet faith makes God to be present to the heart, since the believer assents to God voluntarily, according to the saying of Ephes. iii. 17: *That Christ may dwell by faith in our hearts.* Therefore the knowledge of faith cannot be man's ultimate happiness . . . .

That man's ultimate happiness is not in this life.

Seeing then that man's ultimate happiness does not consist in that knowledge of God whereby he is known by all or many in a vague kind of opinion, nor again in that knowledge of God whereby he is known in science through demonstration; nor in that knowledge whereby he is known through faith, as we have proved above: and seeing that it is not possible in this life to arrive at a higher knowledge of God in His essence, or at least so that we understand other separate substances, and thus know God through that which is nearest to Him, so to say, as we have proved; and since we must place our ultimate happiness in some kind of knowledge of God, as we have shown; it is impossible for man's happiness to be in this life.

Again. Man's last end is the term of his natural appetite, so that when he has obtained it, he desires nothing more: because if he still has a movement towards something, he has not yet reached an end wherein to be at rest. Now, this cannot happen in this life: since the more man understands, the more is the desire to understand increased in him,— this being natural to man,—unless perhaps someone there be who understands all things: and in this life this never did nor can happen to anyone that was a mere man; seeing that in this life we are unable to know separate substances which in themselves are most intelligible, as we have proved. Therefore man's ultimate happiness cannot possibly be in this life.

Besides. Whatever is in motion towards an end, has a natural desire to be established and at rest therein: hence a body does not move away from the place towards which it has a natural movement, except by a violent movement which is contrary to that appetite. Now happiness is the last end which man desires naturally. Therefore it is his natural desire to be established in happiness. Consequently unless together with happiness he acquires a state of immobility, he is not yet happy, since his natural desire is not yet at rest. When therefore a man acquires happiness, he also acquires stability and rest; so that all agree in conceiving stability as a necessary condition of happiness: hence the Philosopher says (1 *Ethic.* x.): *We do not look upon the happy man as a kind of chameleon.* Now, in this life there is no sure stability; since, however happy a man may be, sickness and misfortune may come upon him, so that he is hindered in the operation, whatever it be, in which his happiness consists. Therefore man's ultimate happiness cannot be in this life.

Moreover. It would seem unfitting and unreasonable for a thing to take a long time in becoming, and to have but a short time in being: for it would follow that for a longer duration of time nature would be deprived of its end; hence we see that animals which live but a short time, are perfected in a short time. But, if happiness consists in a perfect operation according to perfect virtue, whether intellectual or moral, it cannot possibly come to man except after a long time. This is most evident in speculative matters, wherein man's ultimate happiness consists, as we have proved: for hardly is man able to arrive at perfection in the speculations of science, even though he reach the last stage of life: and then in the majority of cases, but a short space of life remains to him. Therefore man's ultimate happiness cannot be in this life.

Further. All admit that happiness is a perfect good: else it would not bring rest to the appetite. Now perfect good is that which is wholly free from any admixture of evil: just as that which is perfectly white is that which is entirely free from any admixture of black. But man cannot be wholly free from evils in this state of life; not only from evils of the body, such as hunger, thirst, heat, cold and the like, but also from evils of the soul. For no one is there who at times is not disturbed by inordinate passions; who sometimes does not go beyond the mean, wherein virtue consists, either in excess or in deficiency; who is not deceived in some thing or another; or at least ignores what he would wish to know, or feels doubtful about an opinion of which he would like to be certain. Therefore no man is happy in this life.

Again. Man naturally shuns death, and is sad about it: not only shunning it now when he feels its presence, but also when he thinks about it. But man, in this life, cannot obtain not to die. Therefore it is not possible for man to be happy in this life.

Besides. Ultimate happiness consists not in a habit but in an operation: since habits are for the sake of actions. But in this life it is impossible to perform any action continuously. Therefore man cannot be entirely happy in this life.

Further. The more a thing is desired and loved, the more does its loss bring sorrow and pain. Now happiness is most desired and loved. Therefore its loss brings the greatest sorrow. But if there be ultimate happiness in this life, it will certainly be lost, at least by death. Nor is it certain that it will last till death: since it is possible for every man in this life to encounter sickness, whereby he is wholly hindered from the operation of virtue; such as madness and the like which hinder the use of reason. Such happiness therefore always has sorrow naturally connected with it: and consequently it will not be perfect happiness.

But someone might say that, since happiness is a good of the intellectual nature, perfect and true happiness is for those in whom the intellectual nature is perfect, namely in separate substances: and that it is imperfect in man, by way of a kind of participation. Because he can arrive at a full understanding of the truth, only by a sort of movement of inquiry; and fails entirely to understand things that are by nature most intelligible, as we have proved. Wherefore neither is happiness, in its perfect form, possible to man: yet he has a certain participation thereof, even in this life. This seems to have been Aristotle's opinion about happiness. Wherefore (1 *Ethic.* x.) inquiring whether misfortunes destroy happiness, he shows that happiness seems especially to consist in deeds of virtue, which seem to be most stable in this life, and concludes that those who in this life attain to this perfection, are happy *as men*, as though not attaining to happiness simply, but in a human way.

We must now show that this explanation does not avoid the foregoing arguments. For although man is below the separate substances in the natural order, he is above irrational creatures: wherefore he attains his ultimate end in a more perfect way than they. Now these attain their last end so perfectly that they seek nothing further: thus a heavy body rests when it is in its own proper place; and when an animal enjoys sensible pleasure, its natural desire is at rest. Much more therefore when man has obtained his last end, must his natural desire be at rest. But this cannot happen in this life. Therefore in this life man does not obtain happiness considered as his proper end, as we have proved. Therefore he must obtain it after this life.

Again. The natural desire cannot be void; since *nature does nothing in vain*. But nature's desire would be void if it could never be fulfilled. Therefore man's natural desire can be fulfilled. But not in this life, as we have shown. Therefore it must be fulfilled after this life. Therefore man's ultimate happiness is after this life.

Besides. As long as a thing is in motion towards perfection it has not reached its last end. Now in the knowledge of truth all men are ever in motion and tending towards perfection: because those who follow, make discoveries in addition to those made by their predecessors, as stated in 2 *Metaph.* Therefore in the knowledge of truth man is not situated as though he had arrived at his last end. Since then as Aristotle himself shows (10 *Ethic.* vii.) man's ultimate happiness in this life consists apparently in speculation, whereby he seeks the knowledge of truth, we cannot possibly allow that man obtains his last end in this life.

Moreover. Whatever is in potentiality tends to become actual: so that as long as it is not wholly actual, it has not reached its last end. Now our intellect is in potentiality to the knowledge of the forms of all things: and it becomes actual when it knows any óne of them. Consequently it will not be wholly actual, nor in possession of its last end, except when it knows all, at least these material things. But man cannot obtain this through speculative sciences, by which in this life we know truth. Therefore man's ultimate happiness cannot be in this life.

For these and like reasons Alexander and Averroes held that man's ultimate happiness does not consist in human knowledge obtained through speculative sciences, but in that which results from conjunction with a separate substance, which conjunction they deemed possible to man in this life. But as Aristotle realized that man has no knowledge in this life other than that which he obtains through speculative sciences, he maintained that man attains to happiness, not perfect, but proportionate to his capacity.

Hence it becomes sufficiently clear how these great minds suffered from being so straitened on every side. We, however, will avoid these straits if we suppose, in accordance with the foregoing arguments, that man is able to reach perfect happiness after this life, since man has an immortal soul; and that in that state his soul will understand in the same way as separate substances understand, as we proved in the Second Book.

Therefore man's ultimate happiness will consist in that knowledge of God which he possesses after this life; a knowledge similar to that by which separate substances know him. Hence our Lord promises us a *reward . . . in heaven* (Matt. v. 12) and (Matt. xxii. 30) states that the saints *shall be as the angels*: who always see God in heaven (Matt. xviii. 10).

Human Virtue

Whether human virtue is a habit?

Objection 1. It seems that human virtue is not a habit: For virtue is *the extreme limit of power* (*De Cœlo* i.). But the limit of anything is reducible to the genus of that of which it is the limit; as a point is reducible to the genus of line. Therefore virtue is reducible to the genus of power, and not to the genus of habit.

Obj. 2. Further, Augustine says (*De Lib. Arb.* ii.) that *virtue is the good use of the free-will*. But use of the free-will is an act. Therefore virtue is not a habit, but an act.

Obj. 3. Further, we do not merit by our habits, but by our actions: otherwise a man would merit continually, even while asleep. But we do merit by our virtues. Therefore virtues are not habits, but acts.

Obj. 4. Further, Augustine says (*De Moribus Eccl.* xv.) that *virtue is the order of love*, and (*Qq.* 88) that *the setting in order which is called virtue*

SOURCE: *Summa Theologica*, translated by Fathers of English Dominican Province (New York: Benziger Brothers, 1911), 5, pp. 63–65, 68–71, 87–90, 100–104, 134–137, 146–153. Reprinted with permission of Benziger Brothers and Burns & Oates, Ltd., London.

consists in enjoying what we ought to enjoy, and using what we ought to use.
Now order, or direction, denominates either an action or a relation.
Therefore virtue is not a habit, but an action or a relation.

Obj. 5. Further, just as there are human virtues, so are there natural
virtues. But natural virtues are not habits, but powers. Neither therefore are human virtues habits.

On the contrary, The Philosopher says (*De Prædic.* vi.) that science
and virtue are habits.

I answer that, Virtue denotes a certain perfection of a power. Now a
thing's perfection is considered chiefly in regard to its end. But the
end of power is act. Wherefore power is said to be perfect, according
as it is determinate to its act.

Now there are some powers which of themselves are determinate to
their acts; for instance, the active natural powers. And therefore these
natural powers are in themselves called virtues. But the rational
powers, which are proper to man, are not determinate to one particular
action, but are inclined indifferently to many: and they are determinate
to acts by means of habits, as is clear from what we have said above
. . . . Therefore human virtues are habits.

Reply Obj. 1. Sometimes we give the name of a virtue to that to which
the virtue is directed, namely, either to its object, or to its act: for
instance, we give the name Faith, to that which we believe, or to the
act of believing, as also to the habit by which we believe. When therefore we say that virtue is the limit of power, virtue is taken for the object
of virtue. For the furthest point to which a power can reach, is said to
be its virtue: for instance, if a man can carry a hundredweight and not
more, his virtue is put at a hundredweight and not at sixty. But the
objection takes virtue as being essentially the limit of power.

Reply Obj. 2. Good use of free-will is said to be a virtue, in the same
sense as above (*ad* 1); that is to say, because it is that to which virtue
is directed as to its proper act. For the act of virtue is nothing else
than the good use of the free-will.

Reply Obj. 3. We are said to merit by something in two ways. First,
as by merit itself, just as we are said to run by running; and thus we
merit by acts. Secondly, we are said to merit by something as by the
principle whereby we merit, as we are said to run by the motive power;
and thus are we said to merit by virtues and habits.

Reply Obj. 4. When we say that virtue is the order or setting in order
of love, we refer to the end to which virtue is ordered: because in us
love is set in order by virtue.

Reply Obj. 5. Natural powers are of themselves determinate to one
act: not so the rational powers. And so there is no comparison, as we
have said.

. . . .

Whether virtue is suitably defined?

Objection 1. It seems that the definition, usually given, of virtue, is not suitable: *Virtue is a good quality of the mind, by which we live righteously, of which no one can make bad use, which God forms in us, without us.* For virtue is man's goodness, since virtue it is that makes its subject good. But goodness does not seem to be good, as neither is whiteness white. It is therefore unsuitable to describe virtue as a *good quality*.

Obj. 2. Further, no difference is more common than its genus; since it is that which divides the genus. But good is more common than quality, since it is convertible with being. Therefore *good* should not be put in the definition of virtue, as a difference of quality.

Obj. 3. Further, as Augustine says (*De Trin.* xii.): *When we come across anything that is not common to us and the beasts of the field, it is something appertaining to the mind.* But there are virtues even of the irrational parts; as the Philosopher says (*Ethic.* iii.). Every virtue, therefore, is not a good quality *of the mind*.

Obj. 4. Further, righteousness seems to belong to justice; whence the righteous are called just. But justice is a species of virtue. It is therefore unsuitable to put *righteous* in the definition of virtue, when we say that virtue is that *by which we live righteously*.

Obj. 5. Further, whoever is proud of a thing, makes bad use of it. But many are proud of virtue, for Augustine says in his Rule, that *pride lies in wait for good works in order to slay them.* It is untrue, therefore, *that no one can make bad use of virtue.*

Obj. 6. Further, man is justified by virtue. But Augustine commenting on this passage of St. John (xv. 11): *He shall do greater things than these*, says: *He who created thee without thee, will not justify thee, without thee.* It is therefore unsuitable to say that *God forms* virtue *in us, without us.*

On the contrary. We have the authority of Augustine, from whose writings this definition is gathered, and principally from *De Libero Arbitrio* ii.

I answer that, This definition comprises perfectly the essential notion of virtue. For the perfect essential notion of anything is gathered from all its causes. Now the above definition comprises all the causes of virtue. For the formal cause of virtue, as of everything, is gathered from its genus and difference, when it is defined as *a good quality:* for *quality* is the genus of virtue, and the difference, *good.* But the definition would be more suitable if for quality we substitute habit, which is the proximate genus.

Now virtue has no matter *out of which* it is formed, as neither has any other accident; but it has matter *about which* it is concerned, and matter *in which* it exists, namely, the subject. The matter about which virtue is concerned is its object, and this could not be included in the above definition, because the object fixes the virtue to a certain species, and here we are giving the definition of virtue in general. And so for material cause we have the subject, which is mentioned when we say that virtue is a good quality *of the mind*.

The end of virtue, since it is an operative habit, is operation. But it must be observed, that some operative habits are always referred to evil, as vicious habits: others are sometimes referred to good, sometimes to evil; for instance, opinion is referred both to the true and to the untrue: whereas virtue is a habit which is always referred to good: and so the distinction of virtue from those habits which are always referred to evil, is expressed in the words *by which we live righteously:* and its distinction from those habits which are sometimes directed unto good, sometimes unto evil, in the words, *of which no one makes bad use.*

Lastly, God is the efficient cause of infused virtue, to which this definition applies; and this is expressed in the words *which God forms in us without us.* If we omit this phrase, the remainder of the definition will apply to all virtues in general, whether acquired or infused.

Reply Obj. 1. That which is first seized by the intellect is being: wherefore everything that we apprehend we consider as being, and consequently as one and as good, which are convertible with being. Wherefore we say that essence is being and is one and is good; and that one-ness is being and one and good: and in like manner goodness. But this is not the case with specific forms, as whiteness and health; for everything that we apprehend, is not apprehended with the notion of white and healthy. We must, however, observe that, as accidents and non-subsistent forms are called beings, not as if they themselves had being, but because things are (qualified) by them; so also are they called good or one, not by some distinct goodness or one-ness, but because by them something is good or one. So also is virtue called good, because by it something is good.

Reply Obj. 2. Good, which is put in the definition of virtue, is not good in general which is convertible with being, and which extends further than quality, but the good as defined by reason, with regard to which Dionysius says (*Div. Nom.* iv.) *that the good of the soul is to be in accord with reason.*

Reply Obj. 3. Virtue cannot be in the irrational part of the soul, except in so far as this participates in the reason (*Ethic.* i.). And therefore reason, or the mind, is the proper subject of virtue.

Reply Obj. 4. Justice has a righteousness of its own by which it puts those outward things right which come into human use, and which are the proper matter of justice, as we shall show further on . . .. But the righteousness which denotes order to a due end and to the Divine law, which is the rule of the human will, as stated above . . . is common to all virtues.

Reply Obj. 5. One can make bad use of a virtue objectively, for instance, by having evil thoughts about a virtue, e.g., by hating it, or by being proud of it; but one cannot make bad use of virtue as principle of action, so that an act of virtue be evil.

Reply Obj. 6. Infused virtue is caused in us by God without any action on our part, but not without our consent. This is the sense of the words, *which God works in us without us*. As to those things which are done by us, God causes them in us, yet not without action on our part, for He works in every will and in every nature.

. . . .

Whether there are only three habits of the speculative intellect, viz., wisdom, science and understanding.

Objection 1. It seems unfitting to distinguish three virtues of the speculative intellect, viz., wisdom, science and understanding. Because a species should not be condivided with its genus. But wisdom is a kind of science, as stated in *Ethic*. vi. Therefore wisdom should not be condivided with science among the intellectual virtues.

Obj. 2. Further, in differentiating powers, habits and acts in respect of their objects, we consider chiefly the formal aspect of these objects, as we have already explained . . . . Therefore diversity of habits is taken, not from their material objects, but from the formal aspect of those objects. Now the principle of a demonstration is the formal aspect under which the conclusion is known. Therefore the understanding of principles should not be set down as a habit or virtue distinct from the knowledge of conclusions.

Obj. 3. Further, an intellectual virtue is one which resides in an essentially rational faculty. Now even the speculative reason employs the dialectic syllogism for the sake of argument just as it employs the demonstrative syllogism. Therefore as science, which is the result of a demonstrative syllogism, is set down as an intellectual virtue, so also should opinion be.

On the contrary, The Philosopher (*Ethic*. vi.) reckons these three alone as being intellectual virtues, viz., wisdom, science and understanding.

I answer that, As already stated . . ., the virtues of the speculative intellect are those which perfect the speculative intellect for the consideration of truth: for this is its good work. Now a truth is subject to a twofold consideration—as known in itself, and as known through another. What is known in itself, is as a *principle*, and is at once understood by the intellect: wherefore the habit that perfects the intellect for the consideration of such truth, is called *understanding*, which is the habit of (first) principles.

On the other hand, a truth which is known through another, is understood by the intellect, not at once, but by means of the reason's inquiry, and is as a *term*. This may happen in two ways: first, so that it is the last in some particular genus; secondly, so that it is the ultimate term of all human knowledge. And, since *things that are knowable last from our standpoint, are knowable first and chiefly in their nature* (*Phys.* i.); hence that which is last with respect to all human knowledge, is that which is knowable first and chiefly in its nature. And about these is *wisdom*, which considers the highest causes, as stated in *Metaph.* i. Wherefore it rightly judges all things and sets them in order, because there can be no perfect and universal judgment that is not based on the first causes.—But in regard to that which is last in this or that genus of knowable matter, it is *science* that perfects the intellect. Wherefore according to the different kinds of knowable matter, there are different habits of scientific knowledge; whereas there is but one wisdom.

Reply Obj. 1. Wisdom is a kind of science, in so far as it has that which is common to all the sciences; viz., to demonstrate conclusions from principles. But since it has something proper to itself above the other sciences, inasmuch as it judges of them all, and not merely indeed of their conclusions, but even of their first principles, therefore it is a more perfect virtue than science.

Reply Obj. 2. When the formal aspect of the object is referred to a power or habit by one same act, there is no distinction of habit or power in respect of the formal aspect and of the material object: thus it belongs to the same power of sight to see both colour, and light, which is the formal aspect under which colour is seen, and is seen at the same time as the colour. On the other hand, the principles of a demonstration can be considered apart, without the conclusion being considered at all. Again, they can be considered together with the conclusions, since the conclusions can be deduced from them. Accordingly, to consider the principles in this second way, belongs to science, which considers the conclusions also: while to consider the principles in themselves belongs to understanding.

Consequently, to state the truth about this matter correctly, these three virtues are not on a par with one another, but there is a certain order between them. The same is to be observed in potential wholes, wherein one part is more perfect than another; for instance, the rational soul is more perfect than the sensitive soul; and the sensitive, than the vegetal. For it is thus that science depends on understanding as on a virtue of higher degree: and both of these depend on wisdom, as obtaining the highest place, and containing beneath itself both understanding and science, by judging both of the conclusions of science, and of the principles on which they are based.

Reply Obj. 3. As stated above . . . , a virtuous habit has a fixed relation to good, and is nowise referrable to evil. Now the good of the intellect is truth, and falsehood is its evil. Wherefore those habits alone are called intellectual virtues, that tell the truth and never tell a falsehood. But opinion and suspicion can be about both truth and falsehood: and so, as stated in *Ethic.* vi., they are not intellectual virtues.

. . . .

Whether every virtue is a moral virtue?

Objection 1. It seems that every virtue is a moral virtue. Because moral virtue is so called from the Latin *mos*, i.e., custom. Now, we can accustom ourselves to the acts of all the virtues. Therefore every virtue is a moral virtue.

Obj. 2. Further, the Philosopher says (*Ethic.* ii.) that moral virtue is *a habit of choosing the rational mean.* But every virtue is a habit of choosing: since the acts of any virtue can be done from choice. And, moreover, every virtue consists in following the rational mean in some way, as we shall explain further on . . . . Therefore every virtue is a moral virtue.

Obj. 3. Further, Tully says (*De Invent. Rhet.* ii.) that *virtue is a habit like a second nature, in accord with reason.* But since every human virtue is directed to man's good, it must be in accord with reason: since man's good *consists in that which agrees with his reason*, as Dionysius states (*Div. Nom.* iv.). Therefore every virtue is a moral virtue.

On the contrary, The Philosopher says (*Ethic.* i.): *When we speak of a man's morals, we do not say that he is wise or intelligent, but that he is gentle or sober.* Accordingly, then, wisdom and understanding are not moral virtues: and yet they are virtues, as stated above . . . . Therefore not every virtue is a moral virtue.

I answer that, In order to answer this question clearly, we must consider the meaning of the Latin word *mos*; for thus we shall be able to discover what a *moral* virtue is. Now *mos* has a twofold meaning. For sometimes it means custom, in which sense we read (Acts xv. 1): *Except you be circumcised after the manner (morem) of Moses, you cannot be saved.* Sometimes it means a natural or quasi-natural inclination to do some particular action, in which sense the word is applied to dumb animals. Thus we read (2 Macc. xi. 11) that *rushing violently upon the enemy, like lions, they slew them:* and the word is used in the same sense in Ps. lxvii. 7, where we read: *Who maketh men of one manner (moris) to dwell in a house.* For both these significations there is but one word in Latin; but in Greek there is a distinct word for each, for the word *ethos* is written sometimes with a long, and sometimes with a short *e*.

Now *moral* virtue is so called from *mos* in the sense of a natural or quasi-natural inclination to do some particular action. And the other meaning of *mos*, i.e., *custom*, is akin to this: because custom becomes a second nature, and produces an inclination similar to a natural one. But it is evident that inclination to an action belongs properly to the appetitive power, whose function it is to move all the powers to their acts, as explained above . . . . Therefore not every virtue is a moral virtue, but only those that are in the appetitive faculty.

Reply Obj. 1. This argument takes *mos* in the sense of *custom*.

Reply Obj. 2. Every act of virtue can be done from choice: but no virtue makes us choose aright, save that which is in the appetitive part of the soul: for it has been stated above that choice is an act of the appetitive faculty . . . . Wherefore a habit of choosing, i.e., a habit which is the principle whereby we choose, is that habit alone which perfects the appetitive faculty: although the acts of other habits also may be a matter of choice.

Reply Obj. 3. *Nature is the principle of movement* (*Phys*. ii.). Now to move the faculties to act is the proper function of the appetitive power. Consequently to become as a second nature by consenting to the reason, is proper to those virtues which are in the appetitive faculty.

Whether moral virtue differs from intellectual virtue?

Objection 1. It seems that moral virtue does not differ from intellectual virtue. For Augustine says (*De Civ. Dei*. iv.) *that virtue is the art of right conduct*. But art is an intellectual virtue. Therefore moral and intellectual virtue do not differ.

Obj. 2. Further, some authors put science in the definition of virtues: thus some define perseverance as a *science or habit regarding those things to which we should hold or not hold;* and holiness as *a science which makes man to be faithful and to do his duty to God*. Now science is an intellectual virtue. Therefore moral virtue should not be distinguished from intellectual virtue.

Obj. 3. Further, Augustine says (*Soliloq*. i.) that *virtue is the rectitude and perfection of reason*. But this belongs to the intellectual virtues, as stated in *Ethic*. vi. Therefore moral virtue does not differ from intellectual.

Obj. 4. Further, a thing does not differ from that which is included in its definition. But intellectual virtue is included in the definition of moral virtue: for the Philosopher says (*Ethic*. ii.) that *moral virtue is a habit of choosing the rational mean, even as a prudent man decides*. Now this right reason that fixes the mean of moral virtue, belongs to an intellectual virtue, as stated in *Ethic*. vi. Therefore moral virtue does not differ from intellectual.

On the contrary, It is stated in *Ethic*. i. that *there are two kinds of virtue: some we call intellectual; some, moral*.

I answer that, Reason is the first principle of all human acts; and whatever other principles of human acts may be found, they obey reason somewhat, but in various ways. For some obey reason blindly and without any contradiction whatever: such are the limbs of the body, provided they be in a healthy condition, for as soon as reason commands, the hand or the foot proceeds to action. Hence the Philosopher says (*Polit.* i.) that *the soul rules the body like a despot*, i.e., as a master rules his slave, who has no right to rebel. Accordingly some held that all the active principles in man are subordinate to reason in this way. If this were true, for man to act well it would suffice that his reason be perfect. Consequently, since virtue is a habit perfecting man in view of his doing good actions, it would follow that it is only in the reason, so that there would be none but intellectual virtues. This was the opinion of Socrates, who said *every virtue is a kind of prudence*, as stated in *Ethic.* vi. Hence he maintained that as long as a man is in possession of knowledge, he cannot sin; and that every one who sins, does so through ignorance.

Now this is based on a false supposition. Because the appetitive faculty obeys the reason, not blindly, but with a certain power of opposition; wherefore the Philosopher says (*Polit.* i.) that *reason commands the appetitive faculty by a politic power*, whereby a man rules over subjects that are free, having a certain right of opposition. Hence Augustine says on Ps. cxviii. (*serm.* 8) that *sometimes we understand* (what is right) *while desire is slow, or follows not at all*, in so far as the habits or passions of the appetitive faculty cause the use of reason to be impeded in some particular action. And in this way, there is some truth in the saying of Socrates that so long as a man is in possession of knowledge he does not sin: provided, however, that this knowledge is made to include the use of reason in this individual act of choice.

Accordingly in order for a man to do a good deed, it is requisite not only that his reason be well disposed by means of a habit of intellectual virtue; but also that his appetite be well disposed by means of a habit of moral virtue. And so moral differs from intellectual virtue, even as the appetite differs from the reason. Hence just as the appetite is the principle of human acts, in so far as it partakes of reason, so are moral habits to be considered virtues in so far as they are in conformity with reason.

Reply Obj. 1. Augustine usually applies the term *art* to any form of right reason; in which sense art includes prudence which is the right reason about things to be done, even as art is the right reason about things to be made. Accordingly, when he says that *virtue is the art of right conduct*, this applies to prudence essentially; but to other virtues, by participation, for as much as they are directed by prudence.

Reply Obj. 2. All such definitions, by whomsoever given, were based on the Socratic theory, and should be explained according to what we have said about art . . . .

The same applies to the Third Objection.

Reply Obj. 4. Right reason which is in accord with prudence is included in the definition of moral virtue, not as part of its essence, but as something belonging by way of participation to all the moral virtues, in so far as they are all under the direction of prudence.

. . . .

Whether the moral virtues should be called cardinal or principal virtues?

Objection 1. It seems that moral virtues should not be called cardinal or principal virtues. For *the opposite members of a division are by nature simultaneous* (*Categor.* x.), so that one is not principal rather than another. Now all the virtues are opposite members of the division of the genus *virtue*. Therefore none of them should be called principal.

Obj. 2. Further, the end is principal as compared to the means. But the theological virtues are about the end; while the moral virtues are about the means. Therefore the theological virtues, rather than the moral virtues, should be called principal or cardinal.

Obj. 3. Further, that which is essentially so is principal in comparison with that which is so by participation. But the intellectual virtues belong to that which is essentially rational: whereas the moral virtues belong to that which is rational by participation, as stated above. . . . Therefore the intellectual virtues are principal, rather than the moral virtues.

On the contrary, Ambrose in explaining the words, *Blessed are the poor in spirit* (Luke vi. 20) says: *We know that there are four cardinal virtues, viz., temperance, justice, prudence, and fortitude.*   But these are moral virtues. Therefore the moral virtues are cardinal virtues.

I answer that, When we speak of virtue simply, we are understood to speak of human virtue. Now human virtue, as stated above . . ., is one that answers to the perfect idea of virtue, which requires rectitude of the appetite: for suchlike virtue not only confers the faculty of doing well, but also causes the good deed done. On the other hand, the name virtue is applied to one that answers imperfectly to the idea of virtue, and does not require rectitude of the appetite: because it merely confers the faculty of doing well without causing the good deed to be done. Now it is evident that the perfect is principal as compared to the imperfect: and so those virtues which imply rectitude of the appetite are called principal virtues. Such are the moral virtues, and prudence alone, of the intellectual virtues, for it is also something of a moral virtue, as was clearly shown above . . . . Consequently, those virtues which are called principal or cardinal are fittingly placed among the moral virtues.

Reply Obj. 1. When an univocal genus is divided into its species, the members of the division are on a par in the point of the generic idea; although considered in their nature as things, one species may surpass another in rank and perfection, as man in respect of other animals. But when we divide an analogous term, which is applied to several things, but to one before it is applied to another, nothing hinders one from ranking before another, even in the point of the generic idea; as the notion of being is applied to substance principally in relation to accident. Such is the division of virtue into the various kinds of virtue: since the good defined by reason is not found in the same way in all things.

Reply Obj. 2. The theological virtues are above man, as stated above. . . . Hence they should properly be called not human, but *super-human* or godlike virtues.

Reply Obj. 3. Although the intellectual virtues, except in prudence, rank before the moral virtues, in the point of their subject, they do not rank before them as virtues; for a virtue, as such, regards good, which is the object of the appetite.

Whether there are four cardinal virtues?

Objection 1. It seems that there are not four cardinal virtues. For prudence is the directing principle of the other moral virtues, as is clear from what has been said above . . . . But that which directs other things ranks before them. Therefore prudence alone is a principal virtue.

Obj. 2. Further, the principal virtues are, in a way, moral virtues. Now we are directed to moral works both by the practical reason, and by a right appetite, as stated in *Ethic.* vi. Therefore there are only two cardinal virtues.

Obj. 3. Further, even among the other virtues one ranks higher than another. But in order that a virtue be principal, it needs not to rank above all the others, but above some. Therefore it seems that there are many more principal virtues.

On the contrary, Gregory says (*Moral.* ii.): *The entire structure of good works is built on four virtues.*

I answer that, Things may be numbered either in respect of their formal principles, or according to the subjects in which they are: and either way we find that there are four cardinal virtues.

For the formal principle of the virtue of which we speak now is good as defined by reason; which good can be considered in two ways. First, as existing in the very act of reason: and thus we have one principal virtue called *Prudence*. Secondly, according as the reason puts its order into something else; either into operations, and then we have *Justice;* or into passions, and then we need two virtues. For the need of putting the order of reason into the passions, is due to their thwarting reason: and this occurs in two ways. First, by the passions inciting to something against reason; and then the passions need a curb, which we call *Temperance*. Secondly, by the passions withdrawing us from following the dictate of reason, e.g., fear of danger or toil: and then man needs to be heartened for that which reason dictates, lest he turn back; and to this end there is *Fortitude*.

In like manner, we find the same number if we consider the subjects of virtue. For there are four subjects of the virtue we speak of now: viz., the power which is rational in its essence, and this is perfected by *Prudence;* and that which is rational by participation, and is threefold, the will, subject of *Justice*, the concupiscible faculty, subject of *Temperance*, and the irascible faculty, subject to *Fortitude*.

Reply Obj. 1. Prudence is the principal of all the virtues simply. The others are principal, each in its own genus.

Reply Obj. 2. That part of the soul which is rational by participation is threefold, as stated above.

Reply Obj. 3. All the other virtues among which one ranks before another, are reducible to the above four, both as to the subject and as to the formal principle.

.   .   .   .

Whether there are any theological virtues?

Objection 1. It seems that there are not any theological virtues. For according to *Phys.* vi., *virtue is the disposition of a perfect thing to that which is best: and by perfect, I mean that which is disposed according to nature.* But that which is Divine is above man's nature. Therefore the theological virtues are not virtues of a man.

Obj. 2. Further, theological virtues are quasi-Divine virtues. But the Divine virtues are exemplars, as stated above . . . , which are not in us but in God. Therefore the theological virtues are not virtues of man.

Obj. 3. Further, the theological virtues are so called because they direct us to God, Who is the first beginning and last end of all things. But by the very nature of his reason and will, man is directed to his first beginning and last end. Therefore there is no need for any habits of theological virtue, to direct the reason and will to God.

On the contrary, The precepts of the Law are about acts of virtue. Now the Divine Law contains precepts about the acts of faith, hope, and charity: for it is written (*Ecclus.* ii. 8, *seqq.*): *Ye that fear the Lord believe Him*, and again, *hope in Him*, and again, *love Him*. Therefore faith, hope, and charity are virtues directing us to God. Therefore they are theological virtues.

I answer that, Man is perfected by virtue, for those actions whereby he is directed to happiness, as was explained above . . . . Now man's happiness is twofold, as was also stated above . . . . One is proportionate to human nature, a happiness, to wit, which man can obtain by means of his natural principles. The other is a happiness surpassing man's nature, and which man can obtain by the power of God alone, by a kind of participation of the Godhead, about which it is written (2 Pet.

i. 4) that by Christ we are made *partakers of the Divine Nature.* And because such happiness surpasses the capacity of human nature, man's natural principles which enable him to act well according to his capacity, do not suffice to direct man to this same happiness. Hence it is necessary for man to receive from God some additional principles, whereby he may be directed to supernatural happiness, even as he is directed to his connatural end, by means of his natural principles, albeit not without the Divine assistance. Suchlike principles are called *theological virtues:* first, because their object is God, inasmuch as they direct us aright to God: secondly, because they are infused in us by God alone: thirdly, because these virtues are not made known to us, save by Divine revelation, contained in Holy Writ.

Reply Obj. 1. A certain nature may be ascribed to a certain thing in two ways. First, essentially; and thus these theological virtues surpass the nature of man. Secondly, by participation, as kindled wood partakes of the nature of fire: and thus, after a fashion, man becomes a partaker of the Divine Nature, as stated above: so that these virtues are proportionate to man in respect of the Nature of which he is made a partaker.

Reply Obj. 2. These virtues are called Divine, not as though God were virtuous by reason of them, but because by them God makes us virtuous, and directs us to Himself. Hence they are not exemplar but exemplate virtues.

Reply Obj. 3. The reason and will are naturally directed to God, inasmuch as He is the beginning and end of nature, but in proportion to nature. But the reason and will, according to their nature, are not sufficiently directed to Him in so far as He is the object of supernatural happiness.

Whether the theological virtues are distinct from the intellectual and moral virtues?

Objection 1. It seems that the theological virtues are not distinct from the moral and intellectual virtues. For the theological virtues, if they be in a human soul, must needs perfect it, either as to the intellective, or as to the appetitive part. Now the virtues which perfect the intellective part are called intellectual; and the virtues which perfect the appetitive part, are called moral. Therefore, the theological virtues are not distinct from the moral and intellectual virtues.

Obj. 2. Further, the theological virtues are those which direct us to God. Now, among the intellectual virtues there is one which directs us to God: this is wisdom, which is about Divine things, since it considers the highest cause. Therefore the theological virtues are not distinct from the intellectual virtues.

Obj. 3. Further, Augustine (*De Moribus Eccl.* xv.) shows how the four cardinal virtues are the *order of love.* Now love is charity, which is a theological virtue. Therefore the moral virtues are not distinct from the theological.

On the contrary, That which is above man's nature is distinct from that which is according to his nature. But the theological virtues are above man's nature; while the intellectual and moral virtues are in proportion to his nature, as clearly shown above. . . . Therefore they are distinct from one another.

I answer that, As stated above . . . , habits are specifically distinct from one another in respect of the formal difference of their objects. Now the object of the theological virtues is God Himself, Who is the last end of all, as surpassing the knowledge of our reason. On the other hand, the object of the intellectual and moral virtues is something comprehensible to human reason. Wherefore the theological virtues are specifically distinct from the moral and intellectual virtues.

Reply Obj. 1. The intellectual and moral virtues perfect man's intellect and appetite according to the capacity of human nature: the theological virtues, supernaturally.

Reply Obj. 2. The wisdom which the Philosopher (*Ethic.* vi.) reckons as an intellectual virtue, considers Divine things so far as they are open to the research of human reason. Theological virtue, on the other hand, is about those same things so far as they surpass human reason.

Reply Obj. 3. Though charity is love, yet love is not always charity. When, then, it is stated that every virtue is the order of love, this can be understood either of love in the general sense, or of the love of charity. If it be understood of love, commonly so called, then each virtue is stated to be the order of love, in so far as each cardinal virtue requires ordinate emotions; and love is the root and cause of every emotion, as stated above. . . . —If, however, it be understood of the love of charity, it does not mean that every other virtue is charity essentially: but that all other virtues depend on charity in some way, as we shall show further on. . . .

Whether faith, hope, and charity are fittingly reckoned as theological virtues?

Objection 1. It seems that faith, hope, and charity are not fittingly reckoned as three theological virtues. For the theological virtues are in relation to Divine happiness, what the natural inclination is in relation to the connatural end. Now among the virtues directed to the connatural end there is but one natural virtue, viz., the understanding of principles. Therefore there should be but one theological virtue.

Obj. 2. Further, the theological virtues are more perfect than the intellectual and moral virtues. Now faith is not reckoned among the intellectual virtues, but is something less than a virtue, since it is imperfect knowledge. Likewise hope is not reckoned among the moral virtues, but is something less than a virtue, since it is a passion. Much less therefore should they be reckoned as theological virtues.

Obj. 3. Further, the theological virtues direct man's soul to God. Now man's soul cannot be directed to God, save through the intellective part, wherein are the intellect and will. Therefore there should be only two theological virtues, one perfecting the intellect, the other, the will.

On the contrary, The Apostle says (1 Cor. viii. 13): *Now there remain faith, hope, charity, these three.*

I answer that, As stated above . . . , the theological virtues direct man to supernatural happiness in the same way as by the natural inclination man is directed to his connatural end. Now the latter happens in respect of two things. First, in respect of the reason or intellect, in so far as it contains the first universal principles which are known to us by the natural light of the intellect, and which are reason's starting-point both in speculative and in practical matters. Secondly, through the rectitude of the will which tends naturally to good as defined by reason.

But these two fall short of the order of supernatural happiness, according to 1 Cor. ii. 9: *The eye hath not seen, nor ear heard, neither hath it entered into the heart of man, what things God hath prepared for them that love Him.* Consequently in respect of both the above things man needed to receive in addition something supernatural to direct him to a supernatural end. First, as regards the intellect, man receives certain supernatural principles, which are held by means of a Divine light: these are the articles of faith, about which is faith.—Secondly, the will is directed to this end, both as to the movement of intention, which tends to that end as something attainable,—and this pertains to hope,—and as to a certain spiritual union, whereby the will is, so to speak, transformed into that end,—and this belongs to charity. For the appetite of a thing is moved and tends towards its connatural end naturally; and this movement is due to a certain conformity of the thing with its end.

Reply Obj. 1. The intellect requires intelligible species whereby to understand: consequently there is need of a natural habit in addition to the power. But the very nature of the will suffices for it to be directed naturally to the end, both as to the intention of the end and as to its conformity with the end. But the nature of the power is insufficient in either of these respects, for the will to be directed to things that are above its nature. Consequently there was need for an additional supernatural habit in both respects.

Reply Obj. 2. Faith and hope imply a certain imperfection: since faith is of things unseen, and hope, of things not possessed. Hence faith and hope, in things that are subject to human power, fall short of the notion of virtue. But faith and hope in things which are above the capacity of human nature surpass all virtue that is in proportion to man, according to 1 Cor. i. 25: *The weakness of God is stronger than men.*

Reply Obj. 3. Two things pertain to the appetite, viz., movement to the end, and conformity with the end by means of love. Hence there must needs be two theological virtues in the human appetite, namely, hope and charity.

Whether faith precedes hope, and hope charity?

Objection 1. It seems that the order of the theological virtues is not that faith precedes hope, and hope charity. For the root precedes that which grows from it. Now charity is the root of all the virtues, according to Ephes. iii. 17: *Being rooted and founded in charity.* Therefore charity precedes the others.

Obj. 2. Further, Augustine says (*De Doctr. Christ.* i.): *A man cannot love what he does not believe to exist. But if he believes and loves, by doing good works he ends in hoping.* Therefore it seems that hope precedes charity, and charity hope.

Obj. 3. Further, love is the principle of all our emotions, as stated above. . . . Now hope is a kind of emotion since it is a passion, as stated above. . . . Therefore charity, which is love, precedes hope.

On the contrary, The Apostle enumerates them thus (1 Cor. xiii. 13): *Now there remain faith, hope, charity.*

I answer that, Order is twofold: order of generation, and order of perfection. By order of generation, in respect of which in one same subject matter precedes form, and the imperfect precedes the perfect, faith precedes hope, and hope charity, as to their acts, but not as to their habits (because these are all infused together). For the movement of the appetite cannot tend to anything, either by hoping or loving, unless that thing be apprehended by the sense or by the intellect. Now it is by faith that the intellect apprehends the object of hope and love. Hence in the order of generation, faith precedes hope and charity.—In like manner a man loves a thing because he apprehends it as his good. Now from the very fact that a man hopes to be able to obtain some good through someone, he looks on the man in whom he hopes as a good of his own. Hence for the very reason that a man hopes in someone, he proceeds to love him: so that in the order of generation, hope precedes charity as regards their respective acts.

But in the order of perfection, charity precedes faith and hope: because both faith and hope are quickened by charity, and receive from charity their full complement as virtues. For thus charity is the mother and the root of all the virtues, inasmuch as it is the form of them all, as we shall state further on. . . .

This suffices for the Reply to the First Objection.

Reply Obj. 2. Augustine is speaking of that hope whereby a man hopes to obtain bliss through the merits which he has already: this belongs to hope quickened by and following charity. But it is possible for a man before having charity, to hope through merits not already possessed, but which he hopes to possess.

Reply Obj. 3. As stated above . . . in treating of the passions, hope regards two things. One as its principal object, viz., the good hoped for. With regard to this, love always precedes hope: for good is never hoped for unless it be desired and loved.— Hope also regards the person from whom a man hopes to be able to obtain some good. With regard to this, hope precedes love at first; though afterwards hope is increased by love. Because from the fact that a man thinks that he can obtain a good through someone, he begins to love him: and from the fact that he loves him, he then hopes all the more in him.

Law

Whether law is something pertaining to reason?

Objection 1. It seems that law is not something pertaining to reason. For the Apostle says (Rom. vii. 23): *I see another law in my members,* etc. But nothing pertaining to reason is in the members; since the reason does not make use of a bodily organ. Therefore law is not something pertaining to reason.

Obj. 2. Further, in the reason there is nothing else but power, habit, and act. But law is not the power itself of reason. In like manner, neither is it a habit of reason: because the habits of reason are the intellectual virtues of which we have spoken above. . . . Nor again is it an act of reason: because then law would cease, when the act of reason ceases, for instance, while we are asleep. Therefore law is nothing pertaining to reason.

Obj. 3. Further, the law moves those who are subject to it to act aright. But it belongs properly to the will to move to act, as is evident from what has been said above, . . . Therefore law pertains, not to the reason, but to the will; according to the words of the Jurist (*Lib.* i. *ff.*, *De Const. Prin.*): *Whatsoever pleaseth the sovereign, has force of law.*

On the contrary, It belongs to the law to command and to forbid. But it belongs to reason to command, as stated above. . . . Therefore law is something pertaining to reason.

I answer that, Law is a rule and measure of acts, whereby man is induced to act or is restrained from acting: for *lex* (law) is derived from *ligare* (to bind), because it binds one to act. Now the rule and measure of human acts is the reason, which is the first principle of human acts,

SOURCE: *Summa Theologica*, translated by Fathers of English Dominican Province (New York: Benziger Brothers, 1912), *6*, pp. 1–8, 9–16, 19–21. Reprinted with permission of Benziger Brothers and Burns & Oates, Ltd., London.

as is evident from what has been stated above . . . ; since it belongs to the reason to direct to the end, which is the first principle in all matters of action, according to the Philosopher (*Phys.* ii.). Now that which is the principle in any genus, is the rule and measure of that genus: for instance, unity in the genus of numbers, and the first movement in the genus of movements. Consequently it follows that law is something pertaining to reason.

Reply Obj. 1. Since law is a kind of rule and measure, it may be in something in two ways. First, as in that which measures and rules: and since this is proper to reason, it follows that, in this way, law is in the reason alone.—Secondly, as in that which is measured and ruled. In this way, law is in all those things that are inclined to something by reason of some law: so that any inclination arising from a law, may be called a law, not essentially but by participation as it were. And thus the inclination of the members to concupiscence is called *the law of the members*.

Reply Obj. 2. Just as, in external action, we may consider the work and the work done, for instance the work of building and the house built; so in the acts of reason, we may consider the act itself of reason, i.e., to understand and to reason, and something produced by this act. With regard to the speculative reason, this is first of all the definition; secondly, the proposition; thirdly, the syllogism or argument. And since also the practical reason makes use of a syllogism in respect of the work to be done, as stated above . . . and as the Philosopher teaches (*Ethic.* vii.); hence we find in the practical reason something that holds the same position in regard to operations, as, in the speculative intellect, the proposition holds in regard to conclusions. Suchlike universal propositions of the practical intellect that are directed to actions have the nature of law. And these propositions are sometimes under our actual consideration, while sometimes they are retained in the reason by means of a habit.

Reply Obj. 3. Reason has its power of moving from the will, as stated above . . . : for it is due to the fact that one wills the end, that the reason issues its commands as regards things ordained to the end. But in order that the volition of what is commanded may have the nature of law, it needs to be in accord with some rule of reason. And in this sense is to be understood the saying that the will of the sovereign has the force of law; otherwise the sovereign's will would savour of lawlessness rather than of law.

Whether the law is always directed to the common good?

Objection 1. It seems that the law is not always directed to the common good as to its end. For it belongs to law to command and to forbid. But commands are directed to certain individual goods. Therefore the end of the law is not always the common good.

Obj. 2. Further, the law directs man in his actions. But human actions are concerned with particular matters. Therefore the law is directed to some particular good.

Obj. 3. Further, Isidore says (*Etym.* ii.): *If the law is based on reason, whatever is based on reason will be a law.* But reason is the foundation not only of what is ordained to the common good, but also of that which is directed to private good. Therefore the law is not only directed to the good of all, but also to the private good of an individual.

On the contrary, Isidore says (*Etym.* v.) that *laws are enacted for no private profit, but for the common benefit of the citizens.*

I answer that, As stated above . . . , the law belongs to that which is a principle of human acts, because it is their rule and measure. Now as reason is a principle of human acts, so in reason itself there is something which is the principle in respect of all the rest: wherefore to this principle chiefly and mainly law must needs be referred. Now the first principle in practical matters, which are the object of the practical reason, is the last end: and the last end of human life is bliss or happiness, as stated above . . . . Consequently the law must needs regard principally the relationship to happiness. Moreover, since every part is ordained to the whole, as imperfect to perfect; and since one man is a part of the perfect community, the law must needs regard properly the relationship to universal happiness. Wherefore the Philosopher, in the above definition of legal matters mentions both happiness and the body politic: for he says (*Ethic.* v.) that we call those legal matters *just, which are adapted to produce and preserve happiness and its parts for the body politic:* since the state is a perfect community, as he says in *Polit.* i.

Now in every genus, that which belongs to it chiefly is the principle of the others, and the others belong to that genus in subordination to that thing: thus fire, which is chief among hot things, is the cause of heat in mixed bodies, and these are said to be hot in so far as they have a share of fire. Consequently, since the law is chiefly ordained to the common good, any other precept in regard to some individual work, must needs be devoid of the nature of a law, save in so far as it regards the common good. Therefore every law is ordained to the common good.

Reply Obj. 1. A command denotes an application of a law to matters regulated by the law. Now the order to the common good, at which the law aims, is applicable to particular ends. And in this way commands are given even concerning particular matters.

Reply Obj. 2. Actions are indeed concerned with particular matters: but those particular matters are referable to the common good, not as to a common genus or species, but as to a common final cause, according as the common good is said to be the common end.

Reply Obj. 3. Just as nothing stands firm with regard to the speculative reason except that which is traced back to the first indemonstrable principles, so nothing stands firm with regard to the practical reason, unless it be directed to the last end which is the common good: and whatever stands to reason in this sense, has the nature of a law.

Whether the reason of any man is competent to make laws?

Objection 1. It seems that the reason of any man is competent to make laws. For the Apostle says (Rom. ii. 14) that *when the Gentiles, who have not the law, do by nature those things that are of the law, . . . they are a law to themselves.* Now he says this of all in general. Therefore anyone can make a law for himself.

Obj. 2. Further, as the Philosopher says (*Ethic.* ii.), *the intention of the lawgiver is to lead men to virtue.* But every man can lead another to virtue. Therefore the reason of any man is competent to make laws.

Obj. 3. Further, just as the sovereign of a state governs the state, so every father of a family governs his household. But the sovereign of a state can make laws for the state. Therefore every father of a family can make laws for his household.

On the contrary, Isidore says (*Etym.* v.; and the passage is quoted in *Deocretals, Dist.* 2): *A law is an ordinance of the people, whereby something is sanctioned by the Elders together with the Commonalty.*

I answer that, A law, properly speaking, regards first and foremost the order to the common good. Now to order anything to the common good, belongs either to the whole people, or to someone who is the vicegerent of the whole people. And therefore the making of a law belongs either to the whole people or to a public personage who has care of the whole people: since in all other matters the directing of anything to the end concerns him to whom the end belongs.

Reply Obj. 1. As stated above . . . , a law is in a person not only as in one that rules, but also by participation as in one that is ruled. In the latter way each one is a law to himself, in so far as he shares the direction that he receives from one who rules him. Hence the same text goes on: *Who show the work of the law written in their hearts.*

Reply Obj. 2. A private person cannot lead another to virtue efficaciously: for he can only advise, and if his advice be not taken, it has no coercive power, such as the law should have, in order to prove an efficacious inducement to virtue, as the Philosopher says (*Ethic.* x.). But this coercive power is vested in the whole people or in some public personage, to whom it belongs to inflict penalties, as we shall state further on. . . . Wherefore the framing of laws belongs to him alone.

Reply Obj. 3. As one man is a part of the household, so a household is a part of the state: and the state is a perfect community, according to *Polit.* i. And therefore, as the good of one man is not the last end, but is ordained to the common good; so too the good of one household is ordained to the good of a single state, which is a perfect community.

Consequently he that governs a family, can indeed make certain commands or ordinances, but not such as to have properly the force of law.

Whether promulgation is essential to a law?

Objection 1. It seems that promulgation is not essential to a law. For the natural law above all has the character of law. But the natural law needs no promulgation. Therefore it is not essential to a law that it be promulgated.

Obj. 2. Further, it belongs properly to a law to bind one to do or not to do something. But the obligation of fulfilling a law touches not only those in whose presence it is promulgated, but also others. Therefore promulgation is not essential to a law.

Obj. 3. Further, the binding force of a law extends even to the future, since *laws are binding in matters of the future*, as the jurists say (*Cod.* i., tit. *De lege et constit.*). But promulgation concerns those who are present. Therefore it is not essential to a law.

On the contrary, It is laid down in the *Decretals* (*Append. Grat.*) that *laws are established when they are promulgated*.

I answer that, As stated above . . . , a law is imposed on others by way of a rule and measure. Now a rule or measure is imposed by being applied to those who are to be ruled and measured by it. Wherefore, in order that a law obtain the binding force which is proper to a law, it must needs be applied to the men who have to be ruled by it. Such application is made by its being notified to them by promulgation. Wherefore promulgation is necessary for the law to obtain its force.

Thus from the four preceding articles, the definition of law may be gathered; and it is nothing else than an ordinance of reason for the common good, made by him who has care of the community, and promulgated.

Reply Obj. 1. The natural law is promulgated by the very fact that God instilled it into man's mind so as to be known by him naturally.

Reply Obj. 2. Those who are not present when a law is promulgated, are bound to observe the law, in so far as it is notified or can be notified to them by others, after it has been promulgated.

Reply Obj. 3. The promulgation that takes place now, extends to future time by reason of the durability of written characters, by which means it is continually promulgated. Hence Isidore says (*Etym.* ii.) that *lex* (law) *is derived from legere* (to read) *because it is written* . . . .

Whether there is an eternal law?

Objection 1. It seems that there is no eternal law. Because every law is imposed on someone. But there was not someone from eternity on whom a law could be imposed: since God alone was from eternity. Therefore no law is eternal.

Obj. 2. Further, promulgation is essential to law. But promulgation could not be from eternity: because there was no one to whom it could be promulgated from eternity. Therefore no law can be eternal.

Obj. 3. Further, a law implies order to an end. But nothing ordained to an end is eternal: for the last end alone is eternal. Therefore no law is eternal.

On the contrary, Augustine says (*De Lib. Arb.* i.): *That Law which is the Supreme Reason cannot be understood to be otherwise than unchangeable and eternal.*

I answer that, As stated above . . . , a law is nothing else but a dictate of practical reason emanating from the ruler who governs a perfect community. Now it is evident, granted that the world is ruled by Divine Providence, as was stated in the First Part . . . , that the whole community of the universe is governed by Divine Reason. Wherefore the very Idea of the government of things in God the Ruler of the universe, has the nature of a law. And since the Divine Reason's conception of things is not subject to time but is eternal, according to Prov. viii. 23, therefore it is that this kind of law must be called eternal.

Reply Obj. 1. Those things that are not in themselves, exist with God, inasmuch as they are foreknown and preordained by Him, according to Rom. iv. 17: *Who calls those things that are not, as those that are.* Accordingly the eternal concept of the Divine law bears the character of an eternal law, in so far as it is ordained by God to the government of things foreknown by Him.

Reply Obj. 2. Promulgation is made by word of mouth or in writing; and in both ways the eternal law is promulgated: because both the Divine Word and the writing of the Book of Life are eternal. But the promulgation cannot be from eternity on the part of the creature that hears or reads.

Reply Obj. 3. The law implies order to the end actively, in so far as it directs certain things to the end; but not passively,—that is to say, the law itself is not ordained to the end,—except accidentally, in a governor whose end is extrinsic to him, and to which end his law must needs be ordained. But the end of the Divine government is God Himself, and His law is not distinct from Himself. Wherefore the eternal law is not ordained to another end.

Whether there is in us a natural law?

Objection 1. It seems that there is no natural law in us. Because man is governed sufficiently by the eternal law: for Augustine says (*De Lib. Arb.* i.) that *the eternal law is that by which it is right that all things should be most orderly.* But nature does not abound in superfluities as neither does she fail in necessaries. Therefore no law is natural to man.

Obj. 2. Further, by the law man is directed, in his acts, to the end, as stated above. . . . But the directing of human acts to their end is not a function of nature, as is the case in irrational creatures, which act for an end solely by their natural appetite; whereas man acts for an end by his reason and will. Therefore no law is natural to man.

Obj. 3. Further, the more a man is free, the less is he under the law. But man is freer than all the animals, on account of his free-will, with which he is endowed above all other animals. Since therefore other animals are not subject to a natural law, neither is man subject to a natural law.

On the contrary, The gloss on Rom. ii. 14: *When the Gentiles, who have not the law, do by nature those things that are of the law,* comments as follows: *Although they have no written law, yet they have the natural law, whereby each one knows, and is conscious of, what is good and what is evil.*

I answer that, As stated above . . . , law, being a rule and measure, can be in a person in two ways: in one way, as in him that rules and measures; in another way, as in that which is ruled and measured, since a thing is ruled and measured, in so far as it partakes of the rule or measure. Wherefore, since all things subject to Divine providence are ruled and measured by the eternal law, as was stated above . . . ; it is evident that all things partake somewhat of the eternal law, in so far as, namely, from its being imprinted on them, they derive their respective inclinations to their proper acts and ends. Now among all others, the rational creature is subject to Divine providence in the most excellent way, in so far as it partakes of a share of providence, by being provident both for itself and for others. Wherefore it has a share of the Eternal Reason, whereby it has a natural inclination to its proper act and end: and this participation of the eternal law in the rational creature is called the natural law. Hence the Psalmist after saying (Ps. iv. 6): *Offer up the sacrifice of justice,* as though someone asked what the works of justice are, adds: *Many say, Who showeth us good things?* in answer to which question he says: *The light of Thy countenance, O Lord, is signed upon us:* thus implying that the light of natural reason, whereby we discern what is good and what is evil, which is the function of the natural law, is nothing else than an imprint on us of the Divine light. It is therefore evident that the natural law is nothing else than the rational creature's participation of the eternal law.

Reply Obj. 1. This argument would hold, if the natural law were something different from the eternal law: whereas it is nothing but a participation thereof, as stated above.

Reply Obj. 2. Every act of reason and will in us is based on that which is according to nature, as stated above . . . : for every act of reasoning is based on principles that are known naturally, and every act of appetite in respect of the means is derived from the natural appetite in respect of the last end. Accordingly the first direction of our acts to their end must needs be in virtue of the natural law.

Reply Obj. 3. Even irrational animals partake in their own way of the Eternal Reason, just as the rational creature does. But because the rational creature partakes thereof in an intellectual and rational manner, therefore the participation of the eternal law in the rational creature is properly called a law, since a law is something pertaining to reason, as stated above. . . . Irrational creatures, however, do not partake thereof in a rational manner, wherefore there is no participation of the eternal law in them, except by way of similitude.

Whether there is a human law?

Objection 1. It seems that there is not a human law. For the natural law is a participation of the eternal law, as stated above. . . . Now through the eternal law *all things are most orderly*, as Augustine states (*De Lib. Arb.* i.). Therefore the natural law suffices for the ordering of all human affairs. Consequently there is no need for a human law.

Obj. 2. Further, a law bears the character of a measure, as stated above. . . . But human reason is not a measure of things, but vice versa (*cf. Metaph.* x.). Therefore no law can emanate from human reason.

Obj. 3. Further, a measure should be most certain, as stated in *Metaph.* x. But the dictates of human reason in matters of conduct are uncertain, according to Wis. ix. 14: *The thoughts of mortal men are fearful, and our counsels uncertain.* Therefore no law can emanate from human reason.

On the contrary, Augustine (*De Lib. Arb.* i.) distinguishes two kinds of law, the one eternal, the other temporal, which he calls human.

I answer that, As stated above . . . , a law is a dictate of the practical reason. Now it is to be observed that the same procedure takes place in the practical and in the speculative reason: for each proceeds from principles to conclusions, as stated above . . . . Accordingly we conclude that just as, in the speculative reason, from naturally known indemonstrable principles, we draw the conclusions of the various sciences, the knowledge of which is not imparted to us by nature, but acquired by the efforts of reason, so too it is from the precepts of the natural law, as from general and indemonstrable principles, that the human reason needs to proceed to the more particular determination of certain matters. These particular determinations, devised by human reason, are called human laws, provided the other essential conditions of law be observed, as stated above . . . . Wherefore Tully says in his *Rhetoric* (*De Invent. Rhet.* ii.) that *justice has its source in nature; thence certain things came into custom by reason of their utility; afterwards these things which emanated from nature and were approved by custom, were sanctioned by fear and reverence for the law.*

Reply Obj. 1. The human reason cannot have a full participation of the dictate of the Divine Reason, but according to its own mode, and imperfectly. Consequently, as on the part of the speculative reason, by a natural participation of Divine Wisdom, there is in us the knowledge of certain general principles, but not proper knowledge of each single truth, such as that contained in the Divine Wisdom; so too, on the part of the practical reason, man has a natural participation of the eternal law, according to certain general principles, but not as regards the particular determinations of individual cases, which are, however, contained in the eternal law. Hence the need for human reason to proceed further to sanction them by law.

Reply Obj. 2. Human reason is not, of itself, the rule of things: but the principles impressed on it by nature, are general rules and measures of all things relating to human conduct, whereof the natural reason is the rule and measure, although it is not the measure of things that are from nature.

Reply Obj. 3. The practical reason is concerned with practical matters, which are singular and contingent: but not with necessary things, with which the speculative reason is concerned. Wherefore human laws cannot have that inerrancy that belongs to the demonstrated conclusions of sciences. Nor is it necessary for every measure to be altogether unerring and certain, but according as it is possible in its own particular genus.

Whether there was any need for a divine law?

Objection 1. It seems that there was no need for a Divine law. Because, as stated above . . . , the natural law is a participation in us of the eternal law. But the eternal law is a Divine law, as stated above. . . . . Therefore there is no need for a Divine law in addition to the natural law, and human laws derived therefrom.

Obj. 2. Further, it is written (Ecclus. xv. 14) that *God left man in the hand of his own counsel*. Now counsel is an act of reason, as stated above. . . . Therefore man was left to the direction of his reason. But a dictate of human reason is a human law, as stated above . . . . Therefore there is no need for man to be governed also by a Divine law.

Obj. 3. Further, human nature is more self-sufficing than irrational creatures. But irrational creatures have no Divine law besides the natural inclination impressed on them. Much less, therefore, should the rational creature have a Divine law in addition to the natural law.

On the contrary, David prayed God to set His law before him, saying: *Set before me for a law the way of Thy justifications, O Lord*.

I answer that, Besides the natural and the human law it was necessary for the directing of human conduct to have a Divine law. And this for four reasons. First, because it is by law that man is directed how to perform his proper acts in view of his last end. And indeed if man were ordained to no other end than that which is proportionate to his natural faculty, there would be no need for man to have any further direction on the part of his reason, besides the natural law and human law which is derived from it. But since man is ordained to an end of eternal happiness which is inproportionate to man's natural faculty, as stated above . . . , therefore it was necessary that, besides the natural and the human law, man should be directed to his end by a law given by God.

Secondly, because, on account of the uncertainty of human judgment, especially on contingent and particular matters, different people form different judgments on human acts; whence also different and contrary laws result. In order, therefore, that man may know without any doubt what he ought to do and what he ought to avoid, it was necessary for man to be directed in his proper acts by a law given by God, for it is certain that such a law cannot err.

Thirdly, because man can make laws in those matters of which he is competent to judge. But man is not competent to judge of interior movements, that are hidden, but only of exterior acts which appear: and yet for the perfection of virtue it is necessary for man to conduct himself aright in both kinds of acts. Consequently human law could not sufficiently curb and direct interior acts; and it was necessary for this purpose that a Divine law should supervene.

Fourthly, because, as Augustine says (*De Lib. Arb.* i.), human law cannot punish or forbid all evil deeds: since while aiming at doing away with all evils, it would do away with many good things, and would hinder the advance of the common good, which is necessary for human intercourse. In order, therefore, that no evil might remain unforbidden and unpunished, it was necessary for the Divine law to supervene, whereby all sins are forbidden.

And these four causes are touched upon in Ps. cxviii. 8, where it is said: *The law of the Lord is unspotted*, *i.e.*, allowing no foulness of sin; *converting souls*, because it directs not only exterior, but also interior acts; *the testimony of the Lord is faithful*, because of the certainty of what is true and right; *giving wisdom to little ones*, by directing man to an end supernatural and Divine.

Reply Obj. 1. By the natural law the eternal law is participated proportionately to the capacity of human nature. But to his supernatural end man needs to be directed in a yet higher way. Hence the additional law given by God, whereby man shares more perfectly in the eternal law.

Reply Obj. 2. Counsel is a kind of inquiry: hence it must proceed from some principles. Nor is it enough for it to proceed from principles imparted by nature, which are the precepts of the natural law, for the reasons given above: but there is need for certain additional principles, namely, the precepts of the Divine law.

Reply Obj. 3. Irrational creatures are not ordained to an end higher than that which is proportionate to their natural powers: consequently the comparison fails.

Government

Whether the old law enjoined fitting precepts concerning rulers?

Objection 1. It would seem that the Old Law made unfitting precepts concerning rulers. Because, as the Philosopher says, "the ordering of the people depends mostly on the chief ruler." But the Law contains no precept relating to the institution of the chief ruler, and yet we find therein prescriptions concerning the inferior rulers; firstly: "Provide out of all the people wise men," etc.; again: "Gather unto Me seventy men of the ancients of Israel"; and again: "Let Me have from among you wise and understanding men," etc. Therefore the Law provided insufficiently in regard to the rulers of the people.

Obj. 2. Further, "The best gives of the best," as Plato states (*Timaeus* ii). Now the best ordering of a state or of any nation is to be ruled by a king, because this kind of government approaches nearest in resemblance to the divine government, whereby God rules the world from the beginning. Therefore the Law should have set a king over the people, and they should not have been allowed a choice in the matter, as indeed they were allowed: "When thou . . . shalt say: I will set a king over me . . . thou shalt set him," etc.

Obj. 3. Further, according to Matthew xii. 25: "Every kingdom divided against itself shall be made desolate"—a saying which was verified in the Jewish people, whose destruction was brought about by the division of the kingdom. But the Law should aim chiefly at things pertaining to the general well-being of the people. Therefore it should have forbidden the kingdom to be divided under two kings, nor should this have been introduced even by divine authority, as we read of its being introduced by the authority of the prophet Ahias the Silonite.

Obj. 4. Further, just as priests are instituted for the benefit of the people in things concerning God, as stated in Hebrews v. 1, so are rulers set up for the benefit of the people in human affairs. But certain things were allotted as a means of livelihood for the priests and Levites of the

SOURCE: *Summa Theologica*, translated by the Fathers of the English Dominican Province. (New York: Benziger Brothers, 1915), *6*, pp. 248–253; *8*, pp. 104–109, 113–116, 121–122, 134–135; *10*, pp. 25–27, 35–39. Reprinted with permission of Benziger Brothers and Burns & Oates, Ltd., London.

Law, such as the tithes and first-fruits, and many like things. Therefore, in like manner, certain things should have been determined for the livelihood of the rulers of the people, the more that they were forbidden to accept presents, as is clearly stated in Exodus xxiii. 8: "You shall not take bribes, which even blind the wise, and pervert the words of the just."

Obj. 5. Further, as a kingdom is the best form of government, so is tyranny the most corrupt. But when the Lord appointed the king, He established a tyrannical law, for it is written: "This will be the right of the king, that shall reign over you: He will take your sons," etc. Therefore the Law made unfitting provision with regard to the institution of rulers.

On the contrary, The people of Israel is commended for the beauty of its order: "How beautiful are thy tabernacles, O Jacob, and thy tents, O Israel." But the beautiful ordering of a people depends on the right establishment of its rulers. Therefore the Law made right provision for the people with regard to its rulers.

I answer that, Two points are to be observed concerning the right ordering of rulers in a state or nation. One is that all should take some share in the government, for this form of constitution ensures peace among the people, commends itself to all, and is most enduring, as stated in *Politics* ii. 6. [The other point is one which has to do with the kind of regime, or, in other words, with the forms of government. Of these there are indeed several, as the Philosopher says, but the best ones are two, viz., the *kingdom*, in which one man rules on the strength of his virtue (prudence), and *aristocracy*, that is, the rule of the best, in which few govern, again on the strength of their virtue. Accordingly, the best form of government is to be found in a city or in a kingdom in which one man is placed at the head to rule over all because of the pre-eminence of his virtue, and under him a certain number of men have governing power also on the strength of their virtue]; and yet a government of this kind is shared by all, both because all are eligible to govern and because the rulers are chosen by all. For this is the best form of polity, being partly kingdom, since there is one at the head of all; partly aristocracy, in so far as a number of persons are set in authority; partly democracy, i.e., government by the people, in so far as the rulers can be chosen from the people and the people have the right to choose their rulers.

Such was the form of government established by the divine Law. For Moses and his successors governed the people in such a way that each of them was ruler over all, so that there was a kind of kingdom. Moreover, seventy-two men were chosen, who were elders in virtue; for it is written: "I took out of your tribes men wise and honourable, and appointed them rulers," so that there was an element of aristocracy. But it was a democratical government in so far as the rulers were chosen from all the people; for it is written: "Provide out of all the people wise men," etc.; and, again, in so far as they were chosen by the people; wherefore it is written: "Let me have from among you wise men," etc. Consequently it is evident that [the ordering of the rulers provided for by the Law was the best.]

Reply Obj. 1. This people was governed under the special care of God; wherefore it is written: "The Lord thy God hath chosen thee to be His peculiar people"; and this is why the Lord reserved to Himself the institution of the chief ruler. For this, too, did Moses pray: "May the Lord the God of the spirits of all the flesh provide a man, that may be over this multitude." Thus by God's orders Josue was set at the head [to succeed Moses]; and we read about each of the judges who succeeded Josue that God "raised . . . up a saviour" for the people and that "the spirit of the Lord was" in them. Hence the Lord did not leave the choice of a king to the people, but reserved this to Himself, as appears from Deuteronomy xvii. 15: "Thou shalt set him whom the Lord thy God shall choose."

Reply Obj. 2. A kingdom is the best form of government of the people, so long as it is not corrupt. But since the power granted to a king is so great, it easily degenerates into tyranny unless he to whom this power is given be a very virtuous man; for it is only the virtuous man that conducts himself well in the midst of prosperity, as the Philosopher observes. Now perfect virtue is to be found in few; and especially were the Jews inclined to cruelty and avarice, which vices above all turn men into tyrants. Hence from the very first the Lord did not set up the kingly authority with full power, but gave them judges and governors to rule them. But afterwards when the people asked Him to do so, being indignant with them, so to speak, He granted the making, as is clear from His words to Samuel: "They have not rejected thee, but Me, that I should not reign over them."

Nevertheless, as regards the appointment of a king, He did establish the manner of election from the very beginning, and then He determined two points: first, that in choosing a king they should wait for the Lord's decision, and that they should not make a man of another nation king, because such kings are wont to take little interest in the people they are set over, and consequently to have no care for their welfare. Secondly, He prescribed how the king, after his appointment, should behave in regard to himself—namely, that he should not accumulate chariots and horses, nor wives, nor immense wealth, because through craving for such things princes become tyrants and forsake justice. He also appointed the manner in which they were to conduct themselves toward God—namely, that they should continually read and ponder on God's Law, and should ever fear and obey God. Moreover, He decided how they should behave toward their subjects—namely, that they should not proudly despise them, or ill-treat them, and that they should not depart from the paths of justice.

Reply Obj. 3. The division of the kingdom and a number of kings was rather a punishment inflicted on that people for their many dissensions, specially against the just rule of David, than a benefit conferred on them for their profit. Hence it is written: "I will give thee a king in My wrath"; and: "They have reigned, but not by Me: they have been princes, and I knew not."

Reply Obj. 4. The priestly office was bequeathed by succession from father to son; and this in order that it might be held in greater respect if not any man from the people could become a priest, since honor was given to them out of reverence for the divine worship. Hence it was necessary to put aside certain things for them both as to tithes and as to first-fruits, and, again, as to oblations and sacrifices, that they might be afforded a means of livelihood. On the other hand, the rulers, as stated above, were chosen from the whole people, wherefore they had their own possessions from which to derive a living, and so much the more since the Lord forbade even a king to have superabundant wealth or to make too much show of magnificence; both because he could scarcely avoid the excesses of pride and tyranny arising from such things and because, if the rulers were not very rich and if their office involved much work and anxiety, it would not tempt the ambition of the common people and would not become an occasion of sedition.

Reply Obj. 5. That right was not given to the king by divine institution, rather was it foretold that kings would usurp that right by framing unjust laws and by degenerating into tyrants who preyed on their subjects. This is clear from the context that follows: "And you shall be his slaves," which is significative of tyranny, since a tyrant rules his subjects as though they were his slaves. Hence Samuel spoke these words to deter them from asking for a king, since the narrative continues: "But the people would not hear the voice of Samuel."—It may happen, however, that even a good king, without being a tyrant, may take away the sons and make them tribunes and centurions, and may take many things from his subjects in order to secure the common weal.

. . . .

Whether right is the object of justice?

Objection 1. It would seem that right is not the object of justice. For the jurist Celsus says that "right is the art of goodness and equality." Now art is not the object of justice, but is by itself an intellectual virtue. Therefore right is not the object of justice.

Obj. 2. Further, "Law," according to Isidore, "is a kind of right." Now law is the object not of justice but of prudence, wherefore the

Philosopher reckons "legislative" as one of the parts of prudence. Therefore right is not the object of justice.

Obj. 3. Further, justice, before all, subjects man to God; for Augustine says that "justice is love serving God alone and consequently governing aright all things subject to man." Now right (*ius*) does not pertain to divine things, but only to human affairs, for Isidore says that "*fas* is the divine law, and *ius* the human law." Therefore right is not the object of justice.

On the contrary, Isidore says that "*ius* (right) is so called because it is just." Now the "just" is the object of justice, for the Philosopher declares that "all are agreed in giving the name of justice to the habit which makes men capable of doing just actions."

I answer that, It is proper to justice, as compared with the other virtues, to direct man in his relations with others, because it denotes a kind of equality, as its very name implies; indeed we are wont to say that things are adjusted when they are made equal, for equality is in reference of one thing to some other. On the other hand, the other virtues perfect man in those matters only which befit him in relation to himself. Accordingly that which is right in the works of the other virtues, and to which the intention of the virtue tends as to its proper object, depends on its relation to the agent only, whereas the right in a work of justice, besides its relation to the agent, is set up by its relation to others. Because a man's work is said to be just when it is related to some other by way of some kind of equality; for instance, the payment of the wage due for a service rendered. And so a thing is said to be just, as having the rectitude of justice, when it is the term of an act of justice, without taking into account the way in which it is done by the agent; whereas in the other virtues nothing is declared to be right unless it is done in a certain way by the agent. For this reason justice has its own special proper object over and above the other virtues, and this object is called the "just," which is the same as "right." Hence it is evident that right is the object of justice.

Reply Obj. 1. It is usual for words to be distorted from their original signification so as to mean something else: thus the word "medicine" was first employed to signify a remedy used for curing a sick person, and then it was drawn to signify the art by which this is done. In like manner the word *ius* (right) was first of all used to denote the just thing itself, but afterwards it was transferred to designate the art whereby it is known what is just, and further to denote the place where justice is administered: thus a man is said to appear *in jure*, and yet further, we say even that a man who has the office of exercising justice administers the *ius* even if his sentence be unjust.

Reply Obj. 2. Just as there pre-exists in the mind of the craftsman an expression of the things to be made externally by his craft, which expression is called the rule of his craft, so, too, there pre-exists in the mind an expression of the particular just work which the reason determines, and which is a kind of rule of prudence. If this rule be expressed in writing, it is called a "law," which, according to Isidore, is "a written decree," and so law is not the same as right, but an expression of right.

Reply Obj. 3. Since justice implies equality and since we cannot offer God an equal return, it follows that we cannot make Him a perfectly just repayment. For this reason the divine law is not properly called *ius* but *fas*, because, to wit, God is satisfied if we accomplish what we can. Nevertheless justice tends to make man repay God as much as he can, by subjecting his mind to Him entirely.

Whether right is fittingly divided into natural right and positive right?

Objection 1. It would seem that right is not fittingly divided into natural right and positive right. For that which is natural is unchangeable, and is the same for all. Now nothing of the kind is to be found in human affairs, since all the rules of human right fail in certain cases, nor do they obtain force everywhere. Therefore there is no such thing as natural right.

Obj. 2. Further, a thing is called "positive" when it proceeds from the human will. But a thing is not just simply because it proceeds from the human will, else a man's will could not be unjust. Since then the "just" and the "right" are the same, it seems that there is no positive right.

Obj. 3. Further, divine right is not natural right, since it transcends human nature. In like manner, neither is it positive right, since it is based not on human but on divine authority. Therefore right is unfittingly divided into natural and positive.

On the contrary, The Philosopher says that "political justice is partly natural and partly legal," i.e., established by law.

I answer that, As stated above . . . , the "right" or the "just" is a work that is adjusted to another person according to some kind of equality. Now a thing can be adjusted to a man in two ways: first, by its very nature, as when a man gives so much that he may receive equal value in return, and this is called "natural right." In another way, a thing is adjusted or commensurated to another person by agreement or by common consent, when, to wit, a man deems himself satisfied if he receives so much. This can be done in two ways: first, by private agreement, as that which is confirmed by an agreement between private individuals; secondly, by public agreement, as when the whole community agrees that something should be deemed as though it were adjusted and commensurated to another person, or when this is decreed by the prince who is placed over the people and acts in its stead, and this is called "positive right."

Reply Obj. 1. That which is natural to one whose nature is unchangeable must needs be such always and everywhere. But man's nature is changeable, wherefore that which is natural to man may sometimes fail. Thus the restitution of a deposit to the depositor is in accordance with natural equality, and if human nature were always right, this would always have to be observed; but since it happens sometimes that man's will is unrighteous, there are cases in which a deposit should not be restored, lest a man of unrighteous will make evil use of the thing deposited: as when a madman or an enemy of the common weal demands the return of his weapons.

Reply Obj. 2. The human will can, by common agreement, make a thing to be just provided it be not, of itself, contrary to natural justice, and it is in such matters that positive right has its place. Hence the Philosopher says that "in the case of the legal just, it does not matter in the first instance whether it takes one form or another, it only matters when once it is laid down." If, however, a thing is, of itself, contrary to natural right, the human will cannot make it just, for instance, by decreeing that it is lawful to steal or to commit adultery. Hence it is written: "Woe to them that make wicked laws."

Reply Obj. 3. The divine right is that which is promulgated by God. Such things are partly those that are naturally just, yet their justice is hidden to man, and partly are made just by God's decree. Hence also divine right may be divided in respect of these two things, even as human right is. For the divine law commands certain things because they are good, and forbids others because they are evil, while others are good because they are prescribed, and others evil because they are forbidden.

Whether the right of nations is the same as the natural right?

Objection 1. It would seem that the right of nations is the same as the natural right. For all men do not agree save in that which is natural to them. Now all men agree in the right of nations, since the Jurist says that "the right of nations is that which is in use among all nations." Therefore the right of nations is the natural right.

Obj. 2. Further, slavery among men is natural, for some are naturally slaves, according to the Philosopher. Now "slavery belongs to the right of nations," as Isidore states. Therefore the right of nations is a natural right.

Obj. 3. Further, right, as stated above . . . , is divided into natural and positive. Now the right of nations is not a positive right, since all nations never agreed to decree anything by common agreement. Therefore the right of nations is a natural right.

On the contrary, Isidore says that "right is either natural, or civil, or right of nations," and consequently the right of nations is distinct from natural right.

I answer that, as stated above . . . , the natural right or just is that which by its very nature is adjusted to or commensurate with another person. Now this may happen in two ways: first, according as it is considered absolutely; thus a male by his very nature is commensurate with the female to beget offspring by her, and a parent is commensurate with the offspring to nourish it. Secondly, a thing is naturally commensurate with another person, not according as it is considered absolutely, but according to something resultant from it, for instance, the possession of property. For if a particular piece of land be considered absolutely, it contains no reason why it should belong to one man more than to another, but if it be considered in respect of its adaptability to cultivation and the unmolested use of the land, it has a certain commensuration to be the property of one and not of another man, as the Philosopher shows.

Now it belongs not only to man but also to other animals to apprehend a thing absolutely; wherefore the right which we call natural is common to us and other animals according to the first kind of commensuration. But the right of nations falls short of natural right in this sense, as the Jurist says, because "the latter is common to all animals, while the former is common to men only. " On the other hand, to consider a thing by comparing it with what results from it is proper to reason, wherefore this same is natural to man in respect of natural reason which dictates it. Hence the jurist Gaius says: "Whatever natural reason decrees among all men is observed by all equally, and is called the right of nations." This suffices for the *Reply* to the *First Objection*.

Reply Obj. 2. Considered absolutely, the fact that this particular man should be a slave rather than another man is based, not on natural reason, but on some resultant utility, in that it is useful to this man to be ruled by a wiser man, and to the latter to be helped by the former, as the Philosopher states. Wherefore slavery which belongs to the right of nations is natural in the second way, but not in the first.

Reply Obj. 3. Since natural reason dictates matters which are according to the right of nations as implying a proximate equality, it follows that they need no special institution, for they are instituted by natural reason itself, as stated by the authority quoted above.

. . . .

Whether justice is fittingly defined as being the perpetual and constant will to render to each one his right?

Objection 1. It would seem that lawyers have unfittingly defined justice as being "the perpetual and constant will to render to each one his right." For, according to the Philosopher, justice is a habit which makes a man "capable of doing what is just, and of being just in action and in intention." Now "will" denotes a power or also an act. Therefore justice is unfittingly defined as being a will.

Obj. 2. Further, rectitude of the will is not the will; else if the will were its own rectitude, it would follow that no will is unrighteous. Yet, according to Anselm, justice is rectitude. Therefore justice is not the will.

Obj. 3. Further, no will is perpetual save God's. If therefore justice is a perpetual will, in God alone will there be justice.

Obj. 4. Further, whatever is perpetual is constant, since it is unchangeable. Therefore it is needless, in defining justice, to say that it is both "perpetual" and "constant."

Obj. 5. Further, it belongs to the sovereign to give each one his right. Therefore, if justice gives each one his right, it follows that it is in none but the sovereign, which is absurd.

Obj. 6. Further, Augustine says that "justice is love serving God alone." Therefore it does not render to each one his right.

I answer that, The aforesaid definition of justice is fitting if understood aright. For since every virtue is a habit which is the principle of a good act, a virtue must needs be defined by means of the good act bearing on the matter proper to that virtue. Now the proper matter of justice consists of those things that belong to our intercourse with other men, as shall be shown further on . . . . Hence the act of justice in relation to its proper matter and object is indicated in the words, "Rendering to each one his right," since, as Isidore says, "a man is said to be just because he respects the rights (*ius*) of others."

Now in order that an act bearing upon any matter whatever be virtuous, it requires to be voluntary, stable, and firm, because the Philosopher says that in order for an act to be virtuous it needs first of all to be done "knowingly," secondly to be done "by choice" and "for a due end," thirdly to be done "immovably." Now the first of these is included in the second, since "what is done through ignorance is involuntary." Hence the definition of justice mentions first the "will," in order to show that the act of justice must be voluntary; and mention is made afterwards of its "constancy" and "perpetuity" in order to indicate the firmness of the act.

Accordingly this is a complete definition of justice, save that the act is mentioned instead of the habit which takes its species from that act, because habit implies relation to act. And if anyone would reduce it to the proper form of a definition, he might say that *justice is a habit whereby a man renders to each one his due by a constant and perpetual will;* and this is about the same definition as that given by the Philosopher, who says that "justice is a habit whereby a man is said to be capable of doing just actions in accordance with his choice."

Reply Obj. 1. Will here denotes the act, not the power, and it is customary among writers to define habits by their acts: thus Augustine says that "faith is to believe what one sees not."

Reply Obj. 2. Justice is the same as rectitude, not essentially but causally; for it is a habit which rectifies the deed and the will.

Reply Obj. 3. The will may be called perpetual in two ways. First, on the part of the will's act which endures forever, and thus God's will alone is perpetual. Secondly, on the part of the subject, because, to wit, a man wills to do a certain thing always, and this is a necessary condition of justice. For it does not satisfy the conditions of justice that one wish to observe justice in some particular matter for the time being, because one could scarcely find a man willing to act unjustly in every case; and it is requisite that one should have the will to observe justice at all times and in all cases.

Reply Obj. 4. Since "perpetual" does not imply perpetuity of the act of the will, it is not superfluous to add "constant"; for while the "perpetual will" denotes the purpose of observing justice always, "constant" signifies a firm perseverance in this purpose.

Reply Obj. 5. A judge renders to each one what belongs to him by way of command and direction, because a judge is the "personification of justice," and "the sovereign is its guardian." On the other hand, the subjects render to each one what belongs to him by way of execution.

Reply Obj. 6. Just as love of God includes love of our neighbor, as stated above, so, too, the service of God includes rendering to each one his due.

. . . .

Whether justice is a general virtue?

Objection 1. It would seem that justice is not a general virtue. For justice is specified with the other virtues, according to Wisdom viii. 7: "She teacheth temperance, and prudence, and justice, and fortitude." Now the "general" is not specified or reckoned together with the species contained under the same "general." Therefore justice is not a general virtue.

Obj. 2. Further, as justice is accounted a cardinal virtue, so are temperance and fortitude. Now neither temperance nor fortitude is reckoned to be a general virtue. Therefore neither should justice in any way be reckoned a general virtue.

Obj. 3. Further, justice is always toward others, as stated above (A. 2). But a sin committed against one's neighbor cannot be a general sin, because it is condivided with sin committed against oneself. Therefore neither is justice a general virtue.

On the contrary, The Philosopher says that "justice is every virtue."

I answer that, Justice, as stated above . . . , directs man in his relations with other men. Now this may happen in two ways: first, as regards his relations with individuals; secondly, as regards his relations with others in general, in so far as a man who serves a community serves all those who are included in that community. Accordingly justice in its proper acceptation can be directed to another in both these senses. Now it is evident that all who are included in a community stand in relation to that community as parts to a whole; while a part, as such, belongs to a whole, so that whatever is the good of a part can be directed to the good of the whole. It follows, therefore, that the good of any virtue, whether such virtue direct man in relation to himself or in relation to certain other individual persons, is referable to the common good to which justice directs; so that all acts of virtue can pertain to justice, in so far as it directs man to the common good. It is in this sense that justice is called a general virtue. And since it belongs to the law to direct to the common good, as stated above . . . , it follows that the justice which is in this way styled general, is called "legal justice," because thereby man is in harmony with the law which directs the acts of all the virtues to the common good.

Reply Obj. 1. Justice is specified or enumerated with the other virtues, not as a general but as a special virtue, as we shall state further on. . . .

Reply Obj. 2. Temperance and fortitude are in the sensitive appetite, viz. in the concupiscible and irascible. Now these powers are appetitive of certain particular goods, even as the senses are cognitive of particulars. On the other hand justice is in the intellective appetite as its subject, which can have the universal good as its object, knowledge whereof belongs to the intellect. Hence justice can be a general virtue rather than temperance or fortitude.

Reply Obj. 3. Things referable to oneself are referable to another, especially in regard to the common good. Wherefore legal justice, in so far as it directs to the common good, may be called a general vritue, and in like manner injustice may be called a general sin; hence it is written that all "sin is iniquity."

. . . .

Whether justice stands foremost among all moral virtues?

Objection 1. It would seem that justice does not stand foremost among all the moral virtues. Because it belongs to justice to render to each one what is his, whereas it belongs to liberality to give of one's own, and this is more virtuous. Therefore liberality is a greater virtue than justice.

Obj. 2. Further, nothing is adorned by a less excellent thing than itself. Now magnanimity is the ornament both of justice and of all the virtues, according to *Ethics* iv. 3. Therefore magnanimity is more excellent than justice.

Obj. 3. Further, virtue is about that which is "difficult" and "good," as stated in *Ethics* ii. 3. But fortitude is about more difficult things than justice is, since it is about dangers of death, according to *Ethics* iii. 6. Therefore fortitude is more excellent than justice.

On the contrary, Cicero says: "Justice is the most resplendent of the virtues and gives its name to a good man."

I answer that, If we speak of legal justice, it is evident that it stands foremost among all the moral virtues, for as much as the common good transcends the individual good of one person. In this sense the Philosopher declares that "the most excellent of the virtues would seem to be justice, and more glorious than either the evening or the morning star." But even if we speak of particular justice, it excels the other moral virtues for two reasons. The first reason may be taken from the subject, because justice is in the more excellent part of the soul, viz. the rational appetite or will, whereas the other moral virtues are in the sensitive appetite, whereunto appertain the passions which are the matter of the other moral virtues. The second reason is taken from the object, because the other virtues are commendable in respect of the sole good of the virtuous person himself, whereas justice is praiseworthy in respect of the virtuous person being well disposed toward another, so that justice is somewhat the good of another person, as stated in *Ethics* v. 1. Hence the Philosopher says: "The greatest virtues must needs be those which are most profitable to other persons, because virtue is a faculty of doing good to others. For this reason the greatest honors are accorded the brave and the just, since bravery is useful to others in warfare, and justice is useful to others both in warfare and in time of peace."

Reply Obj. 1. Although the liberal man gives of his own, yet he does so in so far as he takes into consideration the good of his own virtue, while the just man gives to another what is his, through consideration of the common good. Moreover justice is observed toward all, whereas liberality cannot extend to all. Again liberality which gives of a man's own is based on justice, whereby one renders to each man what is his.

Reply Obj. 2. When magnanimity is added to justice it increases the latter's goodness; and yet without justice it would not even be a virtue.

Reply Obj. 3. Although fortitude is about the most difficult things, it is not about the best, for it is only useful in warfare, whereas justice is useful both in war and in peace, as stated above.

. . . .

Whether one man is bound to obey another?

Objection 1. It seems that one man is not bound to obey another. For nothing should be done contrary to the divine ordinance. Now God has so ordered that man is ruled by his own counsel, according to Ecclesiasticus xv. 14: "God made man from the beginning, and left him in the hand of his own counsel." Therefore one man is not bound to obey another.

Obj. 2. Further, if one man were bound to obey another, he would have to look upon the will of the person commanding him as being his rule of conduct. Now God's will alone, which is always right, is a rule of human conduct. Therefore man is bound to obey none but God.

Obj. 3. Further, the more gratuitous the service the more is it acceptable. Now what a man does out of duty is not gratuitous. Therefore if a man were bound in duty to obey others in doing good deeds, for this very reason his good deeds would be rendered less acceptable through being done out of obedience. Therefore one man is not bound to obey another.

On the contrary, It is prescribed: "Obey your prelates and be subject to them."

I answer that, Just as the actions of natural things proceed from natural powers, so do human actions proceed from the human will. In natural things it behooved the higher to move the lower to their actions by the excellence of the natural power bestowed on them by God; and so in human affairs also the higher must move the lower by their will in virtue of a divinely established authority. Now to move by reason and will is to command. Wherefore just as in virtue of the divinely established natural order the lower natural things need to be subject to the movement of the higher, so too in human affairs, in virtue of the order of natural and divine law, inferiors are bound to obey their superiors.

Reply Obj. 1. God left man in the hand of his own counsel, not as though it were lawful to him to do whatever he will, but because, unlike irrational creatures, he is not compelled by natural necessity to do what he ought to do but is left the free choice proceeding from his own counsel. And just as he has to proceed on his own counsel in doing other things, so too has he in the point of obeying his superiors. For Gregory says: "When we humbly give way to another's voice, we overcome ourselves in our own hearts."

Reply Obj. 2. The will of God is the first rule whereby all rational wills are regulated; and to this rule one will approaches more than another, according to a divinely appointed order. Hence the will of the one man who issues a command may be as a second rule to the will of this other man who obeys him.

Reply Obj. 3. A thing may be deemed gratuitous in two ways. In one way on the part of the deed itself, because, to wit, one is not bound to do it; in another way on the part of the doer, because he does it of his own free will. Now a deed is rendered virtuous, praiseworthy, and meritorious chiefly according as it proceeds from the will. Wherefore although obedience be a duty, if one obey with a prompt will one's merit is not for that reason diminished, especially before God, Who sees not only the outward deed but also the inward will.

. . . .

Whether subjects are bound to obey their superiors in all things?

Objection 1. It seems that subjects are bound to obey their superiors in all things. For the Apostle says: "Children, obey your parents in all things"; and farther on: "Servants, obey in all things your masters according to the flesh." Therefore in like manner other subjects are bound to obey their superiors in all things.

Obj. 2. Further, superiors stand between God and their subjects, according to Deuteronomy v. 5: "I was the mediator and stood between the Lord and you at that time, to show you His words." Now there is no going from extreme to extreme, except through that which stands between. Therefore the commands of a superior must be esteemed the commands of God, wherefore the Apostle says: "You . . . received me as an angel of God, even as Christ Jesus"; and: "When you had received of us the word of the hearing of God, you received it, not as the word of men, but, as it is indeed, the word of God." Therefore as man is bound to obey God in all things, so is he bound to obey his superiors.

Obj. 3. Further, just as religious in making their profession take vows of chastity and poverty, so do they also vow obedience. Now a religious is bound to observe chastity and poverty in all things. Therefore he is also bound to obey in all things.

On the contrary, It is written: "We ought to obey God rather than men." Now sometimes the things commanded by a superior are against God. Therefore superiors are not to be obeyed in all things.

I answer that, As stated above . . . , he who obeys is moved at the bidding of the person who commands him by a certain necessity of justice, even as a natural thing is moved through the power of its mover by a natural necessity. That a natural thing be not moved by its mover may happen in two ways. First on account of a hindrance arising from the stronger power of some other mover; thus wood is not burned by fire if a stronger force of water intervene. Secondly, through lack of order in the movable with regard to its mover, since, though it is subject to the latter's action in one respect, yet it is not subject thereto in every respect. Thus a humor is sometimes subject to the action of heat as regards being heated, but not as regards being dried up or consumed. In like manner there are two reasons for which a subject may not be bound to obey his superior in all things. First on account of the command of a higher power. For as a gloss says on Romans xiii. 2, "They that resist the power, resist the ordinance of God. If a commissioner issue an order, are you to comply if it is contrary to the bidding of the proconsul? Again if the proconsul command one thing and the emperor another, will you hesitate to disregard the former and serve the latter? Therefore if the emperor commands one thing and God another, you must disregard the former and obey God." Secondly, a subject is not bound to obey his superior if the latter command him to do something wherein he is not subject to him. For Seneca says: "It is wrong to suppose that slavery falls upon the whole man; for the better part of him is excepted. His body is subjected and assigned to his master, but his soul is his own." Consequently in matters touching the internal movement of the will man is not bound to obey his fellow man, but God alone.

Nevertheless man is bound to obey his fellow man in things that have to be done externally by means of the body; and yet, since by nature all men are equal, he is not bound to obey another man in matters touching the nature of the body, for instance, in those relating to the support of his body or the begetting of his children. Wherefore servants are not bound to obey their masters, nor children their parents, in the question of contracting marriage or of remaining in the state of virginity or the like. But in matters concerning the disposal of actions and human affairs a subject is bound to obey his superior within the sphere of his authority; for instance, a soldier must obey his general in matters relating to war, a servant his master in matters touching the execution of the duties of his service, a son his father in matters relating to the conduct of his life and the care of the household, and so forth.

Reply Obj. 1. When the Apostle says "in all things," he refers to matters within the sphere of a father's or master's authority.

Reply Obj. 2. Man is subject to God simply as regards all things, both internal and external, wherefore he is bound to obey Him in all things. On the other hand inferiors are not subject to their superiors in all things, but only in certain things and in a particular way, in respect of which the superior stands between God and his subjects; whereas in respect of other matters the subject is immediately under God, by Whom he is taught either by the natural or by the written law.

Reply Obj. 3. Religious profess obedience as to the regular mode of life, in respect of which they are subject to their superiors; wherefore they are bound to obey in those matters only which may belong to the regular mode of life, and this obedience suffices for salvation. If they be willing to obey even in other matters, this will belong to the superabundance of perfection, provided, however, such things be not contrary to God or to the rule they profess, for obedience in this case would be unlawful.

Accordingly we may distinguish a threefold obedience: one, sufficient for salvation and consisting in obeying when one is bound to obey; secondly, perfect obedience, which obeys in all things lawful; thirdly, indiscreet obedience, which obeys even in matters unlawful.

Whether Christians are bound to obey the secular power?

Objection 1. It seems that Christians are not bound to obey the secular power. For a gloss on Matthew xvii. 25, "Then the children are free," says: "If in every kingdom the children of the king who holds sway over that kingdom are free, then the children of that King, under Whose sway are all kingdoms, should be free in every kingdom." Now Christians, by their faith in Christ, are made children of God, according to John i. 12: "He gave them power to be made the sons of God, to them that believe in His name." Therefore they are not bound to obey the secular power.

Obj. 2. Further, it is written: "You . . . are become dead to the law by the body of Christ" and the law mentioned here is the divine law of the Old Testament. Now human law whereby men are subject to the secular power is of less account than the divine law of the Old Testament. Much more, therefore, since they have become members of Christ's body, are men freed from the law of subjection, whereby they were under the power of secular princes.

Obj. 3. Further, men are not bound to obey robbers, who oppress them with violence. Now Augustine says: "Without justice, what else is a kingdom but a huge robbery?" Since therefore the authority of secular princes is frequently exercised with injustice or owes its origin to some unjust usurpation, it seems that Christians ought not to obey secular princes.

On the contrary, It is written: "Admonish them to be subject to princes and powers"; and: "Be ye subject . . . to every human creature for God's sake, whether it be to the king as excelling or to governors as sent by him."

I answer that, Faith in Christ is the origin and cause of justice, according to Romans iii. 22: "The justice of God by faith of Jesus Christ"; wherefore faith in Christ does not void the order of justice, but strengthens it. Now the order of justice requires that subjects obey their superiors, else the stability of human affairs would cease. Hence faith in Christ does not excuse the faithful from the obligation of obeying secular princes.

Reply Obj. 1. As stated above . . ., the subjection whereby one man is bound to another regards the body, not the soul, which retains its liberty. Now, in this state of life we are freed by the grace of Christ from defects of the soul, but not from defects of the body, as the Apostle declares by saying of himself that in his mind he served the law of God, but in his flesh the law of sin. Wherefore those that are made children of God by grace are free from the spiritual bondage of sin, but not from the bodily bondage, whereby they are held bound to earthly masters, as a gloss observes on 1 Timothy vi. 1, "Whosoever are servants under the yoke," etc.

Reply Obj. 2. The Old Law was a figure of the New Testament, and therefore it had to cease on the advent of truth. And the comparison with human law does not stand, because thereby one man is subject to another. Yet man is bound by divine law to obey his fellow man.

Reply Obj. 3. Man is bound to obey secular princes in so far as this is required by the order of justice. Wherefore if the prince's authority is not just but usurped, or if he commands what is unjust, his subjects are not bound to obey him, except perhaps accidentally, in order to avoid scandal or danger.

A STUDY GUIDE TO THOMAS AQUINAS' THOUGHT

1. What are Aquinas' five proofs for the existence of God? Is Aquinas' knowledge of God based on some kind of direct perception, or is it based upon what experience teaches us? How is it possible for man to have any kind of knowledge of God when man is so far beneath God?

2. What does Aquinas mean when he says that the intellect is the form of the human body? Why is the intellect a passive power? In what way is intellectual knowledge derived from sensible things? What are three stages of knowledge?

3. What does Aquinas mean when he says that man's ultimate happiness consists in contemplating God? Why cannot man achieve happiness in this life?

4. What is the nature of virtue? What is the difference between moral and intellectual virtue? What are the cardinal virtues? What are the theological virtues?

5. What is the role of reason in regard to law? How many different kinds of law are there? What is the nature of each?

6. Why does Aquinas regard kingship as the best form of government? What are the mutual obligations of the king and his subjects? What is the moral value of the state? In Aquinas' view, what is the right of nations? What are the limits upon the power of the state? Compare Aquinas' view of the moral sanction of the state with Augustine's.

5

MODERN COMMENTARY ON AUGUSTINE

F. Van Der Meer

The great man lived in a small world. He was hardly more than a sort of episcopal dean, and a great deal of his work was that of an ordinary priest; he was the kind of bishop whom the more casual officials cheerfully kept waiting in their anterooms. There was, in fact, beneath the genius, a very humdrum Augustine who lived in what was really a large but very ordinary presbytery and who could be approached by anybody about pretty well any business that his caller fancied.

Viewing him through the perspective of history, we gain the impression that the saint's real home was Carthage and that this was the city from which he dominated Church history in his day. Undoubtedly there were years in which nearly half of his time was spent in the capital, but the truth is that Carthage was still essentially the exception and Hippo the rule. True, Augustine belonged to the Church as a whole; nevertheless his desire was to belong in an especial manner to the Church in Hippo, and it was in the daily cure of souls in that locality that he conceived his first duty to lie.

He was to an exemplary degree a resident bishop, and that in a bishopric considerably the worse for wear. Augustine in Hippo was a figure very like that of Bossuet, but not the Bossuet of the Court who now and then spent a little time in Meaux (and that by preference in the little garden house behind the hornbeams). Rather was he a Bossuet working in Boulogne or Toulon and daily surrounded by beggars and petitioners. Never again did he cross the sea to Italy. Alypius attended to that sort of thing for him; or, if the message he had to send was of minor importance, a simple acolyte or subdeacon performed the service. Nobody at the Court of Ravenna knew what he looked like, and Rome, after thirty years, remained equally ignorant; for the "second founder of the ancient Faith" worked upon the spirits of others by means of his own spirit and not by measures of ecclesiastical policy.

SOURCE: F. Van Der Meer, *Augustine the Bishop* (New York: Sheed & Ward, 1961) pp. xvi–xvii. Copyright Sheed & Ward, Ltd. Reprinted with permission of the publishers.

His was no key position in the Church, yet as he wrote at his desk or spoke from the *cathedra* in the third-rate place which was his home wave upon wave went out over the world. What many readers of Augustine's writings do not realize is that his simple *cathedra* was more important to him than his pen. It was the needs and cares of ordinary Christian folk that supplied both the matter and manner of his loftiest writings, so that the main function of his genius was to serve the pastor of souls. It is not altogether wrong to say that we owe Augustine the saint to the strange and surprising fact that Augustine the genius was little more than a parish priest.

Even that humble task he took on against his will. Indeed, he was literally forced into it, and ultimately, before the end of his life, he handed over this all-too-restricted sphere of his work to a younger man, for the councils of his country now laid greater tasks upon his shoulders. Yet in between these two events there are thirty-five years of humble labour in one of the Lord's less prepossessing vineyards, in that same Hippo where his priestly work began.

From 391 till 426, he was every inch a pastor of souls, and this despite the monastic life which he lived together with his clergy, despite the care for the churches of all Africa which his metropolitan put upon him, and despite his growing literary fame. What ultimately compelled him to travel was the concrete demands which were made upon him by the necessities of the Church. It was the fear of seeing truth clouded over and violence done to the purity of the Church's doctrine, for what was in question was freedom and grace and the unity and holiness of the Church—those very matters which most deeply touched his mind. Of his greater works, one only owes its existence to pure interest in speculation—that on the Trinity. The others all came into being to meet the particular needs of the time.

J. J. O'Meara

To sum up: the book is a confession by Augustine to God of sin, praise, and especially of faith—of faith in the Incarnate Word as against the proud rejection of Christ by the Neo-Platonists. The confession is made to God, but before men and for their edification. It contains in its first nine books the history of Augustine's life up to and including his conversion; in the tenth—a book apparently intercalated after the first publication of the whole work—a history of his present conflicts with the world, the flesh and the devil; and in the last three books a commentary on the first chapter and the first two verses of the second chapter of

SOURCE: J. J. O'Meara, *The Young Augustine* (London: Longmans, Green & Co., 1954), pp. 17–19. Reprinted with permission of the publishers.

Genesis. If there is unity in the *Confessions* it lies, to the exclusion of book ten, in the contrast between the search for Truth under the guidance of Providence in the first part of the work, and the enjoyment of Truth in the Scriptures in the third part. This contrast is the theme of the *Confessions*, the first part of which—seeking for Truth under the guidance of Providence—is of primary importance within the *Confessions* itself and essential for the proper understanding of the second.

Augustine believes that all men have similar experiences in the search under Providence for Truth—up to a certain point. Then they are challenged to accept the authority of Christ: some confess to Christ; others in their presumption reject him. Victorinus, his friend and fellow-countryman, submitted to Christ. So did Augustine, and instantaneously with that submission all his former difficulties were overcome.

The *Confessions* therefore is no autobiography, and not even a partial autobiography. It is the use of Augustine's life and confession of faith in God as an illustration of his theory of man.

The facts of his life are discovered by him in memory and the road of memory he traverses, back and forth, visiting only such places as can be of use in the present purpose. If he has no memory of a particular point which is useful for his theory, he conjectures with easy probability what must have happened. Hence the *Confessions* is not wholly a purely personal history; it is in part typical.

Certain consequences for its historicity can be seen to arise from a book of this nature. To begin with, not all of the facts, not necessarily all the important facts even, of Augustine's life are here related: many are forgotten and many would not fit into the pattern of his theory. The events even as given are presented as seen by the writer at the time of composition and not always as they seemed when they occurred. There are appended, moreover, to the relation of facts many moral disquisitions which again are aimed at interpreting the facts in the light of later beliefs rather than in the light of Augustine's views at the time. Added to all this are a rhetorician's fondness for over-statement on the one hand and under-statement (manifesting itself in deliberate vagueness both in recollection and language) on the other, and the employment of extraordinary means such as dreams, visions and voices for the furtherance of his arguments especially at a crucial juncture.

What is rhetorical, however, is not necessarily false. Where we have a control for certain sections of the *Confessions*, we find that the facts as given there are correct. Where Augustine has recourse to conjecture, he conjectures with reserve. If he does examine events in the light of recent beliefs and add a moral lesson, he is both conscious of what he is doing and occasionally reminds the reader of it. His audience expected him to use the various techniques of rhetoric, and we have only ourselves to blame if we are misled by them; and God, whom Augustine solemnly addressed, is not mocked. It would have been dangerous for him, to put things at their lowest, to attempt to deceive his many friends and enemies.

The *Confessions*, in short, gives a true account of Augustine's life up to the time of his conversion. But since this account is presented in the pattern of a theory and with the methods of a technique, it needs careful elucidation. Neither the theory nor the technique must be considered as unhelpful, much less harmful. They not only reveal to us the facts of Augustine's earlier life, but also give us the clue to their interpretation and to the mind and heart of that towering figure who built upon a city of philosophers and rhetoricians a city of Christian thought.

Herbert Deane

Since Augustine was a profoundly original thinker, his ideas about man, society, and the state exhibit both the power and the limitations of the great vision. He saw man in his fallen condition as completely vitiated by sin. Every human action from the most sublime expression of altruism or patriotism or the highest intellectual or artistic achievement to the most sordid or trivial action is rooted in human sinfulness—in each man's burning desire for self-aggrandizement, whether by the relentless accumulation of material goods and money, the driving lust for power over other men, or the insatiable appetite for fame and glory and, therefore, for the approbation of other human beings. Occasionally, Augustine notes that there are meaningful differences among these sinful actions and among the sinful men who perform them. The patriotic devotion and the desire or glory of the ancient Romans spurred them on to deeds of great bravery and heroic self-sacrifice which enhanced the safety and prosperity of the nation. Although Augustine recognizes that their conduct was "quasi-virtuous" and far more admirable than the materialistic self-indulgence of the later Romans, he does not pursue the idea that there may be "higher" and "lower" forms of sin, better and worse actions. Since his attention is focused on the sinfulness of men's wills and deeds, he sees that even these acts of heroism and self-sacrifice are radically infected with vice—the terrible vices of pride and of vainly seeking immortality by winning the applause of deluded men.

His thought is dominated by the sharp contrast between unredeemed man, whose every action is an exhibition of sin and pride, and the man

SOURCE: Herbert Deane, *The Political and Social Ideas of St. Augustine* (New York: Columbia University Press, 1963), pp. 238–243. Reprinted with permission of the publishers.

who has been saved by the gratuitous gift of God's love, and who is therefore capable of truly virtuous action since not he but the love of God now works within him. In this perspective, the varieties or gradations found in sinful actions, the fact that in the eyes of the world certain sinful deeds are "good" or "honorable," and the fact that the redeemed man may, on occasion, lapse into sinful deeds are all profoundly irrelevant. In Augustine's vision there are two clearly separated types of man —the minority, who love God and do His will, and the great majority, who love themselves and earthly goods, wealth, power, fame, and pleasure. In consequence, there is in his thought no room for the idea that every man is a particular, complex mixture of good and evil impulses, of love and hate, or of egoism and altruism.

His basic idea that most men are sinful and self-seeking leads him directly to the vision of society as a scene of constant strife and mutual injury where each man struggles to satisfy his desires and ambitions at the expense of all other men. It is this vision which constrains him to believe that only the State, with its apparatus of laws, punishments, and coercion, can hold these conflicts within bounds and prevent men from annihilating one another. Because of the violence of men's passions and the strength of their appetites, the peace and order which the State maintains are supremely important and, at the same time, highly precarious. Augustine is so sharply aware of the need to impose a system of order on the conflicting wills of sinful men if human society is to be kept from collapsing into anarchy that he insists that the maintenance of peace is the primary function of the State. He is willing to settle for this one great accomplishment and to ask for relatively little in the way of positive benefits from the political system, because he is so acutely conscious of the importance and the fragility of earthly peace and so deeply impressed by the disastrous consequences of disorder, strife, and war.

As a result of his concentration on the necessity of preserving peace and order (which must always be the first word, though not the last, that is said about the goals of the political system), Augustine insists on absolute obedience to the commands of all rulers, no matter how wicked or corrupt they may be; he allows disobedience, with no attempt a- resistance, only when the ruler's orders run counter to the clear comt mandments of God. Also, he completely ignores the problem of classifying and evaluating different forms of government, as well as the question of how a given system of rule can be changed so as to make it more just or more satisfactory. The worst possible government is far better than anarchy, and in any case it must be endured as a divine punishment for men's sins. Revolution and rebellion, which would destroy the framework of peace and order, would serve only to compound the evil and the suffering.

In addition to his fundamental insight into the essential function of the political order—maintaining peace by the application of coercion—Augustine also gives us penetrating analyses of the complexities of political action and of the pitfalls of ignorance, pride, and cruelty inevitably associated with the exercise of political power. No one who has read Augustine carefully can fail to be impressed by the ambiguities and limitations inherent in political action, and by the enormously difficult tasks and the almost insoluble moral dilemmas that confront the ruler at every turn.

As he surveyed the collapse of ancient institutions and the rising tide of destruction in the world around him, which led many of his contemporaries to the conclusion that the end of the world was at hand, Augustine's keen sense of the perpetual power of human pride and sinfulness compelled him to reject any hope that the future would bring enduring peace or progress. Both his theological beliefs and his experience and observation of men's actions in an age of disorder enforced upon him an attitude of pessimistic realism, which would not allow him to sentimentalize or evade the darker aspects of social and political life.

In our own century, when, once more, men have been compelled to recognize the almost incredible brutalities of which human beings are capable, especially when they struggle for political power and military domination, it is no accident that Augustinian pessimism and realism have enjoyed a considerable revival among both theologians and secular thinkers. As a result of our own experiences, we are much more prepared than our fathers were to give a hearing to the doctrine of original sin and to the view that ceaseless application of coercive power is necessary in order to hold in check human pride and the fruits of pride—aggression, avarice, and lust—and to preserve the fabric of civilization which is constantly imperiled by these forces.

We may have learned our lessons by reading Freud and by observing the new barbarism of our century rather than by listening to Christian realists. Nevertheless, the optimistic beliefs of many nineteenth-century liberals and Marxists—the certainty that the future would inevitably bring a sharp reduction, if not the complete elimination, of the need to employ coercion in social life, and the faith that men could be educated to cooperate voluntarily in a just and harmonious social order—strike us as hopelessly irrelevant as guides to present and future action and shamelessly hypocritical if offered as descriptions of present realities. We know that pride, self-assurance, and a sense of being the instruments of Providence or of historical necessity, as well as the more obvious vices of avarice, lust for domination, and hatred, can lead men and nations to perpetrate enormous crimes. We know too that we must be prepared to use awful weapons to defend ourselves and our civilization from threats of destruction, although we also recognize that our use of these weapons and techniques renders us liable to fall into the same vices. For, like Augustine, we have learned that greed, pride, aggressiveness, and hatred are not simply characteristics of other men and other states. We know that since these impulses dwell in each of us and in our society, we too are capable of translating them into action once the pressures acting upon us rise beyond a certain level.

I believe that these are some of the reasons why pessimistic analysts of human nature and of society and politics have received increasing attention during the last two decades, and why Augustine's views are entitled to our serious consideration. If we are going to preach—or listen to—neo-Augustinianism, we should be willing to examine its doctrines in their original and most compelling forms. My argument is not that grim realism is the only viable political and social doctrine for our age or that the Augustinian version of it is the closest approximation to the truth. I say only that in our era of war, terror, and sharp anxiety about man's future, when, again, a major epoch in human history may be drawing to a close, we cannot afford to ignore Augustine's sharply etched, dark portrait of the human condition. How much of that picture each of us accepts or rejects, how much he modifies it, is a problem that each man must solve for himself. Only one thing is certain. The intellectual equipment that we employ as we face our dilemmas will be needlessly restricted if it has no place for Augustine's powerful and somber vision.

Gerhart Ladner

It is an undeniable fact that Augustine often simply identifies the concepts Ecclesia and Civitas Dei. He does so in *De civitate Dei* as well as in other works, particularly clearly in the *Enchiridion de fide spe et caritate*, which is a little handbook on Christian doctrine and follows the order of the Creed. When Augustine reaches that part of the Creed which expresses the belief in the Church he speaks of her as the House, the Temple, the City of God and says that we must think of her not only in her terrestrial pilgrim's condition but also in her celestial part; this heavenly Church or City of the Angels will at the end of all things have received fulness of its numbers through renewed men. The terms *ecclesia* and *civitas Dei* then can mean the same. And yet, it cannot be an accident that Augustine wrote that incomparable work which he himself called his *magnum* and *ingens opus*, his *grande opus*, around the concept of the City of God. Instead of speaking of the *civitas Dei caelestis* and

SOURCE: Gerhart Ladner, *The Idea of Reform* (Cambridge, Mass.: Harvard University Press), pp. 272–281. Copyright 1959 by the President and Fellows of Harvard College. Reprinted with permission of the publishers.

peregrinans, Augustine might quite conceivably have used at all times and everywhere the terminology of the *ecclesia in gloria et pace* and the *ecclesia in via*, which corresponds to the later terms *ecclesia triumphans* and *ecclesia militans*. Yet he did not do so. The reasons why the idea of the two cities was so essential to him are perhaps less difficult to discover than would at first appear and it is suggested that they are related to his desire for, to his concept of, reform.

First of all, the term *civitas Dei* was "freer" than the term *ecclesia*. It was not as the latter defined dogmatically, liturgically, juridically. The Ecclesia was and is primarily the Corpus Christi, the liturgical communion with and in Christ; on earth it is above all *communio sacramentorum*, it is not yet fully identical with the *communio sanctorum*. The Augustinian concept of the Civitas Dei is much closer to that of the *communio sanctorum;* it differs from the latter chiefly through the fact that in its terrestrial part it is still *in via*, still *peregrinans* and incomplete, whereas the Communion of the Saints envisages only those living and departed souls who at a given time already form a holy company with the angels.

The concept of the Civitas Dei thus could serve admirably to comprehend the heights and the depths of Christian life. St. Augustine saw that the Church of his time was deeply enmeshed in the imperfections of human existence; at the same time he knew that the essence of this same Church was holy and eternal. His idea of the Civitas Dei expressed the unity in this doubleness better than the concept Ecclesia itself does. The Ecclesia being the ever present Body of Christ was both too familiar and too sacred, its situation in the world too sensitive and too vital, to be made the key word of a theology of history, of history even in its relation to eternity; and in fact, no *ex professo* treatise *De ecclesia* was written until the thirteenth century, when the idea and reality of the Church had been securely established over a long period of time.

Another reason why Augustine wrote a *De civitate Dei* and not a *De ecclesia*, is no doubt to be found in the genesis and disposition of the work itself. Augustine's *De civitate Dei*, as his life's work in general, is animated not by one but by two main apologetic motives—not only by his well-known wish to defend Christianity against paganism and heresy, but also by the desire to hold up to the worldly Christians of his day a supreme ideal of life. Augustine himself explains in the *Rectractationes* that, whereas the first ten books of *De civitate Dei* are chiefly a refutation of pagan Rome, the last twelve are an exposition of Christian doctrine in its own right. It was natural, therefore, to start out in terminological and conceptual categories of Roman political thought—*respublica* and *civitas*—and gradually to proceed to an explicit or implicit, often almost casual, identification of Civitas Dei and Ecclesia.

In proceeding from the refutation of paganism to the apology and "self-criticism" of Christendom St. Augustine evidently did not consider it necessary or advisable to change the title and plan of the work or to modify the leading role of the City of God idea in it.

As with all his other writings so also with his books on the City of God Augustine undoubtedly wanted to help in bringing about a change to the better in the condition of the Church of his time. Yet there is also little doubt that to place the Ecclesia in the dead center of his great reckoning with Christians as well as pagans would have been as uncongenial to him as—to judge from earlier and later attempts —it would have been fruitless or disrupting. But, a work on the

> most glorious City of God, be it in this temporal flow, while it is on pilgrimage among the impious and lives in faith (Habac. 2 : 4), be it in that stability of the eternal abode which it now expects with patience (cf. Rom. 8 : 25), "until justice be turned into judgment" (Ps. 93 : 15), and which it will afterwards attain eminently in the last victory and the perfect peace,

a work in other words on those predestined to heavenly happiness and on their counterpart could and actually did set an inspiring standard and suggest that the troubles of Church history are only the heritage of human nature and that contrary to all other human societies the Church, insofar as it is the City of God, will not perish.

A third reason, finally, for the predominant role of the Civitas Dei idea in Augustine's theology of history is most directly related to his conception of reform. Not any more than Christian Antiquity in general does Augustine know of a concept of "Church reform" as such. Everything which pertains to reform is expressed in terms of personal renewal. At any given time the Church, insofar as it *truly was* the Church, was also the Civitas Dei and the *communio sanctorum*, essentially eternal and not in need of reform, whereas the reprobate in the Church —on its surface as it were—would not and could not be lastingly reformed. Yet, the individual elect of God, who on earth form the *civitas Dei peregrinans*, must be constantly reformed until the hour of their death. If then Augustine wanted to indicate the permanent need of reform in the Church, he must express this necessity in terms of a group of men capable of reform; these are the *cives* of the terrestrial Civitas Dei whose salvation will ultimately even "restore" the Kingdom of Heaven, in the sense that they will replenish the angelic hosts whose number was depleted by the fall of the rebel angels.

> And certainly the holy angels taught by God . . . know how great a supplementary number the fulness of that city (i.e., the supernal City of God or the celestial part of the Church) expects out of mankind. Therefore, the apostle said: "To reestablish (*instaurare*) all things in Christ, that are in heaven and on earth, in Him" (Eph. 1 : 10). For, the things that are

in heaven are reestablished when that which in the angels fell from heaven is made up (*redditur*) through men; and the things that are on earth are reestablished when those same men themselves, who are predestined to eternal life, are renewed (*renovati*) from the oldness of corruption.

Commenting in *De civitate Dei* upon the famous verses of the book Ecclesiastes (12:8) concerning the vanity of all things and considering the calamities, the errors of life, the ineluctable lapse of time, the apparent futility of the historical world of becoming Augustine concludes:

> Yet, in the days of his vanity, it makes a very great difference whether [man] resists or obeys truth . . . "Fear God," [Ecclesiastes] says, "and keep his commandments: for this is all man" (Eccl. 12 : 13). For, whosoever is, surely is this, a keeper of God's commandments, because he who is not this, is nothing, for, [such a one] is not reformed to the image of the truth and remains in the likeness of vanity.

That there are in the Church on earth the *mali et ficti*, the wicked and the hypocrites, this may in Augustine's opinion be that *mysterium iniquitatis* of which St. Paul spoke.

> There are not wanting, in fact there are many within who by the loss of all morality torture the hearts of those who live piously, because by them the Christian and Catholic name is blasphemed; and the dearer that name is to those who want to live piously in Christ the more they bear pain that through bad men who are within it comes to be loved less than the minds of those who are pious desire. . . . But the pain itself which arises in the hearts of the pious, who are persecuted by the way of life of bad or false Christians, helps those who bear that pain, because it is derived from their charity in which they do not wish [the bad] to perish or to impede the salvation of others. Finally, great consolations arise also out of the correction [of the bad] (*de correctionibus eorum*) which permeates the souls of the pious with joy as great as had been the pain by which they had been tortured on account of their perdition. Thus, in this world, in these evil days (cf. Eph. 5 : 16) . . . until the end of this world, in between the persecutions of this world and the consolations of God, the Church takes its pilgrim's course.

Correction, reformation of the human person is for Augustine the sole remedy against the evils of history. This means that even in the Church only the saint truly *is* and also that the Church exists truly only in its saints: this is, perhaps, the deepest meaning of the Augustinian City of God, which is the society of the angels and the elect.

Augustine, in *De civitate Dei* and elsewhere, has attempted a solution of the mystery of iniquity by showing that the same Church which has *mali* and *ficti* in her midst, is also the *Civitas Dei peregrinans* whose citizens must again and again be corrected and reformed by the grace of God, if they are to persevere, if they are to remain a part of that Church, of that Civitas which is holy and eternal.

It can never be emphasized too strongly that on the one hand every Christian concept of reform, and so also that of St. Augustine, is primarily individual, personal, and that on the other hand for Augustine, too, the *ecclesia sine macula aut ruga* (Eph. 5:27) exists and will exist notwithstanding the serious imperfections of a part of its members. St. Augustine would no doubt have approved of the assertion that the Church is without sin, though there are sinners in it. . . .

Etienne Gilson

In substantial outline, this is the path followed by the Augustinian soul in its search for God. Such a method unquestionably gives the impression of being slow and tortuous, but the numerous intermediate steps it places between its starting point and conclusion are not indispensable to the mind that has once mastered it. The critical point in the demonstration is evidently the last, wherein God is said to be the only sufficient basis for the truth which is present in the mind. Any truth whatsoever might serve as the starting point of the proof, but best of all is the first of all, namely that I exist. Because, as we have seen, doubt and even error attest the existence of the doubting mind, they can with no less evidence and immediacy bear witness to the existence of God. I doubt; I know that I doubt. Thus I know at least one truth for certain, for I cannot doubt that I doubt. If I am certain of this, am I not so because there is a first truth which illumines every man coming into this world. If I doubt, I exist; if it is true that I doubt, God exists. The certainty of the mind's existence implies the certainty of God's existence.

It will be better to wait until the problem of Augustinian illumination itself has been dealt with before attempting to unfold the full meaning of this proof, but perhaps it will be helpful at this point to remove at once certain difficulties which may obscure its real meaning.

From what has been said, it is quite clear that in Saint Augustine the problem of God's existence cannot be distinguished from the problem of knowledge; knowing how we comprehend truth and knowing the existence of Truth are one and the same thing. Consequently, his proof is effected entirely within the mind without having to take the world of the senses into consideration. However, it would not be an accurate description of the proof to say that it excludes the world of the senses; the fact is that, even though it does not require it, it can make room for it in its own way, if there is need. A well-known passage of St. Paul (Rom. 1, 20) says that one may begin with an examination of the created universe and rise to a knowledge of God's invisible attributes.

SOURCE: Etienne Gilson, *The Christian Philosophy of St. Augustine* (New York: Random House, 1960), pp. 18–24. Copyright © 1960 by Etienne Gilson. Reprinted by permission of Random House, Inc.

Augustine, like everyone else, knew this text and often found inspiration in it. Yet even as he felt its inspiration, he interpreted it in a way that remains typically Augustinian. For him the *invisibilia Dei* are God's Ideas. Thus, to know God by starting with sensible things is to ascend from things to their Ideas. Now, as we have seen, the path leading from bodies to divine truth passes through the mind. So even when it starts with the external world, the Augustinian proof normally proceeds from the world to the soul, and from the soul to God.

Some historians have maintained, however, that Saint Augustine had fully developed proofs of God's existence which are based on an application of the principle of causality to the sensible world and that this was true especially of the proof known to the Middle Ages as the proof *a contingentia mundi*. Of course Augustine often stressed the fact that the mutability of the world of bodies bears witness to its contingency and dependence with respect to a necessary being, namely God. No one can deny that his doctrine contains all the elements necessary for such a proof and, consequently, that such a proof is consistent with the most authentic Augustinism. Moreover, at times he expresses himself in such a way that the mere sight of order in the world seems to be for him the equivalent of a direct proof of God's existence. Now is it possible to reconcile these two methods? In the first place we should note that Augustine himself did not offer such metaphysical reflections, or flights of devotion as proofs, properly so-called, for the existence of God. All the proofs which he developed in full either pass through the mind or begin there. The reason for this is obvious. When we question sensible things about their nature and origin, they show us that they are changeable and answer, as it were: "We have not made ourselves." We must, therefore, transcend them in order to reach their cause. Now we cannot reach the cause of their mutability and contingency, because this is nonbeing; we can reach only the cause of their stability, because this is being. Their number, order, and measure are their stability. Over and above their number is the number of our mind, which knows them. If we transcend the number of the mind, we arrive at the number of Truth, which is God. As soon as Augustinian thought develops, it finds the path of the *De Libero Arbitrio* and the *De Vera Religione*, a path leading from the exterior to the interior and from the interior to the superior.

We may ask the reason for this twofold attitude. If there is only one route for the soul to take towards God, why does he seem to say that there are two? The reason is that Augustine does not follow an abstract dialectic; he uses a dialectic which is merely the actual movement of his own thought. His demonstration of God's existence is really a long meditation; every step must be made in its proper place and time if the mind is to arrive at the goal; but once that goal is reached, the mind is not obliged to stop there. When it turns back and stops at each

step it has taken, it sees that the end of every step *could* have been discovered beforehand, but that it is actually discovered only when the
steps are retraced and after the mind has already reached its goal. Only
then does the proof seem to fall into parts; and each part may appear to
be an independent proof, even though it can be fully justified only if it is
put into its proper place in the whole scheme.

If we look at it from this point of view, it is easy to see how the
Augustinian method of reaching God by way of the mind produced a
symbolic mysticism of the sensible world during the Middle Ages. The
fact is that there is room in Augustinism for a kind of sensible evidence
for God's existence. The world proclaims its author and ever takes us
back to Him. Divine wisdom has left its mark on every thing and we
have but to observe things to be led from them to the soul and from the
soul to God. The path of philosophical reflection passes through the
soul because it is obvious that the numbers of things only exist for us as
numbers which are known; a devout soul or a mind which hurries on
without stopping at every step, because the route is already well known
to it, sees Augustine's universe as the Victorines and St. Bonaventure
were to see it later, i.e. as a clear mirror wherein the mind sees God's
reflection in everything. Let us add: not only can the soul contemplate
Him there, but in a certain sense it must do so. Although it is true that
the supernatural term of contemplating God in the things of nature is a
direct vision of God in His splendor, yet as long as the soul is wandering
far from Him, it can join Him only for brief moments in a dazzling
vision wherein the soul risks blindness in uniting itself to God (*in ictu
trepidantis aspectus*). Then let it return from God Himself to things of
earth; let its sight find rest in the enjoyment of the reflections of that
light it can no longer look upon until a new desire and new graces
raise it to Him once again.

It is true to say, then, that the world's order, beauty, movement and
the contingency they imply form part of the Augustinian proof of God.
But let us suppose that instead of isolating this step in our journey, we
isolate the step which follows it. Then the proof of God's existence
dispenses with the sensible world instead of passing through it and,
although it does not exclude the things it sets aside, it becomes a demonstration based on pure thought. Because it is more abstract and tech-
nical, it is the metaphysician's method; and because it is more spiritual,
it is the mystic's way as he reaches out beyond proof towards union.
As the first aspect of the proof prepares the way for a mediaeval symbol-
ism of the sensible world, this second aspect clears the way for the
metaphysical speculations of an Anselm as he tries to discover God's
existence in the very idea we have of Him. Of course St. Augustine did
not develop such a proof, but he did direct his search along a path that
would normally lead to the proof of the *Proslogion*.

It is important to observe at the outset that Augustinian proofs of God's existence proceed entirely on the level of essence rather than on the plane of existence properly so-called. They do not begin by affirming existences and then proceed to find their first efficient cause. On the contrary, they first observe certain ways of being, and the final explanation of these is sought in a being whose ontological rule, if it may be so termed, is their only possible justification. Whether it is a question of the world of bodies in evolution, or of the life of the mind in search of truth, the basic fact to be explained remains the same. In both cases the philosopher is confronted by that ontological scandal, change. Faithful to the tradition of Plato, St. Augustine thinks less about existence than about being; and since he is convinced that to change is not truly to be, the contingency he tries to explain is not so much the contingency of *existence*, in the proper sense of the word, as the contingency of *beings* which, even though they are not nothing, still do not have a sufficient reason within themselves for being what they are.

Augustinian proofs for God's existence would be understood incorrectly if one tried to interpret them in the same sense as the proofs of St. Thomas Aquinas. The "ways" to God do not follow the same paths in the two doctrines because their terminal points, like their starting points, are not the same. It is true that they have the same God in view, and He is the same God with the same name, but whereas St. Thomas will try especially to prove the existence of a supreme *Esse*, or subsistent act of existing, St Augustine wanted above all else to stress the obligation which the mind has of explaining the spurious *esse* known in experience by a supreme *Vere Esse*, i.e. by a being which fully deserves the title "being." For him, as for Plato, the ὄντως ὄν is by essence that which is identical with itself and consequently, the immutable. This "really real," this *vere esse*, is what Augustine calls *essentia*, and his whole system of proofs is explained by his intention to emphasize the existence of this being, identical with itself, perfectly immutable, and therefore, perfectly existing; the being we call God.

The marked preference Augustine shows for arguments drawn from the presence of truth within us finds its explanation here. In the whole of human experience, truth, and the other transcendentals such as the one, the good and the beautiful which are spontaneously associated with it, are the surest signs of the existence of an immutable, eternal and eternally self-identical being. It is to be noted that all Augustinian meditations on the sensible world are directed towards the same kind of conclusion: "O Truth! *Thou Who truly are!* I find the past and future in every change in things, but in abiding truth I find neither past nor future: nothing but the present, even the incorruptibly present that is not found in the creature. Analyze the changes in things and you will find it *was* and *it will be;* think of God and you will find *He is;* no *was* or *will be* has a place there." Every time Augustine attempts one of these mental ascents he sets out towards the God of *Exodus,* but every path leads him to that which, as far as his reason is concerned, constitutes being in all its fullness: stability in essence, immutability and finally that eternity which for him is not only an attribute of God but His very substance (*Aeternitas, ipsa Dei substantia est*).

It cannot be too strongly emphasized that we are dealing here, not with one aspect of Augustine's doctrine, but with, perhaps, the most profound and most constant element in his metaphysical thought. He never gave any other interpretation of the name God Himself claimed as His own in Scripture: "The angel and, through the angel, the Lord Himself said to Moses when he asked His name: 'I am who am. Thus shalt thou say to the children of Israel: He who is hath sent me to you.' *To be* is the term for immutability (*Esse, nomen est incommutabilitatis*). All mutable things cease to be what they were and begin to be what they were not. Only He Who does not change has true being, pure being, authentic being. He has being of Whom it has been said: 'Thou shalt change things and they shall be changed; but thou art always the selfsame' . . . . What does 'I am who am' mean if not 'I am eternal'? What does 'I am who am' mean except 'I cannot change'?"

We cannot be mistaken here. In a doctrine wherein "I am who am" means, at one and the same time and in exactly the same sense, to be the supreme essence, the supreme being, the supremely immutable and the eternal, the proof of God's existence amounts to showing that the mutable demands something immutable on which it depends by participation. That is why the proofs for the existence of God which are based on the immutability of truth are at the root of all the others, even the cosmological proofs. Truth is immutable, so if we encounter truth in human knowledge, to reach the place where it dwells is to draw near to God Himself. Besides, do we not read in St. John (1, 9) that the Word, Who is God, is the true light which illumines every man coming into this world? Since truth in man is only the reflection of divine immutability, we have but to ascertain the presence of truth in the mind to ascertain God's presence there.

Since Augustinian proofs are intended to show forth God's "essentiality," it was natural that they should tend to follow a shorter route and to look for proof of His perfect essentiality in the content of the divine *essentia* alone. A dialectic quite different from that used by Augustine, one perhaps that he did not care for, made it possible to follow this shorter path. Even though Augustine did not follow it himself, he did construct the ontology on which St. Anselm and his mediaeval successors were to practice their dialectic in order to establish the evidence of God's existence.

It was a metaphysical decision of prime importance to seek God by going, not only beyond man and even the mind of man, but also beyond a datum of that mind which is such that whatever transcends it can only be God. Moreover, although it is true that Augustine did not exactly recommend a direct transition from the idea of God to His existence, truth being the datum of the mind which we have but to transcend in order to attain God, whatever else may be its content, it is true nonetheless that, even in the humblest truth, he sees the reflection of the divine attributes, immutability and eternity, with the result that an Augustinian proof is essentially an act of submission on the part of the mind to the intrinsic necessity of the Divine Essence. We do not prove that God should exist but that He does exist, just as we do not prove that seven plus three should make ten, but that they do make ten. Therefore, the mere presence in man's mind of a datum which obviously transcends man implies the existence of its object. This deep-seated tendency to find in God alone sufficient reason for the idea we have of Him, is the bond which links the metaphysics of Saint Anselm, Saint Bonaventure, Duns Scotus and Descartes to Augustinian metaphysics. But the demonstration of it which Augustine advances far surpasses, in one sense, those it has inspired. It is neither an argument nor a series of arguments, but a complete metaphysics plus an ethics and a mysticism which crowns it. The initial doubt, the appeal to faith, the mind's certitude, the soul's spirituality, the transcendence of truth, each successive step in the proof is the translation of a personal experience which requires meditation for its metaphysical interpretation to become intelligible. But this implicit metaphysics in turn rests on an ethics, because the moment the proof of God's existence is completed, it also becomes a problem. We seek God, but why do we seek One Who gives us the power and the desire to do so? In order to grasp the whole Augustinian demonstration—and this amounts to grasping Augustine's whole teaching and to understanding it in its profound unity—we must walk again and more slowly along the road we have just travelled, stopping at each step as long as may be necessary to justify the route we have traversed.

A STUDY GUIDE

1. What were Augustine's principal occupations in life? And what effect did they have on the nature of his writings?

2. What does O'Meara mean when he says that the *Confessions* is not an autobiography? What is the purpose of the *Confessions* and how is this purpose achieved?

3. According to Deane what are the principal elements in Augustine's conception of the state? Do you agree with his conclusion about the contemporary world?

4. What is the distinction between the two concepts—the Church and the City of God? What is Augustine's idea of reform? What is the relationship between the idea of reform and the theology of history?

5. What is the basic thesis of Gilson's argument? How does one have knowledge of God according to Augustine? Do you think that Gilson is sympathetic to Augustine's position?

6

MODERN COMMENTARY ON THOMAS AQUINAS

M. D. Knowles

St. Thomas's theory of knowledge is that of Aristotle, rendered somewhat more explicit. The mind is a *tabula rasa*. External things impinge upon the senses, which present the individual object to the mind; this strips off all that is individual and accidental, and grasps the essence or nature. We see Smith, and recognize in him manhood, the nature of a rational animal, man. The essence of the individual abstracted by the mind is in one way less real than it is in the individual himself, for it only exists fully and in its own right in the individual. But in another sense it is more real, for to Aquinas, as to the Neoplatonists, immaterial being, spirit and thought, is more real than physical, material being; it is a higher mode of being and is logically prior to anything physical. By reaching the essence we reach the formal cause of a being, the expression in rational shape of the spiritual idea which is ultimately its constitutive agency.

We have alluded to the thorough acceptance of Aristotle by Aquinas. This leads him to assert, or rather to assume, what has been called the primacy of the intellect. Reason and order throughout the universe reflect the unchanging mind and law of God. Hence the celebrated doctrine of the various kinds of Law. Just as with man nothing can be willed before it is known (*nil volitum quin praecognitum*), and therefore reason is of the essence of freedom, so with God it is His knowledge, His unalterable law, that logically precedes His decrees. Consequently Aquinas, like Avicenna and Aristotle before him, has a strong bias towards determinism, and in one of the bitterest of all theological controversies his interpreter, the great Bañez, was accused of near-Calvinism.

SOURCE: M. D. Knowles, *The Evolution of Medieval Thought* (Baltimore, Md.: Helicon Press, Inc.), pp. 264–267. Reprinted with permission of the publishers.

Yet Aquinas's acceptance of Aristotle, though thorough and epoch-making, is neither uncritical nor absolute. He accepts his metaphysics almost in entirety, but his world-system only with reservations, and for all the higher levels of Christian life he repeatedly asserts Aristotles incompetence. Similarly, while taking over bodily from the Jewish Maimonides much of his natural theology, he takes only part (and that with cautious reservation) of his and others' Jewish and Neoplatonist teaching on the information of the heavenly spheres by intelligences or angels, and he firmly rejects the series of creative causes posited by Avicenna, and the emanations of the Neoplatonists. At the same time, Aquinas admits far more from non-Aristotelian sources than appears at first sight. Thus the Platonic ideas, resolutely banished in their familiar form from epistemology and metaphysics, remain "in the heavens" (to use a Platonic phrase) where Augustine had seen them, as the eternal, exemplary, creative ideas in what we call "the mind of God." Moreover, as we have seen, the "exemplary" and participatory function of the ideas is assumed by the Thomist doctrine of essence and existence. Similarly in ethics, alongside the everyday virtues of Aristotle are the four cardinal virtues taken from Plato and the Plotinian specification of all the virtues on the three levels of ordinary life, proficiency in virtue, and the state of perfection. These many undertones and overtones in the thought of Aquinas are important; they give it a richness and a flexibility which it might not otherwise possess.

Indeed, Aquinas makes so much use of ways of thought that are ultimately Platonic that it may almost be said of him that he achieves that fusion of the Academy and the Lyceum that so many of his predecessors and contemporaries were attempting. He accomplishes this, however, not by a synthesis, but by using elements from Platonism mainly in the higher levels of metaphysics. Thus by his use of the principle that all creatures participate in being, though in varying measure, by his use of exemplarism in which the creature reflects the creator, by his doctrine of metaphysical composition, and by his assertion of the self-sufficing being of God, he makes of God the centre and cause of a universe of manifold being, and in ethics the creator, lawgiver and providential Father of each human soul, thus placing the centre of gravity, so to say, at the summit of being, and revealing a radiating centre; a living principle and a final goal where Aristotle points merely to an abstract postulate. In this way he adds all that is true in Plato's idealism, other-worldliness and spirit of love to the common-sense, rationalistic empiricism of Aristotle.

To this copious fund of material taken from older thinkers, and to the many, and as yet not fully catalogued, debts which Thomas owed to his immediate predecessors and masters, another rich source must be added, the self-revelation of God in the Old and New Testaments. This revelation is not indeed philosophy, but, as M. Gilson has finely shown, it gives a clear and simple answer to several of the problems that all philosophers must face; it directs attention to the sovereign importance of others which they might neglect; and it brands as false many conclusions to which some thinkers in every age are prone. In all these ways the Christian religion, in a mind profoundly receptive of its influence, must present the philosopher with a view of the universe different in many respects from that of Plato and Aristotle. Whether this view, and the intuitions and axioms it encourages, are fuller and more true than any purely natural outlook could be, is of course a matter on which universal agreement will never be reached, but it is undoubtedly a constitutive element, and not mere colouring matter, in a philosophical system.

From all these constituents of Aquinas's thought there emerged the first original philosophical system that Christianity had seen—neither Platonism, nor Aristotelianism, nor Augustinism, but Thomism. Henceforward this presentation of the universe of reality could be regarded, not only as a phase in the ever-changing outlook of thinking man, and as a phenomenon of thirteenth-century intellectual life, but as a system to which men could return to study, to adopt and to amend. It is still a common belief, and a common error, that the teaching of Aquinas, besides being the most complete and coherent and in the opinion of many the most intellectually satisfying system of the middle ages, was in addition the most characteristic and the most influential. This belief has been considerably strengthened by the great, though often misrepresented, influence exerted by Aquinas over the single supreme poet of the middle ages. Dante knew his *Summa* well enough, and could apply it to any situation he wished, but he is even less of a pure Thomist than Thomas is a pure Aristotelian. Moreover, Dante speaks for himself, not for his world. When he began to write, and still more when he died, the academic climate had changed from that of the decade of his birth. Thomism, from 1290 to the early sixteenth century, was only a unit, and at times a small unit, in the European pattern of thought. It was only with the counter-Reformation, and still more with the nineteenth century, that the thought of Aquinas came to be regarded as in some respects synonymous with Catholic philosophy. As Gilson remarks with great felicity, at the end of his review of Aquinas, in the thirteenth century "St Thomas may not have been fully acclaimed by his age, but time was on his side: 'These things shall be written in another generation than ours, and a people yet to be created shall praise the Lord'."

F. Copleston

The foregoing outlines of the distinctions between substance and accident, matter and form, essence and existence, all of which illustrate in their several ways the general distinction which runs through all finite being, namely the distinction between act and potentiality, may give the impression that Aquinas' metaphysic consists simply of arid and tortuous discussions, couched in unfamiliar language and without much relevance to the world as we know it. As a conclusion to this chapter, therefore, I want to bring out some implications of his metaphysics, which may perhaps help to render the latter more easily intelligible.

The distinctions between substance and accident and between matter and form draw attention to two features of the world, namely permanence and change. We all speak of things as though they were in some degree permanent. Although a human being is born and dies and although a tree has a certain span of life, we all speak of the human being and of the tree, which each is alive, as an individual entity. Even in the abnormal and pathological case of "split personality" or dual personality we think of the relevant phenomena as happening to a definite human being and as taking place within that human being. We may say, for example, "he is suffering from schizophrenia", attributing the phenomena to a definite and individual being. At the same time we all think and speak of things both as capable of undergoing change and as actually undergoing change. We ourselves change within certain limits, while retaining our identities. The tree changes, though the changes are predicated of the tree considered as a relatively permanent thing. Objects with certain names are changed into objects with other names by chemical action for example. Permanence and change are both features of the world as presented in common experience and described in the ordinary language which reflects and expresses this experience. And these features find abstract expression in Aquinas' distinctions between act and potency, substance and accident, form and matter. He may speak in an unfamiliar way, but he speaks about the familiar. He does not construct a static world like that of Parmenides, nor does he present us with a Heraclitean flux; fundamentally he describes the world as it is known by us in daily experience. He presents us with a world which is shot through, as it were, by form, by intelligible structure, and which is therefore to that extent intelligible On the other hand he presents us with a changing and a developing world. And in emphasizing these aspects of the world he lays too the

Source: F. Copleston, *Aquinas* (Baltimore: Penguin Books, 1965), pp. 108–110. Reprinted with permission of Penguin Books, Ltd., London.

theoretical foundations for the particular sciences. If the world were in no way intelligible, science would not be possible, except as a purely mental and unverifiable construct. On the other hand, emphasis on change and development are characteristic of the sciences. One cannot, of course, deduce the conclusions of the empirical sciences from abstract metaphysical principles; nor did Aquinas think that one could. But there is not that cleavage between the world as presented in Aquinas' metaphysics, when distinguished from the contemporary scientific ideas that he accepted, and modern science which there would be, for example, between the philosophy of Parmenides and modern science. Both Aquinas' metaphysics and modern science presuppose the familiar world of common experience, though Aquinas' metaphysics moves on a more abstract plane than the empirical sciences.

This aspect of Aquinas' metaphysics, namely the presentation of a world combining permanence and change, can be called perhaps the construction of the world. That is to say, it presents an abstract theoretical picture of a developing universe which has at the same time sufficient permanence and intelligibility to make knowledge possible. But there is another aspect, which can perhaps be termed the destruction of the world, if by "world" one here means a self-sufficient Absolute. This aspect is represented by the distinction between essence and existence. There is a natural inclination to imagine all individual things as existing and acting "in the world", as though the world were a kind of containing entity, in which other things are situated. For Aquinas, however, the world is the system of interrelated finite substances and not something different from them; and in each finite substance he finds what may be called a radical existential instability, expressed abstractly in the essence-existence distinction. Under this aspect his metaphysic goes in a sense beyond the familiar workaday world, even though he thought of the distinction as reflected in ordinary language. It also forms a transition to his metaphysical theory about God, to the knowledge of whom metaphysics is, he insists, essentially orientated. This aspect of his metaphysics can be linked, of course, with the systems of other metaphysicians who have concerned themselves with the reduction of multiplicity to unity, of the dependent to the independent or absolute. But it is to be noted that in making the transition from the world to God Aquinas does not, as it were, annul the world of finite substances or turn them into accidents or modes of the Absolute: he relates the finite substances of experience to God, and it is in these concrete things that he finds a relation to a ground of their existence. His 'destruction' of the world is a critique of the idea of the world as a quasi-entity, as a pseudo-Absolute, and not of the things which in their inter-relatedness form the world. How he makes the transition from finite beings to God will be considered in the following chapter.

Etienne Gilson

St. Thomas' position is clearly marked out in advance by his theory of knowledge, and never for an instant do we find him trying to evade its necessary consequences. Our intellect forms all its concepts by the aid of sense intuition, wherefore, in its present state, it can have no object that is unattainable by means of such intuitions. But there is nothing at all to be alarmed about in this. St. Paul says that we can rise to the knowledge of God from our knowledge of creatures, and it is thus clear that an epistemology that binds itself to proceed by way of sense will always find at least one way open to God: that, namely, which finds its starting-point in the spectacle of creation. Sensible empiricism, therefore, entails no agnosticism in the field of natural theology; but if it does not close the way to God we may still ask what knowledge of God it gives us?

If we start from the sensible, God is not to be attained except as the creative cause of the world of bodies; and all our natural knowledge of God will be limited to what we can know of such a cause through the medium of its effects. That is very far from nothing, nor is it even a little, but it certainly is not all. We can, in fact, reason from the existence of contingent beings and conclude to the existence of a necessary being. We know therefore that He is, and that He is the first cause of all the rest; and that knowledge is enough, as we have seen, to effect a complete transformation in our philosophic interpretation of the universe. This term once attained, it is still possible to circumscribe, in a measure, the divine essence thus posited in existence; for if God is the first cause in the order of being, we can be sure that He altogether transcends every given being and, indeed, every being conceivable by a created mind. In the intellectual effort to deny to God all those limits that we find inscribed in the sensible being that we know, we are led to posit the existence of a supereminent essence, entirely distinct from all the effects it causes. That said, all that man can say is said. The human intellect knows this essence as existing, it does not penetrate it as such, and as we have already seen, we know that by its own powers it will never do so. Dionysius had good reason then to say that the God Whom our reason reaches remains, so to speak, an unknown God: *Deo quasi ignoto conjungimur;* for we know, indeed, that He is, and we know what He is not, but what He is remains wholly unknown to us: *de Deo quid non sit cognoscimus, quid vero sit penitus manet ignotum.* Certainly the distance between the intellect and God is immense in Thomism; it is, if

SOURCE: Etienne Gilson, *The Spirit of Medieval Philosophy*, pp. 258–263. Copyright 1936 Charles Scribner's Sons; renewal copyright © 1964 Etienne Gilson. Reprinted with permission of the publishers.

one may say so, a "*distantia maxima*"; nevertheless, it is not such that God Himself could not overcome.

It is to be noted in the first place, that however feeble the intellect may be, it is and remains an intellect; that is to say a capacity to become, in a manner, all things by way of representation. It is due to its lowly estate among intellects that it can assimilate only the intelligible enclosed in the sensible; but what it seeks in the sensible is precisely the intelligible, and nothing will quench its thirst for that as long as there remains any intelligibility to be assimilated. This is clear enough if we consider only the scientific or philosophic life of the mind. Limited as we are by the natural object of our investigation, at least we can never rest until we have attained its limits; that is, until we have gathered up all the actually acquired material of knowledge under a small number of first intelligible principles. It is as if the whole life of the mind were animated from within by a natural desire for the fullest possible unification; or rather, this natural desire is merely another name for the life of the mind itself; it is, we might say, the contingent mind itself, striving to actualize its latent possibilities, to fulfil and realize itself. That, moreover, is why no natural desire can be in vain; for the mere fact that it exists supposes an active possibility—one which is aware of itself in the case of an intellect—and the desire simply expresses its tendency to self-actualization. But note that we say "possibility," and nothing other than possibility, for the success of the effort does not depend only on the subject that puts it forth, it depends also on the accessibility of the object. Something more than an effort is required for success. But an effort arrested *en route* is no vain effort; it fails of its object, but that does not prove that it has no object. Quite the contrary: even when it is proved that he who desires will never by his own powers attain the whole end of desire, and even if he has no reason to hope for any help that could make him capable of it, the desire experienced remains there still, not in the least extinguished, but rather exasperated into anguish by the very sense of its own impotence. This anguish St. Thomas knew; and Alexander of Aphrodisias knew it, and Averroes, and Aristotle: *in quo satis apparet quantam angustiam patiebantur hinc inde eorum praeclara ingenia;* for this is the anguish of the human intellect itself which has in itself the power to become all things, and, grasping the existence of Being from the starting point of sense, would become *that;* and cannot.

Here, and only here, the familiar formula St. Thomas so often repeats in connection with this question attains its full meaning: *impossibile est naturale desiderium esse inane.* That the desire to see God is natural the whole history of philosophy proves, and, we may add, the personal experience of every man who, from the consideration of the world, rises to the consideration of its cause. The world of sense is given, and we would know the reason of its existence, and the answer is that things are because God is. Knowing that God is we then desire to know what He is; and there philosophy is brought to a standstill. But far from being suppressed, the desire is only sharpened by its own repulse. Whether it can be satisfied or not, yet as many men as there are to know that God exists so many men will there be to desire to know His nature; so many souls will there be to know neither rest nor beatitude while deprived of this knowledge, and even to suffer worse miseries than other men, because those who are unaware of their own ignorance are also unaware of what transcendent good they lack. The last word of philosophy is the assured affirmation of the existence of a supreme good and of our impotence to partake of it; or rather, this would be the last word did not our knowledge of God's existence, and our desire to behold His essence, bear witness at the same time that the vision is possible. The anguish of the pagan soul measures the distance that divides the human intellect from the sole Object that can satiate it; and that is why the divine promise delivers that soul from anguish, for now, knowing the nature of the intellect and its own immortality, it knows also that, by the grace of God, His beatitude may become our beatitude, because our truth will be perfected by His truth. Let us be more precise on this last point.

Even in the philosophy of St. Thomas there is a point for the insertion of a divine gift which, since it is added as a grace to nature, by no means destroys nature, fulfils it rather, brings it to the highest perfection of which it is capable. That the intellect can receive such a perfection is quite evident, it results from its very nature; which is a capacity for the apprehension of the intelligible. Between what it is, and what God is, there is no incompatibility as regards the order of knowledge, and for this reason St. Thomas can write that the divine substance is not entirely alien to the created intellect. Certainly it is entirely beyond its reach, but that is only because it is infinitely above it, not because it is formally unknowable: *divina substantia non sic est extra facultatem intellectus creati, quasi aliquid omnino extraneum ab ipso*. The active *power* of the intellect in respect of its proper object, whereby it may be led to order all its knowledge with respect to Being, is thus accompanied by a complementary *possibility*, a possibility of apprehending even this Being itself which it posits as existing without in any way attaining to its nature. We say *possibility*, because, since the proper object of the intellect lies in the sensible, it has no power in itself to rise above that level. And, further, even were the pure intelligible its proper object, yet, since it is itself but a being by participation, it could never naturally attain to Being; this would still infinitely transcend all its forces. But this possibility is no merely abstract one; it is a real capacity of a subject, which, although altogether without the means to actualize itself, can nevertheless be actualized by God. It could never be actualized by Aristotle's God. The natures that strive to know him do not owe him their existence; such as they are such they remain, that is to say in so far as they do remain before disappearing for ever. It can be actualized, nevertheless, by the Christian God, for since He created these natures He can also perfect them. He Who gave them being and made them immortal remains both able and willing to add to His gifts. He can give all there is to give—provided only that they are capable of receiving. Since, then, in itself, the intellect is capable of the total intelligibility, God can bestow it if He wills, and it is in this sense that, while firmly maintaining the truth of the epistemology of Aristotle, St. Thomas leaves open perspectives on to the supernatural that will profoundly modify its significance.

His natural theology, in fact, legitimizes the whole ambit of the Christian hope, but at the same time it remains as modest as can possibly be. That of Duns Scotus is the only one which, with similar firmness of thought, has ventured to grant us a little more in this life without authorizing us in the least to make God the primary object of the intellect. It is a doctrine equally received by both philosophers, in which for the rest they simply follow Aristotle, that being is the first intelligible concept attained by our minds. We can perceive nothing or conceive nothing otherwise than as a being; and it is only after we have done that that we determine the nature of the object thus apprehended. That is why St. Thomas affirms that being is the first intelligible, and the proper object of our intellect: *ens est proprium objectum intellectus, et sic est primum intelligible*. Only, when he expresses himself thus, St. Thomas always considers that our concept is and remains an abstraction from the sensible, so that if we try to apply it to a pure intelligible, such as God, it is attributable only by way of analogy, and becomes available only when corrected by all the necessary negations.

Jacques Maritain

This brief treatise on existence and the existent may be described as an essay on the existentialism of St. Thomas Aquinas. It is important to obviate from the beginning any risk of confusion on this point. The "existentialism" of St. Thomas is utterly different from that of the "existentialist" philosophies propounded nowadays. If I say that it is, in my opinion, the only authentic existentialism, the reason is not that I am concerned to "rejuvenate" Thomism, so to speak, with the aid of a

SOURCE: Jacques Maritain, *Existence and the Existent* (New York: Pantheon Books, Inc., 1948), pp. 11–13. Reprinted with permission of Pantheon Books, a Division of Random House, Inc.

verbal artifice which I should be ashamed to employ, by attempting to trick out Thomas Aquinas in a costume fashionable to our day. (The word "costume," in this connection, would certainly be a euphemism.) I am not a neo-Thomist. All in all, I would rather be a paleo-Thomist than a neo-Thomist. I am, or at least I hope I am, a Thomist. For more than thirty years I have remarked how difficult it is to persuade our contemporaries not to confuse the philosopher's faculty of invention with the ingenuity that inspires the art of the dress designer.

A Thomist who speaks of St. Thomas's existentialism is merely reclaiming his own, recapturing from present-day fashion an article whose worth that fashion itself is unaware of; he is asserting a prior right. I shall add, for the sake of greater precision, that in my view, what distinguishes authentic Thomism from the many non-Thomist, or allegedly Thomist currents in Scholasticism, into which the spirit of Plato, Descartes, or Wolff has insinuated itself (a spirit of which the so-called Thomism taught to-day has not yet been completely purged), is precisely the primacy which authentic Thomism accords to existence and to the intuition of existential being. It would be an excellent thing if, as a result of the stimulus given by the contemporary systems of existentialism, attention was unmistakably directed to this point. Even before these systems appeared, I had already repeatedly pointed out the error of conceiving the philosophy of *being* as a philosophy of *essences* or as a dialectic of essences (what I call thumbing through a picture-book) instead of seeing that philosophy for what it really is, what constitutes its peculiar advantage over all other philosophies and gives it its unique and eminent place among them, namely, the fact that it is the philosophy of existence and of existential realism, the confrontation of the act of existing by an intelligence determined never to disown itself.

As to vocabulary, it is commonly known that it is chiefly owing to the influence of Kierkegaard that the word 'existential' has become part of current speech, particularly in Germany. Twenty years ago there was a good deal of talk about existential Christianity, and I remember an eloquent lecture in which Romano Guardini explained to a number of slightly bewildered prelates that the existential meaning of the Gospel of St. John had been revealed to him by the character of Prince Muyshkin in Dostoevski's *Idiot*. Many philosophers, from Jaspers and Gabriel Marcel to Berdyaeff and Chestov, were already calling themselves "existential" philosophers. It was some time later that the word "existentialism" passed into common usage, and with such success indeed that to-day, as M. Sartre remarked recently, "it no longer signifies anything at all." Apart from this incidental disadvantage, it is in itself a useful, nay an excellent word. As regards Thomist philosophy, it has this in common with the word realism, that it is not to be found in Peter of Bergamo's index. St. Thomas never proclaimed himself either an existentialist or a realist—though for that matter he never said he was a Thomist. The fact remains however that these things are consubstantial with his thought . . . .

A STUDY GUIDE

1. In Knowles' view what is the extent of Aquinas' debt to Aristotle? In what ways does Thomas depart from Aristotelian doctrine? What is the general role of Thomism in Christian thought?

2. What does Copleston mean when he speaks of Thomas' "construction" and "destruction" of the world?

3. In Gilson's view, how does Thomas Aquinas "legitimize the whole ambit of the Christian hope"? Do you agree with Gilson's enthusiastic appraisal of Thomas' achievement?

4. How does Maritain evaluate Thomism in terms of twentieth-century modes of thought? Is this view justified?

A B C D E F G H I J   5 4 3 2 1 7 0 6 9